MEN BEHIND THE MEDALS

MEN BEHIND THE MEDALS

by
Air Commodore Graham Pitchfork

LEO COOPER

First published in Great Britain in 1998 by Leo Coop
Reprinted in this format in 2003 by
LEO COOPER
an imprint of
Pen & Sword Books Ltd
47 Church Street, Barnsley,
South Yorkshire
S70 2AS

ISBN 1 84415 007 0

A CIP record of this book is available from
the British Library

Printed in England by
CPI UK

Contents

Foreword

by Air Marshal Sir Ivor Broom
KCB, CBE, DSO, DFC & two bars, AFC, RAF (Retd).

Approximately 150,000 men were trained to fly in various categories in the Royal Air Force in the Second World War. A few names have become household legends, but the vast majority are largely unknown outside their squadrons and circle of family and friends.

In this book Air Commodore Graham Pitchfork has focused on a number of relatively unknown aircrew personalities of that war and carried out extensive research into their service, decorations and campaign medals. His research has revealed fascinating stories of cool, calm reaction to adversity and tales of great gallantry and devotion to duty. The aircrew concerned never shrank from carrying out their allotted tasks regardless of their personal safety and were typical of the squadron members of the Second World War. They were the bedrock of the wartime Royal Air Force, but are largely unknown.

The lack of navigational facilities and the consequential danger imposed by poor weather conditions often created particularly hazardous operational sorties in the early years, but the stories reveal the enormous changes in the operational capability as the war developed.

The wide cross-section of the Royal Air Force covered by these fascinating stories involve all aircrew categories, all major aircraft roles, and all theatres of war. They will particularly appeal to those who are interested in the exploits of typical aircrew who fought in that war and the decorations and awards which they received.

It is worth reminding readers of the average age of aircrew mentioned in this book in order to put their performance into perspective. 20, 21, 22 years of age would be very typical with more action packed into those early years than in a normal lifetime. As the author so clearly highlights, when the challenge came they were not found wanting.

Rickmansworth
May 1997   IVOR BROOM

Acknowledgements

To write a book about people, particularly those with an abundance of courage, is immensely fascinating and satisfying. Indeed, it is an honour. Of course, to know your subjects well enough to write about them involves discovering those who knew them, worked with them, loved them and flew with them. This huge, and essential task has been particularly rewarding and it has been an enormous privilege to meet them and to establish new friendships which have developed over the last three years. To the very many who have patiently offered me their help, support and their friendship, I owe a deep debt of gratitude and I thank them all most sincerely. There are too many to mention individually but I feel compelled to single out a number.

First I want to thank Air Marshal Sir Ivor Broom for so kindly agreeing to writing the Foreword to this book. No one could be better qualified to write of courageous airmen and I feel privileged that he agreed to contribute.

The Director of the Air Historical Branch, Sebastian Cox, and his excellent and friendly staff have given me a great deal of help and I am particularly grateful to Graham Day for his unfailing and expert advice and assistance. Mrs Jean Buckberry at the RAF College Cranwell Library, the staff of the Central Flying School and the members of the Halton Aircraft Apprentices Association have given me invaluable help. Bob Coppock of the Naval Historical Branch has introduced me to the fascination of foreign naval documents and has been a great help. When I have been unable to trace documents in the Public Record Office, Dave Morris has come to my rescue and provided me with some crucial information and John Foreman gave me a great deal of help with *Luftwaffe* claims and losses. Wing Commander Jim Routledge gave his expert advice for which I am very grateful. Special mention must be made of Group Captain Chris Morris who has proof-read every chapter as it came off the production line. His constructive comments, skill in the use of the English language and advice have been invaluable. That he has carried out these 'duties' in conjunction with being in command of one of the largest and busiest RAF flying stations makes my admiration even greater.

It was my RAF colleague and friend Ken Delve, the Editor of *Flypast*, who encouraged me to write a series of articles about 'The Men Behind the Medals' which he published in his excellent magazine. He and his staff have given me a great deal of help and he has allowed me to use his extensive library and collection of photographs. I am grateful to Ken for agreeing to continue the series after the publication of this book. I also want to thank Duncan Cubitt who took the photographs of the medals which appear in full colour in the '*Flypast*' articles.

Photographs are an essential aspect of a book relating history. Without the help of my good friends Andy Thomas and Peter Green this book would be incomplete. Squadron Leader Peter Singleton of the Air Historical Branch and Chris Ashworth have also given me a great deal of assistance and I thank them all most sincerely. Many others helped with individual photographs and these are acknowledged in the pages that follow and I trust that they will accept this as my thanks for their help.

I want to reserve a special thankyou to the many wartime aircrew and the members of numerous Squadron Associations who have given me so much help. I had the privilege of meeting many of them and listening to their accounts which they related in such modest terms. I was thrilled to receive letters from Canada, Australia, Kenya and Zimbabwe; they were of immense help and serve to illustrate only too well the prodigious contribution made by the aircrew who came from the Commonwealth. All these men shared the experiences of those whose exploits are recorded in this book. Indeed, they could just as easily have been the subjects.

A number of my friends have given me a great deal of support over the past three years. In particular, I thank my close friend Air Chief Marshal Sir 'Sandy' Wilson and his wife Mary. To Derek Read, David Bancroft, Ian Tavender and David Haller I offer a sincere thankyou. They all gave me unfailing encouragement and advice and boosted my morale during the difficult periods.

Finally, I have a special thankyou for my family. Had my dear wife been well enough to help, she would have given me all the inspiration and support needed. It fell to my three children and my brother to sustain me and without their love, support and encouragement, this project could not have been completed.

Preface

The stories that make up this book relate the flying exploits of twenty-one men who were decorated for their gallantry in the air during the Second World War. The selection has been chosen in an attempt to cover a wide cross-section of the roles of the Royal Air Force during that war and I have also attempted to include as many theatres of operation as possible. With the exception of the Victoria Cross, all the British gallantry medals awarded for flying are included and I have endeavoured to give recognition to all the main aircrew categories. To encompass all these aspects in so few stories has proved to be a complex task but I hope that I have achieved the right balance and, in doing so, have created a series of stories that highlight the wide variety of flying activities undertaken by the Royal Air Force, in addition to paying tribute to the courage of the men who flew on operations.

With just twenty-one stories, inevitably there are a few omissions. I would like to have given deserved recognition to the gallant aircrew who flew with the Air-Sea Rescue squadrons, those who supported the Special Operations Executive and to those who flew in smaller, but equally important, roles.

Since it has been my intention to ensure that each story stands on its own and is a comprehensive account of each individual's flying career, there is inevitably some overlap. For example, two of the 'Men Behind the Medals' took part on the Eindhoven low-level raid and two others dropped paratroopers from Dakotas on the night of D-Day. In other respects, their stories are very different and would have been incomplete if I had merely abbreviated those few aspects that have appeared in an earlier chapter.

Notwithstanding an interest in the activities of the Royal Air Force during the Second World War which goes back many years, I have found the detailed research necessary to complete this book to be one of the most fascinating and rewarding projects that I have ever undertaken. I have learned a great deal and discovered many new aspects of the 'Air War'. However, the over-riding impression is one of the greatest admiration for the thousands of aircrew who flew with the Royal Air Force during the last great war and it is to 'The Many' that I dedicate this book.

CHAPTER ONE

The Medals

Introduction

This book tells the story of the exploits and service of gallant aircrew whose courage was recognised by the award of medals. Some knowledge of the medals referred to in the chapters that follow will, I believe, be useful. However, it is not my intention to treat the reader to a detailed study of British medals. This is a vast and fascinating topic and there are some outstanding works that the enthusiast can study, none more so than *British Gallantry Awards* by Abbott and Tamplin and *British Battles and Medals* by Gordon, recently up-dated, both of which are strongly recommended.

The medals referred to in this book are British and, in general terms, can be split into four categories; gallantry, campaign service, long service and commemorative. This chapter will concentrate on the background to the medals awarded to members of the Royal Air Force for gallantry and for service in the Second World War.

Readers should be aware that there have been some recent major changes made to the Honours system and some well known gallantry medals have disappeared, for example the Distinguished Flying Medal. Others have been introduced such as the Conspicuous Gallantry Cross. Since all the stories that follow relate to the Second World War, these changes will not be covered in this chapter and all reference to medals will be based on the pre-1995 changes.

The exploits of those awarded the Victoria Cross, the nation's ultimate award for gallantry, have been told many times so I have chosen not to include a story of one of the recipients. To those with a specific interest in this award, I recommend they read Chaz Bowyer's book '*For Valour. The Air VCs.*'

The descriptions outlined below are general and do not go into the numerous warrants, minor changes and styles of naming that have been made over the years. Clearly, all the awards reflect the appropriate cypher and crown but we are concerned only with those awarded during the reign of His Majesty King George VI. The gallantry medals which appear in the following chapters are listed in order of precedence.

Distinguished Service Order

The Distinguished Service Order (DSO) was instituted in 1886, is only awarded to Commissioned Officers and is available to members of all three services for 'distinguished services under fire'. This might include a specific act of gallantry or for distinguished service over a period of time. A good example of the former was the immediate award made to the then Pilot Officer Leonard Cheshire for safely bringing back to base his Whitley bomber of 102 Squadron which had been severely damaged by enemy fire over Cologne.

The silver gilt and white enamelled cross with the crown on the obverse and the cypher on the reverse hangs from a laureled suspender and a red ribbon with narrow blue borders which is attached to a similar laureled bar and brooch. The year of award is engraved on the back of the suspender. Bars are awarded for subsequent acts of distinguished service or gallantry and these are similar in design to the brooch and suspender bars.

Some 870 orders and 72 bars were awarded to members of the Royal Air Force during the Second World War. A further 217 orders and 13 bars were awarded to members of the Commonwealth Air Forces and a further 38 Honorary Awards to foreign (non-Commonwealth) officers.

Distinguished Flying Cross

Following the formation of an independent Royal Air Force on 1 April, 1918, specific awards for gallantry in the air were instituted on 3 June, 1918. These included the Distinguished Flying Cross (DFC) awarded to Officers and Warrant Officers 'for exceptional valour, courage and devotion to duty whilst flying in active operations against the enemy'. The award was extended to equivalent ranks in the Royal Navy on 11 March, 1941.

The silver cross flory is surmounted by another cross of aeroplane propellors with a centre roundel within a wreath of laurels with an Imperial Crown and the letters RAF. The reverse is plain with the Royal Cypher above the date 1918. The cross is attached to the ribbon by a clasp adorned with two sprigs of laurel. Since July, 1919, the ribbon has been violet and white alternate stripes running at an angle of forty five degrees from left to right. The year of award is engraved on the reverse. Bars are awarded for further acts of gallantry and the year of award is engraved in a similar fashion.

During the Second World War, just over 20,000 awards were made with a further 1592 bars. Among the latter were 42 second bars. Officers of the Royal Artillery engaged in flying duties during 1944 and 1945 were awarded 87 crosses.

Air Force Cross

The Air Force Cross (AFC) was introduced at the same time as the DFC. It too is awarded to Officers and Warrant Officers for an act or acts of valour, courage and devotion to duty whilst flying, though not in active service against the enemy.

The cross is silver and consists of a thunderbolt in the form of a cross, the arms conjoined by wings, the base bar terminating with a bomb surmounted by another cross composed of aeroplane propellers, the four ends inscribed with the letters G.V.R.1. The roundel in the centre represents Hermes mounted on a hawk in flight bestowing a wreath. The reverse is plain with the Royal Cypher above the date 1918. The date of the award is engraved on the reverse. The suspension is a straight silver bar ornamented with sprigs of laurel. The ribbon is in the same style as the DFC with red and white diagonal stripes. Bars are awarded for further acts of gallantry or duty.

Conspicuous Gallantry Medal

Until 1942 the Royal Air Force did not have a medal for Warrant Officers, Non-commissioned officers and men which ranked between the Victoria Cross and the Distinguished Flying Medal. The Royal Navy had the Conspicuous Gallantry Medal and the Army had the Distinguished Conduct Medal. A Royal Warrant of 10 November, 1942, extended the Conspicuous Gallantry Medal to members of the Army and Royal Air Force for 'conspicuous gallantry whilst flying against the enemy'. The medal was called the Conspicuous Gallantry Medal (Flying), but abbreviated to CGM, and it had its own distinctive ribbon.

The medal is silver and has the Sovereign's effigy on the obverse with the words 'For Conspicuous Gallantry' surrounded by a laurel wreath and surmounted by a crown on the reverse. The medal is suspended from a straight silver swivel and hangs from a light blue ribbon with a narrow dark blue marginal stripe. Bars could be awarded but none were made. The medal is named on the edge with the recipient's number, rank, name and service.

During the Second World War there were just 109 awards including one to a pilot in the the Glider Pilot Regiment. This small number makes it by far the rarest of the flying gallantry awards.

Military Medal

Although the Military Medal (MM) is not awarded for flying operations, a number of awards have been made for gallantry to members of the Royal Air Force and the Women's Auxiliary Air Force. A brief description is included here since a later chapter will relate the story of Pilot Officer D. Bebbington who was awarded the medal in 1943.

The medal is awarded to Non-commissioned officers and men of the British Army for bravery in the field. It was instituted in 1916 and extended by a 1920 Warrant to include other ranks of 'any of Our Military Forces.' A Warrant in

1931 refined this statement further with a new provision that it could be given to other ranks of 'Our Air Forces' for services on the ground. The silver medal carries the Sovereign's effigy on the obverse and the words 'For Bravery in the Field' surrounded by a laurel wreath surmounted by the Royal Cypher and a crown on the reverse. The medal is suspended by an ornate scroll bar suspender hanging from a dark blue ribbon with three white and two crimson narrow stripes down the centre. The medal is named in a similar way to the CGM.

During the Second World War 129 medals were awarded to the Air Forces including six to members of the Women's Auxiliary Air Force. Surprisingly, some medals were awarded to Royal Air Force personnel for engagements at sea.

Distinguished Flying Medal

The Distinguished Flying Medal (DFM) was instituted at the same time as the DFC and is awarded to Non-commissioned officers and other ranks for 'an act or acts of valour, courage or devotion to duty performed whilst flying in operations against the enemy.'

The silver medal is oval and carries the Sovereign's effigy. The reverse is more ornate, showing Athena Nike seated on an aeroplane with a hawk rising from her right hand. Below are the words FOR COURAGE and the G VI issue contains the date 1918 in the top left segment. The medal is suspended by a straight silver suspender fashioned in the form of two wings, all hanging from a ribbon of very narrow violet and white stripes at an angle of 45 degrees from left to right. The medal is named on the edge. Bars are awarded for subsequent acts of valour and the date is engraved on the reverse.

During the Second World War 6637 medals were awarded with just 60 bars and one second bar (the latter to Flight Sergeant Don Kingaby who was later commissioned and awarded the DSO and AFC as well). The small number of awards of the Bar is explained by the fact that many recipients of the DFM were subsequently commissioned. Many were decorated again as officers.

Air Force Medal

The Air Force Medal (AFM) was the fourth of the 'flying' medals to be instituted by the Warrant of 3 June,1918, following the formation of the Royal Air Force. As with the AFC, the AFM is awarded for 'valour, courage, or devotion to duty performed whilst flying not in active operations against the enemy'. The medal is awarded to Non-commissioned officers and other ranks.

The silver medal is very similar to the DFM with the exception of the reverse and the ribbon. The reverse shows Hermes mounted on a hawk and bestowing a wreath. The G VI issue has the date 1918 placed at the centre left. The ribbon is the same design as the DFM but with the colours red and white. The medals are named on the edge. Bars are awarded for additional acts of valour or duty.

There have been about 850 awards of the AFM since the award was instituted almost eighty years ago. Of these, 259 were awarded in the Second World War including two to the Army Air Corps. The AFM is the second rarest of the awards for flying.

Mention in Despatches

The practice of mentioning subordinates in despatches is of long standing. During the Second World War and in recent years, a Mention in Despatches was normally awarded only for gallantry or distinguished services in operations against the enemy for services which fell just short of the award of a gallantry medal. Until recently, the only medal to be awarded posthumously was the Victoria Cross. Posthumous 'Mentions' invariably indicated that the recipient would have earned a gallantry award had he survived but, with the exception of the Victoria Cross, the statutes of the day denied posthumous recognition.

The emblem is single-leaved being approximately three-quarters of an inch long. For the Second World War the emblem is worn on the ribbon of the War Medal and for other actions it is worn on the appropriate Campaign medal ribbon. Recommendations are submitted for the Sovereign's approval and a certificate is issued.

Air Efficiency Award

The Air Efficiency Award is not a gallantry award but is included here because it is an award made specifically to members of the Royal Air Force's Auxiliary and Volunteer Reserve Forces. It was instituted in 1942 and can be awarded to all ranks who have completed ten years of service. War service reduced the qualifying period depending on the type of service.

The silver medal is oval with the Sovereign's effigy on the obverse. The reverse is plain with the words Air Efficiency Award. The suspender is an eagle with wings outspread and the medal hangs from a green ribbon with two pale blue central stripes. Bars can be awarded for additional service.

Second World War Campaign Stars and Medals

Eight campaign stars were awarded for services during the Second World War. The six-pointed stars were made of a copper zinc alloy and were identical except for the name of the campaign in an outer circle surrounding the Royal Cypher and crown. All the medals were issued un-named. The maximum number of stars that could be awarded to one individual was five. Nine clasps were issued but only one could be worn with each star.

The qualifying periods for the campaign stars varies greatly and the reader who wishes to verify specific awards should consult one of the authoritative books mentioned in the Introduction to this Chapter.

The 1939–45 Star. This star was awarded for service in an operational area between 3 September, 1939, and 2 September, 1945. The colours of the ribbon represents the three services with the navy blue of the Senior Service on the left, the red of the Army in the centre and the pale blue of the RAF on the right. Fighter aircrew who took part in the Battle of Britain between 10 July and 31 October, 1940, were awarded the clasp 'Battle of Britain'.

The Atlantic Star. The Atlantic Star was awarded to those involved in operations during the Battle of the Atlantic from 3 September, 1940, to 8 May, 1945. The watered ribbon of blue, white and green represents the mood of the Atlantic. The clasps 'Air Crew Europe' and 'France and Germany' can be worn with this star.

The Air Crew Europe Star. The Air Crew Europe Star was awarded for operational flying over Europe from airfields in the United Kingdom between the outbreak of war and the invasion of Normandy on 6 June, 1944. The ribbon of 'Air Force' blue, with black edges and two yellow stripes represents continuous operations by day and night. The clasps 'Atlantic' and 'France and Germany' were awarded with this star.

The Africa Star. This star was awarded for one or more days service in numerous areas of Africa, primarily North Africa, between the entry of Italy in the war on 10 June, 1940, and 12 May, 1943. Other qualifying areas included Abyssinia, Somaliland, Sudan and Malta. The ribbon is pale buff representing the desert with a central red stripe flanked by a single navy blue and light blue stripe. These represent the three services. The clasp 'North Africa 1942–43' was awarded to qualifying members of the RAF.

The Pacific Star. The Pacific Star was awarded for service in the Pacific area of operations between 8 December, 1941, and 2 September, 1945. These areas included those invaded by the enemy, Malaya and the Pacific Ocean. The ribbon is dark green with red edges with a central yellow stripe flanked by thin lines of dark and light blue. These colours represent the jungle and desert and the involvement of all three services. The clasp 'Burma' was issued with this star.

The Burma Star. This star was awarded for service in the Burma Campaign between 11 December, 1941, and 2 September, 1945, and for service in parts of India, China and Malaya over certian periods. The ribbon is dark blue with the wide red stripe down the middle. The latter represents the Commonwealth forces. The blue edges each have a central orange stripe representing the sun. A clasp 'Pacific' was worn with this star by those eligible for both.

The Italy Star. This star was awarded from the beginning of the Italian campaign for operational service in Sicily or Italy from 11 June, 1943, to 8 May, 1945. Air crew service between these dates over Yugoslavia, Greece, the Dodecanese, Sardinia and Corsica also qualified for this star. The ribbon represents the Italian colours of green, white and red in equal stripes with the red on the outside and the green in the middle of the white centre. There are no clasps with this star.

The France and Germany Star. This star was awarded for service in France, Belgium, Holland and Germany after D-Day on 6 June, 1944, to VE Day on 8 May, 1945. Operations mounted from Italy did not qualify for this star. The ribbon is red, white and blue representing the national flags of Great Britain, France and Holland. The colours are in equal stripes with the blue on the outside and the red in the centre. The clasp 'Atlantic' can be awarded with this star.

The Defence Medal. The Defence Medal is made of cupro-nickel and shows the uncrowned head of King George VI on the obverse. The reverse has the Royal Crown resting on the stump of an oak tree with the years 1939 and 1945 at the top left and right. The words 'THE DEFENCE MEDAL' are at the base. The ribbon is flame-coloured with green edges and two thin black stripes down the centre of the green ones. These colours represent our green land and the fires during the night blitz. Qualification for this medal is complex but it was basically issued to reward those in a non-operational but threatened area and the qualifying period was three years at home and one year in certain areas overseas. The medal was issued un-named.

The War Medal. The medal is also made of cupro-nickel but the obverse has the crowned head of King George VI. The obverse shows a lion standing on a dragon with two heads with the years 1939 and 1945 above. The colours are symbolic of the Union Jack. All personnel with a minimum of 28 days were eligible for the award. The War Medal was also issued un-named.

Campaign Medals

Since the early nineteenth century, medals have been awarded to those who have taken part in the countless campaigns that have involved British forces overseas. Where there may have been numerous actions within a campaign, individual clasps have been awarded which are attached to the ribbon of the campaign medal. For example, during the early part of the twentieth century there were numerous actions in the North of India and a total of twelve clasps were awarded for the Indian General Service Medal. There are very many British campaign medals but the reader will only encounter the General Service Medal in the chapters that follow and a brief description follows.

General Service Medal   To commemorate other 'minor' wars following the end of the First World War, a General Service Medal was instituted in 1923 and, by the time it was replaced in 1962, sixteen clasps had been authorised. Some will be covered in the stories that follow. The medal has been issued with three different obverse effigies and several different legends. The crowned head of the Sovereign appears on the obverse. On the reverse is the standing winged figure of Victory holding a trident and placing a wreath on the emblems of the two services. The ornamental suspender and the medal hangs fron a purple ribbon with a central green stripe. The recipient's name is impressed on the edge. Recipients of a Mention in Despatches wear a bronze oak leaf emblem on the ribbon.

CHAPTER TWO

Air-Drop Ace – Lew Cody

Just after midday on 2 September 1939, Sergeant Alfred 'Lew' Cody climbed into the observer's seat of his 40 Squadron Fairey Battle at Abingdon. As his pilot, Flight Lieutenant W. G. Moseby, started the Merlin engine, fifteen other Battles burst into life. Together with the other nine squadrons of the Advanced Air Striking Force, 40 Squadron was heading for a landing ground in Northern France. However, Lew Cody and his crew would be late arrivals. Half-way across the Channel their aircraft suffered an engine failure and Moseby ditched alongside the Cross Channel Ferry.

Five-and-half-years later, on the last day of the European war, and in the meantime having re-trained as a pilot, Flight Lieutenant Lew Cody DFC, AFC, DFM brought home from captivity in Germany thirty-five recently liberated prisoners of war. Between these two significant flights, Lew Cody remained on continuous operations; few can have had a more adventurous or action-packed war.

London-born Cody had joined the Royal Air Force in November, 1938, to train as an air observer, having previously served for a few months with the RNVR. On completion of his flying training and the award of his brevet, he was posted to 40 Squadron, based at Abingdon, and equipped with the Fairey Battle. The Battle had replaced the last of the biplane light bombers in the RAF inventory and its cruising speed of 210 knots was considered to be quite good when it first entered service in 1937. A mere two years later it would prove to

The medals awarded to 'Lew' Cody. Distinguished Flying Cross, Air Force Cross, Distinguished Flying Medal, 1939-45 Star, Aircrew Europe Star (France and Germany Clasp), Africa Star (North Africa 1942-43 Clasp), Italy Star, War Medal with Mention in Despatch emblem.

be wholly inadequate. However, as the ten squadrons were mobilised at the end of August and prepared to leave for France, Lew Cody and his colleagues were in a confident mood.

After his involuntary ditching, Cody arrived in France four days after the Squadron. The 'airfield' at Betheniville could best be described as basic and it was a few days before the the first operational sorties were flown. Throughout September the Squadron was engaged in flying reconnaissance sorties which included short-range penetrations into German airspace. On 26 September, 1939, Cody flew the first of his very many war sorties when he took off on a reconnaissance of the Saarbrücken and Neunkirchen areas in Battle K 9361, piloted by the Squadron Commander, Wing Commander 'Cecky' Barlow. Within a few days other Battle squadrons had suffered heavy casualties at the hands of the Me 109s and such unescorted recce sorties were abandoned.

After two frustrating months of training and waiting on two hour's standby, it was decided to re-equip 40 Squadron with the Blenheim and on 1 December, the Squadron flew back to Wyton. The first of the Blenheim IVs began to arrive at the Huntingdonshire airfield a few days later.

The early part of 1940 was taken up with training and preparations to move overseas. Speculation was rife since a number of the Squadron's aircraft had recently been prepared for transfer to the Finnish Air Force, but in the event the Squadron was to remain at Wyton. With the German attack in the west on 10 May, 1940, the Squadron was finally to go to war in earnest. It was to be a fierce and tragic baptism as four aircraft failed to return from the first sortie.

Five days later, on 15 May, the Squadron Commander led three aircraft on a bombing raid to Dinant. Flying as No 3 was Sergeant Jim Higgins in P 4909 with Lew Cody as observer. As the formation dropped their bombs they were attacked by Me 109s and the Blenheims dived for the ground. Taking advantage of the terrain, Higgins flew at tree-top height with his gunner returning the enemy fire. Eventually they escaped and returned to Wyton to discover that they were the only survivors. The popular Wing Commander Barlow was among those killed.

Within eight days the Squadron lost a second CO when Wing Commander J. G. Llewellyn failed to return from a sortie in support of the beleaguered British Expeditionary Force. Cody was flying on the same sortie to bomb mechanised forces near Boulogne. Over the next seven days, which led up to the evacuation from Dunkirk, Cody and his pilot Higgins were to fly every day, attacking enemy columns, bridges and choke-points on roads. With mounting

Blenheim IV – R 3612 – of 40 Squadron (A Thomas)

Lew Cody (left) with his pilot 'Big Jim' Higgins at RAF Wyton February 1940. (R Higgins)

losses, fighter escorts were provided whenever possible and this gave some respite to the Squadron.

Early June saw the intensity of operations continue as desperate attempts were made to stem the German advances. Cody and his crew did not fly on 6 June as twelve aircraft took off to bomb Abbeville. Three hours later he watched as just seven returned. Among those lost was the acting CO. Four sorties later, on 14 June, Cody and his crew were one of nine to attack bridges near Ivry. Three aircraft failed to return, including the acting CO of eight days. With fourteen operational sorties in four weeks, Cody and his crew found themselves as one of the most experienced and longest serving crews on the Squadron; a graphic indication of the tragic loss rate in the 2 Group Blenheim squadrons.

With the fall of France, 40 Squadron directed its attacks against enemy airfields in France and the Low Countries in an effort to disrupt the *Luftwaffe's* attacks on England. In addition, the Squadron carried out numerous photographic reconnaissance missions. With fighters in such short supply, many of the recce sorties were unescorted and, as a matter of routine, they were abandoned if there was insufficient cloud cover. During June and July Cody bombed

Blenhein IVs of 40 Squadron set off on a raid. (MOD)

the airfields at Evere, Amiens, Waalhaven, and Eelde. Losses continued, including a fifth CO in eight weeks, and by mid-July just five crews of the original eighteen remained.

As the intensity of fighting in the Battle of Britain increased, attacks against airfields became a priority. On 15 August, Cody attacked Chartres airfield but two crews failed to return. A week later it was the airfield at St Brieuc and on the 25th three crews attacked the airfield at Le Treport but only Cody and his crew returned.

With the increasing likelihood of a German seaborne invasion, 40 Squadron switched attacks in early September to the Channel ports where the invasion fleet was gathering. On 8 September, Cody and his pilot Jim Higgins flew together for their twenty-seventh consecutive sortie as they bombed the barges in Ostend harbour. After three dummy runs over the target, Cody finally released the bombs, much to his pilot's relief as he was due to be rested after this sortie.

Cody was to fly a further six sorties against the Channel ports during September. On 8 October, with his Flight Commander, Squadron Leader E. J. Little, at the controls of Blenheim 'O', he bombed the docks at Boulogne on his thirty-fifth and final operational sortie. At the time of his posting, Cody was one of a very few survivors of those aircrew who had deployed to France a year earlier.

Shortly after leaving 40 Squadron, it was announced that Sergeant A.Cody had been awarded the Distinguished Flying Medal. The citation commented on his accuracy and reliability as a navigator who '*inspires the remainder of the formation with great confidence. He has at all times shown great courage and determination and remains calm in the face of the enemy, setting an excellent example to the rest of the squadron.*' The *London Gazette* also announced the award of the Distinguished Flying Cross to his recent pilot Jim Higgins.

After six months as an instructor at the Blenheim OTU at Upwood, during which time he was 'Mentioned in Despatches', Cody decided that training to be a pilot would be more exciting than continuing with his instructional duties. Within a few months he was back at Upwood, but this time on a Blenheim pilot's conversion course. Having finished his training with 17 OTU he was posted to 139 Squadron at nearby Oulton where he was commissioned as a Pilot Officer.

Lew Cody's wartime flying career was littered with 'incidents' and his operational career as a pilot ran true to form. On 13 October he was at the controls of Blenheim IV (Z 7297) flying the first sortie of his second tour when his aircraft was badly damaged by intense *flak* as he bombed the ship lift at Arques from 13,000 feet. With damaged controls and no hydraulics he returned to make a belly landing on the airfield at Horsham St Faith. After two 'shipping beat' sorties over the North Sea, he converted to the Hudson aircraft and, soon after, joined a pool of pilots who left for the Middle East to reinforce the build-up of the multi-engined squadrons in the theatre.

In July,1942, Cody joined the newly formed Hudson Flight on 216 Squadron, a transport squadron that had seen long and distinguished service in the Middle East equipped initially with the Valentia and then the Bombay. The Hudson Flight operated from Khanka before moving to Cairo West airfield. The gun turret had been removed and the aircraft converted for troop carrying, and the Flight was ready to start operating in August.

Over the next twelve months Cody flew countless re-supply and casualty evacuation sorties in support of the 8th Army operating into the many forward Landing Grounds. On numerous occasions he landed just hours after the withdrawal of German forces and after hasty mine-clearing operations had been completed. In addition, the Hudsons established routine weekly runs to Lydda, Habbaniya, Cyprus and to the Sudan. Regular flights to Kufra Oasis in support of the Long Range Desert Group were started and Cody was to fly in support of the Special Forces on numerous occasions.

On the night of 23/24 October, Cody was at the controls of Hudson EW 881, the second of four aircraft to take off on a diversion operation in support of

Hudson VI-EW 970 – of 216 Squadron at a Desert Advance Landing Ground with a captured Ju 87 'Stuka' in RAF markings. (A Thomas)

General Montgomery's breakout from El Alamein. The aircraft took off at five minute intervals for the enemy-held Fuka airfield. Each aircraft carried eight self-destroying dummy 'parachute troops' which were dropped with the object of diverting attention from the main battle area and causing disruption among the German and Italian troops in the area. Over a period of thirty minutes each aircraft released flares and dropped their 'parachutists' between Fuka airfield and its nearby satellite. The close attention of light flak confirmed that the enemy was well aware of the 'airborne landing'. All aircraft returned safely to be congratulated by the AOC on having completed efficiently an important operation.

As the Allied Armies advanced rapidly through Mersa Matruh towards Tobruk, in mid-November it was necessary to establish a fighter wing well behind enemy lines and Cody flew in to LG 125 with supplies for the secret fighter unit. The routine for the rest of the year and the early part of 1943 was to re-supply the rapidly advancing armies and the airfields at Castel Benito, Benina and Marble Arch were soon to become regular stopping places. During February and March detachments of Hudsons operated from these forward Landing Grounds in support of the Army who were preparing to attack the enemy stronghold of the Mareth Line.

With final victory in North Africa, there was a continuous and demanding requirement for air transport over a huge area which now included routes to Casablanca, Algiers and Gibraltar. In addition, routes were established to Karachi in the east and to Khartoum and Takoradi in the south and west. This massive requirement coincided with the arrival of Dakota aircraft, and on 6 May, Lew Cody flew his first sortie in FD 832 taking supplies to Monastir and returning with a load of casualties to Cairo West.

By mid-July Cody had flown over 700 hours in his year with 216 Squadron and was due for a rest. He was posted to 4 Middle East Training School at Ramat David to fly Dakota aircraft. The primary task of the School was to train parachutists of the British, French and Greek parachute battalions. In mid-September Cody's rest came to an abrupt end. He was one of a few pilots who had gained considerable experience in the parachute dropping role and his skills were needed for operations being planned in the Greek Islands.

With the Allies having established a firm foothold in Italy, it was decided to open a second front with the capture of the main Greek Islands in the Eastern Aegean Sea. The priority was to capture the island of Rhodes and to establish an airfield. However, before the attack could be mounted the German garrison was reinforced and it was decided to avoid Rhodes and capture instead the islands of Cos, Leros and Samos. The key was the capture of Cos which would effectively isolate the enemy garrison on Rhodes. Cos was to be taken by a combined assault of all three arms which included an airborne landing to capture the airfield at Antimachia which would then be used by the Dakotas to fly in reinforcements and supplies.

For this operation Cody returned to 216 Squadron. On 14 September, an Advanced Air Headquarters had been established at Nicosia in Cyprus for Operation Microbe and six Dakotas flew into the airfield during the day in preparation for operations later that night. With men of A Company of the 11th Battalion the Parachute Regiment on board, the six aircraft took off at two-minute intervals from 2200 hours, Cody taking off second, flying FD 778. The weather was fine and clear and there was a full moon. The aircraft flew along the southern coast of Turkey and remained below 3,000 feet in order to be sheltered by the Turkish hills and below the cover of the German radar on Rhodes. As the aircraft reached the dropping zone just outside the main town, each fired a red Very cartridge which was answered by a green. With the landing 'T' illuminated, each of the six Dakotas dropped thirty troops and their equipment before setting a direct course for base, reached after a six-hour flight. The

Hudsons embark troops at a desert airfield (Author's collection)

operation had been a complete success.

Over the next few days the Dakotas of 216 Squadron made numerous landings on the airfield at Cos delivering more troops and supplies for the fighter squadrons which had deployed to provide air cover for the troops. The German response to the invasion was immediate and a vigorous air campaign was activated to regain the island. With local air superiority, the Germans rapidly gained the initiative and the garrison on Cos prepared to hold the island unaided. As the position of the Allied forces became untenable, Cody and his colleagues flew five Dakotas at night into the badly cratered airfield with urgent supplies, returning with casualties. After a mere three weeks the island of Cos was back in German hands.

The next island to be regained by the enemy was Leros a few miles north of Cos. Throughout the second half of October the Dakota crews made great efforts to maintain the garrison. Flying on moonless nights and having approached the islands at very low level, the aircraft dropped supplies without lights or signals from the dropping zone and facing light flak.

Finally, on 30 and 31 October, Cody flew two sorties of almost nine hours each as he dropped men of the Greek Sacred Squadron on Samos, the last island in Allied hands. On both nights five Dakotas carrying 100 troops set off from Cairo West at fifteen-minute intervals. Both nights were moonless and the narrow and short dropping zone was situated in a steep valley, making it the most difficult parachute drop of the campaign. However, the ground lights were good and all the men were dropped successfully. A few days later the island had to be evacuated.

In his summary of the Aegean operations, the official RAF historian commented, 'In this unhappy story the gallantry of the Dakota crews of No 216 Squadron must not be forgotten. The outstanding achievement of the squadron was the dropping of the men of the Greek Sacred Squadron on to the island of Samos.' As one of the senior and most experienced of the 216 Squadron pilots, Cody had played a major role in this unique and little known air supply operation.

After a further two months flying transport support operations throughout the Mediterranean region, Cody returned to England in February, 1944, and shortly afterwards it was announced that he had been awarded the Distinguished Flying Cross for '*displaying the greatest determination and unshakeable courage*' during his twelve months in the Middle East, during which time he had flown over 700 hours and participated in some of the most hazardous transport operations in that theatre of war.

During early 1944 many experienced Dakota aircrew were brought back to the United Kingdom from overseas to create the backbone of the rapidly expanding Dakota force being formed in 46 Group. In March Cody was posted to 233 Squadron at Blakehill Farm, one of three newly constructed airfields built near Swindon in preparation for Operation Overlord, the re-occupation of North West Europe. Teaming up with two very experienced aircrew, navigator Alan Hollingsworth and wireless operator G Goodfellow, the Cody crew would spend almost eighteen months together and would fly some of the most demanding operations undertaken by the Squadron.

The period leading up to D-Day was devoted to intensive training which included glider towing, parachute dropping and huge exercises involving large formations of transport aircraft on long-range sorties for mass parachute drops of men and equipment of the 6th Airborne Division. Some of these training flights were conducted at night with 233 Squadron generating as many as twenty-two aircraft for each exercise. On 24 April, a Corps Exercise (Operation Mush) took place as a dress rehearsal for the air-drop phase of the Invasion. During this build-up period, most crews also flew a 'Nickelling' mission to drop propaganda leaflets over Northern France and these sorties afforded an excellent opportunity to practise the navigation procedures and use the aids over the terrain that would soon be the scene of the greatest invasion in history. On 1 June, Cody's Squadron was brought to a state of immediate readiness for Operation Tonga, the air-drop phase of Overlord.

Following the final briefing on the evening of 5 June, the crews of 362 transport aircraft drawn from fifteen RAF squadrons boarded their aircraft at eight airfields in the south of England. Cody and his crew started up their Dakota III KG 448 loaded with men of the 3rd Parachute Brigade and their containers.

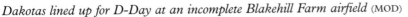

Dakotas lined up for D-Day at an incomplete Blakehill Farm airfield (MOD)

Six 233 Squadron aircraft towing gliders took off first at 2250 hours and were quickly followed by the twenty-four Dakotas carrying the paratroopers. The aircraft were routed over Littlehampton to a point off the French coast immediately north of Merville before turning for the drop zone. For the transit phase the navigators used the GEE navigation aid and homed to the drop zones using EUREKA beacons which had been positioned by the pathfinders of 22 Independent Parachute Company who had been dropped just before the main body.

Cody and his crew were assigned to Drop Zone 'K' near Toufreville, the most southerly of the drop zones used. Crossing the French coast at 45 minutes past midnight on 6 June, Cody turned his Dakota on to the final run. Using the specially prepared target map, and homing onto the EUREKA beacon, the aircraft settled at 800 feet and, five minutes later, the troops were successfully dropped with their containers ready to attack the major enemy gun battery at Merville and to demolish bridges inland from the main invasion beaches. Two hours later Cody landed back at base but two crews from 233 Squadron failed to return. In this massive operation no less than 95.8% of the para-drop aircraft dropped their troops successfully.

Twenty-four hours later Cody took off again in KG 448 on Operation Rob Roy a re-supply mission to the 6th Airborne Division east of the Rive Orne and using Drop Zone 'N' east of Ranville. Twenty-one Dakotas took off with 371 panniers containing food, ammunition, petrol and radio sets. Crossing the French coast, the aircraft were engaged by intense light flak, thought to be from friendly vessels which had just been attacked by enemy aircraft, and the leader and his No 2 were hit and seen to go down in flames. Others were damaged, but the remainder dropped their supplies on target.

Ten days after the invasion 233 Squadron were the first transport squadron to land in France and the first to bring out casualties. Cody took supplies to Airfield B 2 and brought out twenty-five wounded from the hastily constructed pierced-steel-planking landing strip built near Bayeux. To assist with the 'casevac' task, each aircraft carried an Air Ambulance Orderly, probably the first time that women had flown into the combat zone as members of aircrew. All these gallant ladies were volunteers. For the next two months Cody and his crew flew many re-supply sorties to the Advanced Landing Grounds in France, returning with the wounded. Towards the end of August the Squadron was heavily committed to flying food into the airfield at Orleans/Bricy for the Relief of Paris and Cody flew three sorties as the Squadron delivered 230 tons of food.

Cody's third major airdrop operation was the ill-fated Operation Market at Arnhem. On the second day of the operation, 18 September, he took off in KG 448 with a Horsa glider in tow but the tow parted over East Anglia and both the Dakota and the glider landed safely at Andrews Field near Ipswich.

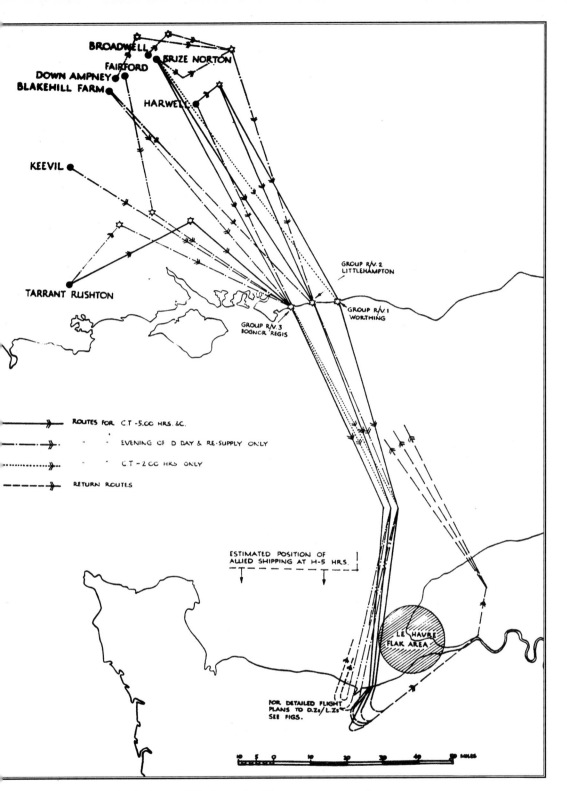

The route map for the D-Day airlift Operation Neptune *was complex*

The following day Cody tried again as the only Dakota/glider combination and he joined behind a stream of Stirlings and successfully released his glider over the drop zone. The German ground defences had been reinforced considerably and the barrage of flak that greeted the glider dropping force was intense. Cody's aircraft was damaged in the port wing and the fuselage and it spent a week being repaired. As a result, he and his crew did not fly to Arnhem on the following day, when the Squadron lost four aircraft.

On 21 September, 233 Squadron dropped supplies to the now desperate and beleaguered First Airborne Division. Two hundred and forty panniers were dropped on or near the Drop Zone. The enemy opposition was even greater than on previous sorties and included attacks by Focke Wulf 190s. Of the eighteen aircraft despatched by the Squadron, three failed to return. Most aircraft were damaged and after a five-hour flight leading the second formation, Cody landed his Dakota (FZ 681) back at Blakehill Farm. The high spirits and banter which normally accompanied a completed mission were absent from the final day of Operation Market.

For the remainder of 1944, Cody flew many re-supply and casevac sorties in support of the advancing armies with Brussels a frequent destination. By early 1945, sorties were being flown to the forward Allied airfields being established in Holland. On 9 January, Cody took off from Eindhoven in his faithful KG 448 and on the climb out in poor visibility his aircraft collided with another Dakota and most of the port outer wing was lost. At 5 foot 5 inches and with the build of a flyweight boxer, Cody could only control the aircraft by standing up and getting his co-pilot to place both feet on the starboard rudder pedal. In this precarious position he completed an immaculate emergency landing.

At the end of February, it was announced that Flight Lieutenant A Cody DFC, DFM had been awarded the Air Force Cross. The citation stated: '*This officer has taken part in the airborne operations and in every case has shown great determination and endurance by carrying out his tasks in an exemplary manner. He is second in command of his Flight and the example he has set for skill, keenness, courage and determination has been an inspiration to all the other pilots of the Squadron.*' The citation concluded by making specific mention of his great skill in landing his damaged aircraft after the mid-air collision. Since much of his transport flying was conducted 'in the face of the enemy' and against intense enemy fire, many would think that Cody should have received the operational award of a Bar to his DFC.

After two months of intensive re-supply sorties, often in marginal weather, Lew Cody embarked on his final major airborne operation. With the Allied Armies pressing towards Germany, it was decided to establish a bridgehead on the east bank of the River Rhine north of the town of Wesel. To achieve surprise, Operation Varsity was to be a 'One Lift' operation, the complete force from the

6th British Airborne Division and the 17th US Airborne Division being put down on D-Day. The lifting of the British force was shared between the RAF and the IX US Transport Command with the seventeen RAF squadrons allotted the glider-towing task and all operating from airfields in East Anglia. This huge air armada called for 683 transport aircraft and 440 gliders. Additionally, countless bombers, ground attack and fighter aircraft flew in support in order to achieve the essential air superiority.

Cody and his colleagues positioned twenty-four Dakotas at Birch airfield in Essex and at dawn on the morning of 24 March, each with a Horsa glider in tow, they took off with 357 troops of the Oxfordshire and Buckinghamshire Light Infantry. There was very little enemy opposition and the gliders were released successfully. Flying his now repaired KG 448, Cody had his most uneventful sortie on an airborne operation.

By early May, 1945, the war in Europe was almost over but the tasks placed on the transport squadrons did not diminish. The rapid advance of the Armies across North Germany called for maximum effort from the re-supply Dakotas and Cody found himself flying daily supplies of petrol into the forward airfields at Celle, Rheine and Luneburg. On the last day of the war Cody and his long-standing crew of Hollingsworth and Goodfellow took off for a routine sortie to Brussels. On arrival they were immediately despatched to Kastrup airfield near Copenhagen to take reinforcements and supplies to the Danish Resistance who were still engaging the remnants of the *SS*. In Dakota FZ 688, Cody was the first Allied pilot to land at Kastrup, where he was met by a number of high-ranking German officers who were anxious to surrender to the British before the Danish Resistance captured them. On the return flight over Schleswig Holstein, the aircraft came under fire from pockets of resistance on the ground

RAF Dakotas approach the drop zone for Operation Varsity, the Rhine Crossing. (MOD)

so Cody hedge-hopped back to Allied lines. Thirty-five British prisoners of war were picked up at Luneberg and returned that evening to the reception airfield at Wing in Buckinghamshire. After a long and eventful day Lew Cody's action-filled war was over.

How does one summarise Lew Cody's war effort? With difficulty. However, there can be few who spent so long on operational flying and who made such a significant personal contribution. To complete a full tour with a 2 Group Blenheim Squadron during the period of crippling losses in 1940 required courage, and perhaps an element of luck. His reaction was typical of such a pugnacious and spirited man; he volunteered to be a pilot. He went on to fly countless hours in support of the Armies in North Africa and in support of the Special Forces, including spectacular and hazardous night parachute drops in the abortive Aegean operations. Finally, he played a major part in the three great airborne operations of the Second World War, flying in the first wave on D-Day, three sorties over Arnhem and then taking a glider on the Rhine crossing. Some record.

Lew Cody remained in the RAF after the war. He served at the Headquarters of Transport Command and in movements control at the Ministry of Defence during the Berlin Airlift. He attended the Central Flying School in 1950 prior to a tour at 5 FTS in Rhodesia as a flying instructor. Returning to England in 1953, he joined 1 FTS at Moreton-in-Marsh where he instructed on Harvards. In 1955 he returned to transport flying duties with 31 Squadron flying Ansons at Hendon. Shortly after his arrival, the Squadron was re-named the Metropolitan Communications Squadron.. After a three-year period as a flying instructor training the embryo German Air Force at Memmingen, he trained in 1961 as a photographic interpreter and retired from the Royal Air Force four years later.

Instructors of 1 FTS at Moreton-in-Marsh, Spring 1954. Lew Cody is seated second from right.
(Gerry Tyack)

CHAPTER THREE

Coastal Patrol Pilot – Nelson Webb

On the day following the outbreak of the Second World War, Nelson Webb strapped himself into the pilot's seat of his Avro Anson K 8829 and took off from St Eval in Cornwall on the first of his many coastal patrol sorties. Although one of the least glamorous roles of the Royal Air Force, it was, nevertheless, a vital and arduous one. Surrounded by the sea, Britain relied on secure sea lines of communication and the monotonous and unspectacular work of reconnaissance and convoy protection was absolutely crucial if the country was to survive. Webb and his colleagues on 217 Squadron would play a major role in maintaining the vigil that would ensure ultimate victory.

Nelson Henry Webb was born and educated in Bradford-on-Avon in Wiltshire. Having decided to join the Royal Air Force as an aircraft apprentice he reported to Halton in September, 1932, and elected for training in the wireless trade. Within a week he had moved to Cranwell to join the Electrical and Wireless School where he would spend three years before graduating as a wireless mechanic.

After a brief spell with 9 Squadron, he was posted to Abingdon to join 214 (B) Squadron equipped with the Virginia bomber. Almost immediately he

Nelson Webb's medals. Distinguished Flying Medal, 1939-45 Star, Altlantic Star, War Medal with Mention in Despatch

Pilot Officer Nelson Webb

Nelson Webb (centre) *with two colleagues and 70 Squadron Valentia – Iraq 1937* (Mrs E Godfrey)

volunteered as an air gunner and started to draw 'crew pay', being officially re-mustered as a wireless operator mechanic/air gunner. After eighteen months with 214 Squadron he embarked for Iraq just two weeks before the birth of his only daughter.

Once in Iraq he joined 70 Squadron, equipped with Valentia transport aircraft flying first from Hinaidi and then Habbaniya. The aircraft did sterling work in the desert areas and amassed an impressive total of flying hours. Webb took every opportunity to fly and, with almost 200 hours in his log book, he was selected for training as an airman pilot in late 1937. After twelve months with 70 Squadron he returned to England to start pilot training.

Two days after reporting to 11 EFTS at Perth he took off with his instructor in a Tiger Moth (G-ADON) for his first training flight. After just eight hours his instructor, Flight Lieutenant Rowe, sent him on his first solo flight. With a further sixty hours in his log-book, he completed his initial training at Perth and was assessed as 'Above Average' and sent in June, 1938, to 9 FTS at Hullavington for multi-engine training. Whilst there, he was able to spend the next few months just a few miles from his family in nearby Bradford-on-Avon.

With the clouds of war gathering, the pace of training was fast. He was awarded his 'wings' at the end of September and was promoted to Sergeant.

Remaining at Hullavington he completed his advanced training, which concentrated on photography, reconnaissance, bombing and gunnery, with an above average assessment as an NCO and the rarely awarded 'Distinguished Pass' as a pilot. After completing the Navigation and Reconnaissance Course at the School of General Reconnaissance at Thorney Island, he was posted to 217 (Exeter) Squadron based at St Eval, arriving in May, 1939.

At the outbreak of war the Coastal Command force was small and it was equipped, in the main, with obsolescent aircraft. All but one of the eleven general reconnaissance squadrons were equipped with the Anson. Although highly reliable, the Anson was slow and had a limited radius of action and a small bomb load. The 100 lb anti-submarine bombs proved to be very ineffective, even with a direct hit, and self-defence armament consisted of one fixed forward-firing .303 machine gun and another mounted in a turret. With such limited operational capabilities, the aircraft was fit only for general reconnaissance and convoy protection.

There was to be no 'Phoney War' for the crews of the Coastal Command squadrons. From the outbreak of war there was a real threat to British shipping, not only from German surface warships, but also from submarines and mines. There were continuous patrols to be flown over the Western Approaches with convoys to be escorted, fishing fleets to protect and general reconnaissance for enemy mines and patrolling aircraft. With a small force spread widely around the coasts of Britain, allied to a slow build-up of trained crews, the Anson squadrons had to operate from the very beginning at intensive rates. With ever-worsening weather as winter approached, and the monotony of many hours' patrolling, the flying was arduous and difficult, with little excitement to stimulate the crews, but it was crucial.

In this early phase of coastal operations the Anson carried two pilots, a wireless operator and a gunner. Both pilots had been trained as air navigators and they flew alternate sorties as pilot and as navigator, a procedure that continued well into 1940.

From the outset Webb displayed great enthusiasm and flew at every opportunity, so it was no surprise when his name appeared in an early list of wartime honours. After he had completed thirty-three convoy patrols, the *London Gazette* of 20 February, 1940, announced that he had been awarded a Mention

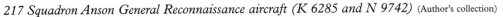

217 Squadron Anson General Reconnaissance aircraft (K 6285 and N 9742) (Author's collection)

in Despatches for *'gallantry and devotion to duty in the execution of air operations'*.

Following the fall of France in the Spring of 1940, the Battle of Britain and the possibility of a German invasion occupied most people's minds, but there was another and equally dangerous aspect of the German assault on Britain – the economic blockade prosecuted by an ever-growing and capable U-boat fleet. Throughout this period Webb and his Coastal Command colleagues flew many convoy escort sorties and the occasional anti-submarine patrol in an attempt to safeguard the sea lanes to the south west of England.

By the beginning of June the evacuation from Dunkirk was nearing completion and enemy U-boats had been active in trying to disrupt the operation, particularly at the western end of the English Channel. At 1530 hours on 4 June Webb and his crew took off in Anson N 9888 to rendezvous with Convoy HCF 32. Flying at 1,000 feet and in three miles visibility, Webb intercepted the convoy and he set up his patrol, remaining on station for the next two hours. Just before 1800 hours another Anson arrived to take over the escort duties and Webb set heading for base. Shortly afterwards a surfaced U-Boat was sighted on a northerly course forty miles south-west of Falmouth and Webb immediately set up an attack. Taken by surprise, the U-boat crash dived just as two 100 lb anti-submarine bombs were released. One hit and one near miss were estimated by the Anson crew. Some four minutes after the attack a large quantity of bubbles rose to the surface but the crew were unable to assess the damge.

Webb had attacked *U-101 (Kapitänleutnant* Fritz Frauenheim) whose log shows that the submarine had just surfaced when the Anson attacked. The poor visibility and low sun had prevented the aircraft being seen until it was 3,000 yards away. Although the bombs landed close to the submarine, there was no significant damage. Frauenheim, who went on to earn the Knight's Cross, survived the war.

By mid-June the shortage of pilots led to the introduction of a full-time navigator to replace the second pilot and Webb acted as first pilot and captain throughout the remainder of his time on 217 Squadron. He had a reputation as an aggressive pilot who sought out the enemy. This characteristic was once again strongly in evidence on 11 July when he was scrambled at 0900 hours to search for an enemy aircraft located by a Direction Finding (DF) bearing twenty miles south-east of Start Point. Arriving in mid-Channel forty minutes later he sighted an enemy seaplane with the letter markings D-AGIO on the fuselage and upper main plane. The aircraft was a He 59 with Red Cross markings and it was heading for the recently occupied island of Guernsey.

Over the previous few weeks the He 59 had been appearing more frequently round the British coast and in the vicinity of coastal convoys and it was suspected that these 'Red Cross' aircraft were being used for reconnaissance and convoy spotting. Following the interception of two of these aircraft by

The He 59 shot down by Webb on 11 July 1940 showing the crew boarding dinghy. (Mrs E Godfrey)

Hurricanes in early July, scrutiny of their log books highlighted entries relating to reconnaissance duties. Accordingly, the Air Ministry issued a warning that these 'ambulance seaplanes' could not be given immunity and would be shot down 'if they are being employed for purposes which H.M. Governmeat cannot regard as being consistent with the privileges generally accorded to the Red Cross.'

With this recent policy in mind, Webb gave chase and he opened fire with the front gun at 500 yards and the enemy aircraft immediately slowed up on being hit and turned to land on the sea. Webb banked the Anson to port to allow the gunner to open fire. With a damaged wing and port float, the aircraft crash landed on the sea and the three-man crew were seen boarding a dinghy. The Anson remained circling overhead as the enemy aircraft finally heeled over and sank, but shortly afterwards Webb was forced to return to base with engine trouble. Before other aircraft arrived on the scene, the crew from *Seenotflugkommando 1* were rescued by a German launch.

It is interesting to note that Webb shot this enemy aircraft down 24 hours after the start of the qualifying period for the 'Battle of Britain' Clasp for the 1939–45 Star, but he was not entitled since he did not belong to a Fighter

The He 59 rolls over and sinks. (Mrs E Godfrey)

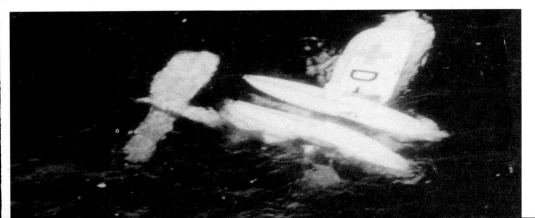

Squadron! This was one of the many strange anomolies in the award of medals for service in the Second World War.

Three weeks later Webb's fighting qualities were once more in evidence. Flying Anson N 9888 again, he took off at 1230 hours to escort Convoy SA 12. As he neared the convoy 100 miles to the south-west of Land's End he sighted a surfaced U-boat and closed in to attack. The submarine dived and Webb aimed his bombs ahead of the wake with little expectation of causing any serious damage with the inadequate 100 lb bombs. Nevertheless, he pressed home his attack. He resumed his escort duties and was on the point of returning to St Eval when he sighted a fully surfaced U-boat. Having used his only bombs, he immediately attacked with his single forward-firing machine gun from 300 feet. The submarine crashed dived, the stern lifting well clear of the water.

On both occasions Webb had attacked *U 57* whose Captain, *Oberleutenant zur See* Erich Topp, would survive the war as one of the U-boat 'Aces' with the Knight's Cross with Oak Leaves and Swords. Topp reported no damage from either attack but admitted that he had been surprised by the second attack and his boat had been straddled by machine-gun fire. After the boat had dived a noise was heard that caused Topp mistakenly to believe that a bomb had hit the sides but failed to explode. On the formation of the post-war Federal German Navy Topp rejoined and eventually retired as an Admiral.

Shortly after this most gallant attack with his puny weapons, and not knowing if he would face return fire, it was announced that Flight Sergeant N Webb had been awarded the Distinguished Flying Medal. The recommendation for this award drew attention to his continuous devotion to duty and keenness and concluded : '*The determined spirit of this pilot to carry out his tasks regardless of personal safety is worthy of reward.*' Shortly afterwards he was commissioned as a Pilot Officer.

In September the Ansons adopted a more aggressive posture. At midnight on the 23rd nine aircraft, led by the Squadron Commander, took off at two-minute intervals to bomb shipping in Brest Harbour. Webb and his crew were second to take off and the Squadron aircraft bombed from heights varying between 4,000 and 10,000 feet. With half cloud cover and intense flak, results could not be observed. Landing after a four-hour flight, this was to be Webb's 108th and final operational Anson sortie. A few days later he started a training course on the Beaufort I aircraft.

The Beaufort was designed to meet an Air Ministry requirement for an Anson replacement to be used primarily as a torpedo bomber, although the aircraft was employed in the early days mainly as a light bomber. The aircraft had a much better performance than the Anson, with a greater range and, most important, a much better bomb-load. After some initial teething troubles with the Taurus engines, the aircraft entered service in the middle of 1940, 217

Beaufort I of 217 Squadron at St Eval. (MOD)

Squadron being one of the first Squadrons to replace its 'Faithful Annies'.

Nelson Webb was one of the first of 217 Squadron's pilots to convert to the Beaufort and by the end of November, 1940, the Squadron had sufficient aircraft and crews to begin operations. Almost all the early Beaufort raids were bombing and mining operations against the Atlantic coastal ports of north-west France where elements of the formidable surface and submarine fleets of the German Navy were based for their forays into the Atlantic. For these early raids the aircraft carried either the 250 lb bomb or the 1,600 lb Time Impact Mines known as the TIM bomb. The latter was a cylinder full of high explosive with a small parachute to provide some stabilisation during the bomb's fall. They had to be dropped from 1,000 feet with a delay fuse which allowed the aircraft to fly clear of the impact area before the bomb detonated. The bomb had poor ballistics, making aiming difficult, and it could best be described as an area blast weapon, albeit a powerful one. A slightly different version was used against shipping with much success. Dropped from low level in the mouth of harbours and estuaries and along known shipping lanes, it rested on the sea bed until activated magnetically by ships passing overhead. Such minelaying operations carried the codename 'Gardening'.

On 1 December, Webb and his crew of Sergeants C. Tiplady, P. Milligan and W. Plant took off for their first operational Beaufort sortie in L 4474 as part of a six-aircraft attack against Brest. This was followed over the next two weeks by six similar attacks against the Atlantic ports. On the 7th and 12th Brest was attacked again and on the 15th it was the turn of Lorient where TIMs were dropped on the docks.

The most significant of the early raids was mounted on 17 December when six aircraft took off to bomb installations at Bordeaux, a target well out of the range of the old Ansons. Intelligence had indicated a build-up of submarines in the port area. The moon was bright, making target identification straight-forward although the earlier aircraft had alerted the flak batteries and one aircraft was seen to go down in flames. Webb pressed home his attack from low level and saw his bombs bursting in the target area. Turning for the coast, Webb flew over the airfield at Merignac where a number of four-engined aircraft were lined up. He attacked these with his forward-firing guns, seeing hits on at least two of them. As the Beaufort swept over the airfield his gunner fired into the line up of aircraft (almost certainly FW 200 Condors) registering further hits. Two hours later they arrived back at St Eval elated with their success. Returning from this sortie, Nelson Webb was interviewed by the BBC and the transcript still exists. He described the heavy flak as 'spiralling flaming onions and the tracers rising from all directions'.

Two nights later, on the 20th, Nelson Webb took off at 0325 hours in L 4474 loaded with a TIM to attack the military port facilities at Lorient. It was his 115th operational sortie. After take off nothing further was heard from his aircraft.

Nelson Webb is commem
on the war memorial in h
town of Bradford-on-
Wiltshire. (Author)

On this raid three of the five aircraft failed to locate the target due to bad weather and returned early. A further aircraft dropped its TIM successfully. It transpired later that Nelson Webb had reached the target despite the poor weather that had forced the return of other aircraft. He was heard by the local French population searching for the target when he was engaged by the flak batteries. Shortly afterwards the aircraft crashed at Lanester near Lorient with the loss of all four crew members.

At daybreak the following morning many visitors paid homage at the crash site and, a few days later, crowds of people with flowers followed the four airmen to their final resting place in Lanester Cemetery where they were buried with full military honours.

Today Nelson Webb is commemorated in his home town of Bradford-on-Avon and remembered as the brave and determined young man who knew no fear. He lies in a foreign field alongside his gallant crew where the staff of the Commonwealth War Graves Commission and the local population tend their graves with great care and devotion.

Nelson Webb and his crew are buried at Lanester Cemetery near Lorient. (Mrs E

CHAPTER FOUR

Leaflets, Bombs and Testing
Welch Foster

At 1430 hours on the afternoon of the second day of the Second World War, Sergeant Bickerson lifted his Whitley Mk III (K 8942) from the grass runway of RAF Linton-on-Ouse, the home base of 51 Squadron. He and his crew were en route to Rheims where they were to position and await dusk before setting off for the Ruhr on the squadron's first 'Nickel' raid during which they were to drop 1,200 lbs of propaganda leaflets. Flying as the observer in Bickerson's five-man crew was Sergeant Welch Foster. And so began the distinguished operational career of the quiet, regular airman from Cookstown in County Tyrone.

Foster had enlisted into the Royal Air Force as an aircraft hand/wireless operator in August, 1935, being posted to Martlesham Heath to join 64(F) Squadron flying the Demon. Within twelve months, he had re-mustered to be a WOP/Air Gunner and his long flying career had begun. Flying training took place on the squadron and after six weeks and just twenty-three hours, his Squadron Commander, Squadron Leader F. V. Beamish, signed his flying log book and awarded him his air gunner's badge, the coveted winged

Welch Foster's medals. Air Force Cross, Distinguished Flying Medal, 1939-45 Star, Aircrew Europe Star, Africa Star (North Africa 1942-43 Clasp), Defence Medal, War Medal.

Flight Lieutenant Welch Foster
(Author's collection)

Foster (standing left) *on his observers' course at Linton on Ouse – 1939 (51 Squadron)*

bullet worn on the right sleeve of his tunic. After eighteen months of formation attacks, interception exercises with 49(B) Squadron and squadron practice drills for Empire Air Day, Foster was selected for Air Observer training and left his first squadron for the Flying Training School at Perth with eighty hours in his log book. Completing his training at West Freugh, he joined 51 Squadron and, within eight days, he took off on his first operational sortie.

The initial rate of sorties over enemy territory was slow, with just six missions by the end of February, 1940. The hazardous nature of these early sorties in ill-equipped aircraft from rudimentary forward landing grounds was soon apparent. Foster was navigator to Flight Sergeant Wynton, flying K 9008, one of five Whitleys to take off on 27 October loaded with leaflets for what became commonly known as a 'Nickel sortie'. The aircrew had a less complimentary description and referred to them as 'bumph bombing'. With a meteorological forecast of solid cloud from 1,000 to 15,000 feet and a freezing level of 1,500 feet, one aircraft turned back with icing problems, one had to be abandoned on the return from Munich and another landed with frozen-up instruments. Foster's target was Frankfurt and, after dropping the leaflets, problems began to mount on the return flight. The mid-upper turret became jammed and the exertion to free it, allied to the dwindling oxygen supply and the intense cold, reduced Foster to near collapse, but he remained at his post. The starboard engine then caught fire, causing the vacuum pumps which powered the blind flying instruments to fail. With six inches of ice covering the wings, the aircraft entered a steep dive. The two pilots regained some limited control just as the aircraft cleared cloud and they levelled out just in time to smash through the top branches of a wood and execute a successful crash landing at night near Triaucourt, not far from Verdun. Remarkably, all the crew escaped unharmed. Foster's crew, together with the two others who also reached their targets, were

Leaflet 'bumph' bombing (51 Squadron)

Whitley V – N 1503 – of 51 Squadron at Dishforth. (MOD)

commended by the Commander in Chief for 'their determination and fortitude'.

With the Squadron operating from Dishforth and equipped with the Merlin-
engined Whitley Mark V, Foster found himself crewed with Squadron Leader
P Gilchrist, the Flight Commander, and they were to complete their tour of
operations together. Their first sortie in a Mark V (N1407) was a Nickel and
flare drop over Berlin on 27 February, 1940, when they were the only aircraft
over the 'Big City'. After a nine-hour sortie in the intense cold, they landed at
the forward landing ground at Villeneuve in France before returning to base the
following day. A few days later Foster and his crew participated in a 'bombing
first' when they attacked the German seaplane base at Hornum where heavy
flak was encountered on this, the first occasion when bombs fell on German
soil in the Second World War.

After bombing attacks against the *Luftwaffe*-occupied Fornebu Airfield at
Oslo, Foster and his crew were to be involved in another first on the night of
11/12 May. They joined the attack against the railway network near München
Gladbach, the first time that bombs had fallen on the German mainland. With
Hitler's attack in the West a few days later, the 'Phoney War' was over and
bombing missions became the routine. At the opening of the five-year-long
Strategic Offensive against Germany on 15/16 May, Foster and his crew
bombed the oil refineries at Bremen from 6,500 feet flying their new Whitley
P 4982 which was to see them safely through the remainder of their tour of
operations. As the military situation in France became inceasingly critical, the
Whitleys of 4 Group were tasked to support the British Expeditionary Force in
France which had come under heavy attack following the German Blitzkreig.
Attacks on river crossings were ordered and Foster and his crew bombed the
bridge over the River Oise at Ribemont.

Within a few days the 'heavies' resumed their attacks against German communications and oil targets but the Whitleys were still occasionally called on to support the British ground forces as they retreated towards the Channel and 51 Squadron attacked road and rail communications at Abbeville, Bapaume and Givet in Northern France. Bombing was with 500 and 250 lb bombs at night by individual aircraft from heights between 7,000 and 10,000 feet. Although target identification was difficult and the use of flares was common, crews regularly reported successful attacks.

With the fall of France, attacks against targets in Germany continued on an increasing scale. Foster and his crew flew seventeen sorties in a six-week period to targets which included Cologne, Soest, Frankfurt and Rheydt. Marshalling yards, river traffic, airfields and oil installations were the priority, but the small bomber force was thinly spread and achievements were very limited. However, much valuable experience was gained for the future conduct of bomber operations. On 30 June, Foster took off in P 4892 on his thirty-first and final sortie to bomb petroleum works at Bremen, but poor weather prevented a successful attack and four 250 lb bombs were dropped on the alternative target at Norderney Airfield.

So ended Welch Foster's first operational tour which had begun on the second day of the war, saw him over Berlin within a few weeks, attacking targets in Norway and Northern France and finally taking part on the earliest bombing sorties over German towns that were to become household names. Although the early bomber crews did not have to face the formidable German night fighter arm of later years, they still faced considerable odds. The increasing threat posed by the rapidly developing anti-aircraft fire, accompanied by intense searchlight activity, caused losses to mount. Sorties of seven or eight hours, flown by Foster and his colleagues in the ill-equipped, noisy Whitley with its wholly inadequate heating sysem and lacking the performance of their successors, were the routine. Added to these problems the elements, particularly icing and adverse winds, were a constant danger. The courage and fortitude of these early bomber crews can only be admired.

Shortly after starting an instructional tour with 19 OTU at Kinloss came news of the award of the Distinguished Flying Medal. In the words of the citation accompanying the award, Sergeant Welch Foster: *'had continued to show*

Bombing up at Dishforth – 1940. (51 Squadron)

remarkable courage, determination and zeal following the very bad experience of crashing in a badly iced up aircraft. His bombing and navigation have been of a very high order indeed, and he has materially assisted the successes obtained by the crew with whom he has flown.'

The recommendation was endorsed by Air Commodore 'Mary' Coningham, the AOC of 4 Group who commented on Foster's courage and determination and strongly reommended him for the award. On 1 March, 1941, Foster attended an Investiture at Buckingham Palace where His Majesty The King presented him with his Distinguished Flying Medal.

Commissioned in January, 1941, Foster continued his duties as an armament instructor at Kinloss for a further year before completing a conversion course to the Wellington at 15 OTU at Harwell. On 2 January, 1942, he set out, with Sergeant Gunning as captain, to deliver Wellington DV 419 to 108 MU in Egypt, transiting through Gibraltar. After a week's delay in Gibraltar, the crew set off for Barce in Algeria, but after being airborne for eleven hours they had to make a forced landing at Tolmeta short of fuel and, for a number of hours, they were posted as missing. Having organised themselves and contacted the nearest airfield, they had to wait while repairs were carried out and these took a week to complete before they were able to make the twenty-minute flight to complete the trip to Barce

Joining 148 Squadron at Kabrit, flying the Wellington Mk Ic, Foster under-took the first operation of his second tour in DV 655, but bad weather over the target at Benghazi resulted in a fruitless eight-hour sortie. Four days later a successful sortie was flown from ALG 106. The pattern of operations for the rest of April was set with six to seven-hour flights to Benghazi and Maturba from ALG 106.

At midnight on 29 May, Flight Lieutenant J. E. Watts, the pilot of Wellington Z 8974, took off from ALG 106 to bomb Tmimi with Welch Foster as his navigator. At 0230 hours the 4,000 lbs of bombs were dropped from 6,500 feet on the landing ground at Tmimi. A very large fire started in the petrol and oil storage area and two photographic runs were carried out. On the second the starboard engine failed, the aircraft started to lose height and was turned immediately onto an easterly course towards base. All removable items were jettisoned, but the aircraft continued to descend and a successful belly landing was made three miles north of Bir Hacheim. Classified items were destroyed, flimsies eaten (reported to be not very palatable!), water and survival items salvaged and the aircraft set on fire. After walking for a few hours the uninjured

Wellington Ic on a desert airfield. (via A Thomas)

crew came across a tented camp, but they were immediately fired on. As the fire became more accurate and intensified, they decided to surrender, only to discover that they had run into a Free French patrol cut off behind enemy lines. The following night a patrol of the King's Royal Rifle Corps broke through to the French position and twenty-four hours later the whole party was able to regain the British lines. The crew returned to the squadron to be enrolled as members of the 'Never Too Late Club'.

Foster returned to operations in mid-June at the height of Rommel's sustained efforts to enter Egypt, and this kept the Wellington crews of 205 Group busy, as they flew by night to supplement the daylight efforts of the light bombers and fighter bombers. Crews were cheered to be released from the 'Benghazi Milk Run' and to start attacking enemy troop concentrations and lines of communication. Flying initially with Squadron Leader Tom Prickett (later Air Marshal Sir Thomas) and then with Flight Lieutenant Gane, Foster was to fly intensive operations over the next hectic six weeks. Falling back to Kabrit in the Canal Zone, the Wellingtons of 148 Squadron were flying nightly long-range sorties against enemy troop and MT concentrations. Captured German documents acknowledged the success of the British night bombers against their supply columns. With Rommel recognising in early July that his advance had been halted, the Air Officer Commander in Chief, Air Marshal Arthur Tedder, ordered his bombers against the Libyan ports and their installations.

During the latter half of July, Foster was to fly nine sorties averaging seven hours duration including seven attacks against Tobruk harbour and shipping. During this period of intense activity against Tobruk, Foster and his crew also attacked the runways at Heraklion airfield on Crete, with 250 lb bombs, fragmentation bombs and incendaries scoring hits on the south-east runway. On 4 August he took off in Wellington HX 483 on his fifty-fourth and last operational bombing sortie of the war. The target once again was Tobruk and, despite heavy flak and the attention of fourteen searchlights, he dropped his bombs on the target. Landing after a seven- and-a-half-hour flight, he had flown no less than eighty five operational hours during his final month on 148 Squadron. Although this signalled the end of Welch Foster's operational career, his contribution to the war effort was far from over.

After twelve months instructing at 30 OTU at Hixon, he was posted in December, 1943, as a test observer and bomb aimer to the Royal Aircaft Establishment at Farnborough. Joining the Armament and Guided Weapons Flight, he remained at Farnborough for the next seven years, during which time he flew 900 hours in thirty aircraft types ranging from the Halifax to the Avenger and the Albemarle to the Meteor. He participated in an immense range of trials concentrating initially on the dropping of flares and incendaries for the

Barracuda II – MX 613 – with lifeboat. Foster flew a number of lifeboat-dropping trials in this aircraft. (Flypast)

Pathfinder force. On the 14 April, 1944, he dropped two Tallboy bombs at Orfordness from Lancaster JB 415 followed a few days later by the trial-dropping of an airborne lifeboat from Warwick HF 957. Photo flash trials over Cannon Heath from Wellington HE 442, Radiosonde meteorological trials at 30,000 feet over Pawlett in Mosquito XVI MM 363 and further boat trials over Queen Mary Reservoir from Barracuda MX 613 are but a small sample of the type of wartime trials recorded by Foster. Post-war work included much work in association with the Mark IX Airborne Interception Radar, on bomb fuzing, the dropping of various parachute stores and sonobuoy and marine markers. With guided weapons trials entering the test programme early in 1950, Welch Foster's long and distinguished service at Farnborough came to an end.

In recognition of his outstanding service to experimental flying, Flight Lieutenant Welch Foster was awarded the Air Force Cross in the New Year's Honours List on 1 January, 1948. The citation drew attention to the wide range of trials he had participated in and the variety of stores he had tested, and concluded by saying: *'The success of a great deal of the research and development has depended upon the co-operation and skill which Flight Lieutenant Foster has shown in all these trials. His exceptional ability and unselfish devotion to duty have been an essential contribution to the success of the work.'*

Welch Foster finished his flying career at the Central Signals Establishment at Watton, flying Lincolns. His final tour in the RAF was in charge of the Recruiting Office at Brighton and, although grounded, he managed to find time to fly sixty hours in Ansons and Chipmunks from Kenley. He retired from the RAF on 27 June, 1957, after twenty-two years of almost continuous flying.

CHAPTER FIVE

Spitfire Auxiliary – 'Buck' Casson

As 'Buck' Casson settled himself into the cockpit of his Spitfire I on the morning of 19 August, 1940, he looked across the airfield at Leconfield to see fourteen of his 616 Squadron colleagues also preparing for take off. The South Yorkshire Auxiliary Squadron was departing to join the 11 Group Sector at Kenley as the Luftwaffe raids built up over Southern England. Just fifteen days later he would return north but only five other pilots would still be with the Squadron.

Lionel Casson, known throughout his RAF career and ever since as 'Buck', was living in his native Sheffield in 1938 when he learned that the last of the twenty-one Auxiliary Squadrons was to form in South Yorkshire. Believing that war with Germany was inevitable, he decided to apply for one of the vacancies and was soon asked to present himself at the Squadron Headquarters in Ellers Road, Doncaster. In early 1939 he joined the Squadron as one of the first three volunteer pilots, the others being Ken Holden from Selby and Hugh 'Cocky' Dundas from the nearby Bawtry Hall; it proved to be a formidable trio.

Spending his weekdays working in one of the great steel foundries in Sheffield, Casson's weekends were spent learning to fly in the Squadron's Tutor. Shortly after receiving his commission on 28 July, 1939, as an Acting Pilot Officer, and with seven-and-a-half hours' dual instruction, he flew his first solo in a Tutor. As war approached, all the Auxiliary Squadrons were 'embodied' into the Royal Air Force and 'Buck' Casson decided to join the Regular RAF notwithstanding his reserved occupation status. He was sent to 2 FTS at Brize Norton to complete his flying training on the Harvard. Passing out second on

Buck Casson's medals are Distinguished Flying Cross, Air Force Cross, 1939-45 Star with Battle of Britain Clasp, Aircrew Europe Star, War Medal, Coronation Medal (EIIR), Air Efficiency Award with Clasp.

'Buck' Casson at the time of the Battle of Britain. (L H Casson)

the course with an assessment of above average he returned to 616 who had re-equipped with Spitfires at Leconfield. However, within a few days he was posted to 6 OTU at Sutton Bridge where he converted to the Hurricane and was initiated into fighter tactics.

Posted on 15 May, 1940, to the Advanced Air Striking Force at Arras in Northern France, Casson spent a few fruitless days trying to make contact with his new unit before finding himself at Cherbourg on a ferry back to England. After reporting to Uxbridge, Casson was sent to join 79 Squadron at Biggin Hill and, after a few days at readiness, he flew in Hurricane P 2609 on his first operational sortie escorting light bombers to Abbeville. Attacked by some Me 109s, he became separated, but he chased and fired at a lone aircraft which he last saw diving for Cherbourg streaming black smoke. A few days later he attacked a He 111 while on an offensive patrol in the Le Treport region but, running short of fuel, he was forced to land on the small grass airfield at St Andre de l'Eure in Northern France. Assisted by a local Frenchman, he refuelled his aircraft with the only available 'gasolin' and, after an adventurous take off, he finally returned to Biggin Hill.

Throughout the rest of June and early July he flew numerous patrols over Hawkinge and Dungeness and bomber escort sorties to Calais and Merville. The highlight of his short stay with 79 Squadron at Biggin Hill was to command A Flight on a parade in honour of HM King George VI who was visiting the Squadron to present gallantry medals to some of the pilots. A few days later, Casson drove north to rejoin 616 Squadron at Leconfield, still equipped with the Spitfire.

616 Squadron A Flight – Battle of Britain, Casson standing second from right. Other pilots include Denys Gillam (standing centre) *and 'Cocky' Dundas* (standing second from left)*. Three pilots are wearing 'mock' DFCs as a show of one-upmanship against their Flight Commander, Gillam who had just been awarded an AFC. Ironically, all were subsequently awarded the DFC.* (L H Casson)

The fighter squadrons of 12 Group based in the north of England spent much of the summer practising air-to-air firing on the ranges off Acklington, battle drills and tactics, with an occasional scramble against single German bombers harassing east coast convoys. There were a number of engagements and the Squadron scored a few successes.

The first significant action for the Squadron occurred on 15 August when the Germans mounted a major attack on the north of England to coincide with large-scale raids in the south. The northerly raiders from *Luftflotte 5* based in Denmark were unescorted. Unknown to German intelligence, the few northern squadrons were at maximum readiness to protect an important convoy sailing up the east coast. The raid was picked up by the radar site at Staxton Wold and 616 Squadron was ordered to scramble. The aircrew were in the process of changing duty flights when the alarm sounded and so all the Squadron were launched. Flying N 3275, Casson scrambled with Green Section led by 'Cocky' Dundas and they soon intercepted a large force of Junkers 88 bombers heading for the Yorkshire airfields. Casson attacked a lone bomber which had turned away and he emptied his ammunition into the enemy which was last seen just above the water with dense smoke streaming from the port engine.

As the Spitfires straggled back to Leconfield it soon became apparent that the Squadron had achieved a major victory with eight enemy aircraft claimed destroyed and a further six damaged. Undoubtedly some claims may have been duplicated, but the combined efforts of the northern-based squadrons were so successful that the *Luftwaffe* never again attacked the north in strength, thus allowing the bulk of Fighter Command to meet the major threat in the south.

Within a few days the Squadron received orders to proceed south to Kenley to join the main Battle and fifteen aircraft departed Leconfield on 19 August. No sooner had Casson arrived than he was loaned to 615 Squadron who were desperately short of Hurricane pilots. His stay was to be short, just two days. In that time 616 had been so badly mauled that he was ordered to return to the Squadron at Kenley. The Squadron had lost nine pilots, including three who were killed. After two quiet days to recover, the half-decimated Squadron spent the next week flying at intensive rates.

On 28 August, Casson flew for over five hours on three 'X' raids patrolling over the Thames Estuary and Manston, but his friend Jack Bell, who was one of the longest-serving squadron members, was killed while attempting an emergency landing at West Malling in his damaged Spitfire. Led by their fearless Flight Commander, Denys Gillam, the remaining ten pilots scrambled as many as five times each day and the Squadron score mounted. A large force of Heinkel 111s with a Me 110 escort was intercepted over the Thames Estuary on 30 August and Casson was credited with a probable and a damaged.

On 1 September, the Squadron was scrambled to patrol behind Hawkinge but en route they intercepted about thirty Me 109s which were engaged. One was destroyed and three probables were claimed, including one by Casson. Within minutes of landing Gillam led five aircraft against an incoming formation of bombers. Casson attacked a Dornier 215 which had its fuselage ripped open before stalling and disappearing. Return fire had knocked a large hole in the port wing and oil tank of his Spitfire (R6778) but he successfully crash landed at base although his aircraft was a write-off. This was his fifth sortie of the day. With the loss of his aircraft, he was allocated Spitfire X 4184 which would be his permanent aircraft for the next six months.

After two more days of intensive operations, the exhausted remains of 616 Squadron were withdrawn from the battle. Of the original twenty-one pilots who had departed for Kenley ten days earlier just seven remained, and Denys Gillam was immediately promoted and posted to be awarded a Distinguished Flying Cross a few days later. Fifteen enemy aircraft had been shot down with a further six claimed as probables and at least nine damaged. However, the price had been very high.

Under a new Commanding Officer, the Cranwell Sword of Honour winner Squadron Leader Billy Burton, the Squadron moved to Kirton in Lindsey to re-group. The few experienced pilots, including Casson, were detached to the Bader Wing at Duxford for a few days in mid-September and they participated in a number of Big Wing operations before returning north to train the large influx of newly arrived pilots. These included Pilot Officer Johnnie Johnson and 'Cocky' Dundas (who was returning after recovering from the wounds received when he baled out shortly after arriving at Kenley a month earlier).

The next three months were taken up with the training of the new pilots and Casson soon found himself leading and instructing, even though he had just over 300 hours in his own log book. Fighter pilots soon became experienced during the Battle of Britain! There were occasional scrambles against lone raiders and on one night Casson saw a Junkers 88 over Barnsley and gave chase as far as Middlesbrough but it escaped at sea level before he could get into a firing position. Following the major blitz on his home city early in December,

Casson's Spitfire 'Pampero One' – P 7753 at Tangmere March 1941. He baled out of this aircraft over Chichester Harbour on 5 May, 1941. (L H Casson)

Casson flew over Sheffield and the other South Yorkshire towns leading a 'Xmas Goodwill' formation.

After a further two months of training, 616 returned to the front-line on 26 February, 1941, when they moved to Tangmere. The Squadron exchanged aircraft with the departing 65 Squadron and Casson was allocated Spitfire II P7753 (QJ-X). The aircraft had been presented by the British community of Buenos Aires and was christened 'Pampero One'. In early March Wing Commander Douglas Bader arrived as the new Wing Leader and he led the Wing, with the South Yorkshire Squadron using the callsign 'Dogsbody'.

Channel sweeps and patrols over the South Coast gave the Wing ample opportunities to develop tactics, including the recently introduced 'finger four' formation. In April the Squadron started bomber escort and offensive patrols over Northern France, and a few weeks later moved to the nearby satellite airfield at Westhampnett. The tempo of operations quickly picked up and successes mounted. On 5 May, Casson took off in company with his great friend Roy Marples. Over Portsmouth at 15,000 feet they intercepted a reconnaissance Junkers 88 which immediately dived to sea level. Casson closed and silenced the rear gunner with his eight Brownings, but in the engagment his engine was hit by return fire. With glycol escaping and the engine temperature rising, he headed for the coast . At 1,000 feet, and with the cockpit full of smoke, Casson rolled his Spitfire 'X' onto its back and baled out, landing in Chichester Harbour and bringing the brief career of 'Pampero One' to an end.

Led by its dynamic leader, Douglas Bader, the Tangmere Wing was continually in action over Northern France during the early summer of 1941. Bader led with 616 Squadron, 610 providing the middle airspace cover and 145 giving top cover. Almost all the patrols were escort missions for the RAF's light bomber force and, during these 'Wing Circus' sorties, successes against the enemy mounted, but losses also increased. On 22 June, Casson was flying in company with Roy Marples when they each destroyed a Me 109 in a dogfight over Hazebrouck. He followed this up a few days later with a 'damaged' Me 109. This heralded a period of almost daily engagements with the German fighters and four days later Johnnie Johnson claimed the first of his many kills. Soon the Squadron achieved its fiftieth victory and Bader received a bar to his Distinguished Service Order and there was a Distinguished Flying Cross each for Billy Burton, 'Cocky' Dundas and Ken Holden.

During July the Squadron re-equipped with the cannon-firing Spitfire Vb and Wing sweeps over Abbeville, St Omer and Gravelines brought further success. However, Colin Macfie, one of the Flight Commanders, was lost and Casson was promoted to take over B Flight with his old friend Dundas in charge of A Flight. During July the Squadron was credited with fourteen kills and many probables and damaged, almost all the victims being Me 109s. Casson was

A Spitfire V of 616 Squadron being prepared for a sortie. (Johnnie Johnson)

credited with two probables and one damaged.

On 9 August, following some poor weather, the Wing was tasked with bomber escort over Béthune, but the sortie went badly from the outset. Bader's radio was faulty and the top cover squadron, flying its first operation since relieving the experienced 145 Squadron, failed to make the rendezvous. Crossing the coast, Me 109s were spotted below and 616 dived to attack with Ken Holden's 610 Squadron remaining to give limited top cover. More Me 109s of JG 26, led by the German Ace *Oberstleutnant* Adolph Galland, pounced on the Spitfire squadrons and a great melee developed. All formation cohesion was lost and it was every pilot for himself as the Spitfires tried to disengage and return home. In the resulting dogfights Douglas Bader was shot down and took to his parachute to spend the rest of the war as a prisoner.

Casson was leading B Flight in his new Spitfire Vb (W 3458) and dived to attack a number of Me 109s. His shots sent one of the enemy fighters down inverted. Finding himself alone he spotted four Spitfires circling with numerous 109s around and joined the formation. Seeing a lone Spitfire in trouble below, and failing to attract the leader's attention with his radio calls, he left the formation to assist his colleague expecting the remainder to follow. They did not.

Hauptmann Gerhard Schopfel, the *Gruppenkommandeur* of III/JG26 and his wingman spotted the lone diving Spitfire and closed for an attack. Casson heard shells hitting his aircraft, saw the two Me 109s in his mirror and realised that the other Spitfires had not followed him. His engine was hit and he dived to tree-top height hoping to cross the Channel at low level. The German fighters followed and with his engine overheating and running rough, the Me 109s soon gained on him and began firing again, hitting his armour plating, instruments and fuel tank. With the cockpit filling with fuel he tried one more desperate attempt to shake off the enemy fighters but his engine seized. He made a hasty forced landing near St Omer and, with the German fighters circling overhead, he set light to his Spitfire which destroyed the centre section. He was soon captured and marched off to captivity as Schopfel returned to base to record his thirty-third victory.

The loss of Bader and Casson, one of only two of the original twenty-four pilots still serving on the Squadron, cast a great gloom over Tangmere. 'Cocky' Dundas and Johnnie Johnson immediately organised a search and took off with two others to scour the French coast and the Channel returning as night fell unaware that the two pilots were already in captivity.

Casson spent the night under guard before leaving for Frankfurt and *Dulag Luft*. A few days later he was surprised, but delighted, to see Douglas Bader stomp through the gate. Within a few days they were split up and Casson left for Lübeck and *Oflag Xc* where he was reunited with his old Flight Commander, Colin Macfie who had recently been awarded the Distinguished Flying Cross in his absence. A few days later Casson learnt that he too had been awarded the DFC. The citation highlighted his service from Dunkirk through the Battle of Britain and the *'large number of offensive patrols over Northern France. His efficiency, leadership and courage have set an excellent example.'* This award created a hat-trick for the Squadron as the DFC had now been awarded to the three original Auxiliary members, Ken Holden and 'Cocky' Dundas having received their awards a few weeks earlier whilst also serving on the Squadron.

Buck Casson's time as a prisoner of war for almost four years justifies an article in its own right. He spent time at *Oflag XXI* at Schubin. In April 1943, he was transferred to the infamous *Stalag Luft 3* at Sagan where, twelve months later, he stood on a special parade as the Senior British Officer announced that fifty of their colleagues had been shot by the Gestapo following the 'Great Escape'.

As the Russians closed towards Sagan in January 1945, the German authorities decided to evacuate the camp. In bitterly cold weather on 28 January, and with improvised haversacks, Casson and his fellow prisoners from the East compound each collected a food parcel and set off on 'The March'. Tolstoy's *War and Peace* had been a favourite book in the camp and, with heavy snow on the ground, the analogy between the scenes during Napoleon's retreat from

Buck Casson managed to destroy his Spitfire after his crash landing in Northern France and before he was captured. (via Don Caldwell)

Moscow and those the prisoners experienced was striking. After eight days of marching and travelling in cattle trucks, the long column arrived at a former Navy prison camp at Tarmstedt where they would spend the next two months. Early in April it was time to evacuate Tarmstedt and 'The March' was resumed. In contrast with the privations experienced in January, this march was undertaken in glorious weather and was classed as a 'picnic'.

The column moved almost daily camping overnight in the fields and villages, heading towards Lübeck, until 27 April when they arrived at a large estate and established a camp. Four days later there was great excitement as Casson and his friends welcomed a British Army Lieutenant and his two Comet tanks. The prisoners were free. On 8 May, Casson travelled to Rheine airfield and the following day he climbed aboard a Lancaster to return to England, landing at Dunsfold. Within a few days he was back home in Sheffield for the first time in almost four years.

'Buck' Casson's involvement with the South Yorkshire Auxiliary Squadron was far from over. As soon as the Squadron re-formed at Finningley in June 1946, under the leadership of his old friend Ken Holden, he rejoined as a Flying Officer. Initially the Squadron was equipped with Mosquito NF XXX aircraft which were retained for two years, but a policy that all the Auxiliary Squadrons would fly in the day fighter role saw the Squadron re-equip with the Meteor III,

As a Prisoner of War in Stalag Luft III. Casson is in back row, second from the right with his 616 Squadron colleague Colin Macfie on his left. (L H Casson)

Casson (second right) returns from a sortie in his Meteor IV – EE 348. Finningley 1950. (L H Casson)

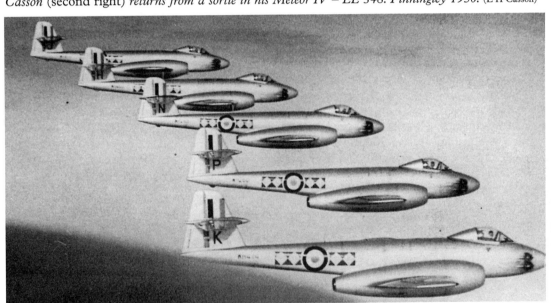

Casson leads 616 Squadron Meteor F 8s back to Acklington after a gun-firing exercise 1952. (L H Casson)

A 616 Squadron Meteor F 8 is 'turned around' during the 1953 summer camp at Takali, Malta. (L H Casson)

the first arriving in January, 1949. Within a few weeks, Casson flew his first jet solo flight in EE 348.

The routine of weekend flying and annual summer camps became a feature of Casson's spare time until December 1950, when he became the Squadron's second post-war Auxiliary Air Force Commanding Officer. Almost immediately, he and his Squadron were called up as the Korean War broke out and this heralded a three-month intensive period of training including air-to-air firing on the ranges off Acklington in Northumberland. The Squadron Commander led the way, achieving the highest score with 40% hits on the 'banner'. Under Casson, 616 Squadron achieved a high level of efficiency during 1951 and this was recognised with the award of the coveted Esher Trophy, presented annually to the most efficient of the twenty-one Auxiliary Squadrons.

With an ever-demanding managerial job in the precision small tools industry and command of a top fighter Squadron, 'Buck' Casson was a very busy man. When the new town headquarters was due for opening, his old Wing Leader and fellow prisoner, Douglas Bader, arrived to perform the opening ceremony which provided the perfect excuse for a reunion of the old Tangmere Wing with appropriate celebrations.

Returning from Summer Camp at Oldenburg, Casson's time as an Auxiliary was running out. However, before handing over command of the Squadron to a regular officer, it was announced that Squadron Leader L. H. Casson had been awarded the Air Force Cross for his *outstanding leadership and devotion to duty*. In June 1954, after 16 years service with 616 Squadron, it was time for 'Buck' Casson to hang up his flying helmet. Did anyone ever serve a single squadron more loyally? Almost certainly not. Notwithstanding his DFC and AFC, the Air Efficiency Award with an additional clasp is testimony to his devoted service.

616 Squadron pilots at Buckingham Palace for the 50th Anniversary of the Battle of Britain. 'Cocky' Dundas is second from left with Denys Gillam on his left. 'Buck' Casson is second from right. (Author)

CHAPTER SIX

Low Level Attacker – Dickie Gunning

The morning of Sunday 6 December, 1941, was cloudy with slight drizzle as Dickie Gunning settled into the spacious and comfortable cockpit of his Boston light bomber at Oulton airfield close to the Norfolk Broads. Together with the crews of Ventura and Mosquito squadrons based nearby, thirty-five other Boston crews were also preparing to take off on what would be recognised as one of the most famous and daring bomber operations of the Second World War; the low-level daylight attack against the Philips radio factory at Eindhoven. Apprehension of the dangers ahead was nothing new to the aggressive and experienced Gunning; he had already completed a full tour flying Blenheims during some of the most bitter air fighting of the war.

With the expansion of the Royal Air Force gathering pace during 1936, London-born 'Dickie' Gunning exchanged his role as a part-time gunner with the City of London Yeomanry and enlisted as a pilot. After completing pilot training and the award of his wings at 7 Flying Training School, Gunning joined 49 (B) Squadron based at Worthy Down. Within a few months he was posted in March 1937, to fly Hind light bombers with the recently re-formed 107 Squadron based at Harwell and part of 2 Group the tactical bombing element of Bomber Command. During the next three years Gunning experienced the dramatic changes that saw the end of the 'halcyon years' of armament practice

Dickie Gunning's medals are Distinguished Flying Cross, Distinguished Flying Medal, 1939-45 Star, Aircrew Europe Star, Defence Medal, War Medal.

A Blenheim IV - R 3816 - of 107 Squadron pictured at Leuchars in March 1941. (via A Thomas)

camps, participation in the Empire Air Day Pageants and annual exercises with the Army on Salisbury Plain replaced by the early war years when such horrific losses would be sustained by the low-level bombers.

With the gathering of war clouds, 107 exchanged its delightful but wholly inadequate and out-dated Hind bi-plane bombers for the Blenheim. Initially the Squadron was equipped with the Mark I but, with a move to Wattisham, these were exchanged for the Mark IV in July, 1939. Tension mounted throughout 1939 and the 2 Group Squadrons practised low and high-level bombing raids and long cross-country flights with mock raids simulating likely operational ranges. There were also formation flights over France 'showing the flag', giving further long-range navigation practice over unfamiliar terrain.

By the time of the major annual home defence exercise held in August Sergeant Gunning was becoming one of the most experienced pilots on the Squadron. By the end of the month readiness D had come into force, aircraft were dispersed around the airfield perimeters and flying was restricted to essential air tests. There was apprehension among the aircrew, together with the realisation that the performance of their 'wonder bomber', advertised as 'faster than the fighter', left something to be desired.

Just prior to the opening of hostilities, Bomber Command had issued orders that the priority for operations would be attacks on enemy shipping in the Heligoland Bight area, on electricity generating stations and on oil and refining plants, but it would be some time before attacks were mounted against the latter two categories. Five Blenheims of 107 Squadron took part in the first bombing sortie of the war on 4 September, 1939, an attack on enemy shipping in the Schilling Roads. Four of the aircraft failed to return, a stark indication of the dangers that lay ahead for the 2 Group low level bomber crews. If the morale of Gunning and his colleagues had suffered a setback, it was soon restored by the arrival of their dynamic new leader, Wing Commander Basil Embry DSO.

Immediately after the initial raid, the Blenheim crews had little activity as the Phoney War became established. A few armed reconnaissance sorties were flown, but Gunning had to wait until New Year's Day, 1940, before flying his first war sortie. Taking off in his Blenheim IV (N 6183), he carried out an uneventful armed sweep over the North Sea. His next sortie was to bring a great deal more excitement.

Operational activity increased significantly in March. On 4 March, Gunning and his crew of Sergeant W. Brinn and LAC J. Bartley were on standby for strike and reconnaissance duties when his was one of two aircraft ordered to take off at 1300 hours to search for flak ships. Flying N 6183 again, he arrived off the Schilling Roads one-and-a-half hours later and sighted a number of merchant ships. Shortly afterwards he was leaving a bank of cloud at 2,500 feet when he sighted a U-boat on the surface. He immediately set up an attack from directly astern and dived to 1,400 feet before dropping four 250 lb bombs. The air gunner observed the last bomb hit the submarine between the stern and the conning tower and, as Gunning turned his aircraft to starboard, the crew saw an explosion and a 'mass of seething foam' around the conning tower as the U-boat crash dived. A reconnaissance sortie by an aircraft of 82 Squadron later confirmed that the Germans had placed four wreck marker buoys at the estimated position.

Basil Embry commented on the valuable effect this attack had on the morale of the Squadron and, within a few days, Air Chief Marshal Sir Edgar Ludlow-Hewitt, the Commander-in-Chief of Bomber Command, approved the immediate award of the Distinguished Flying Medal to Sergeant Gunning. Post-war analysis shows that the same submarine was sunk by Squadron Leader M V Delap of 82 Squadron on 11 March, the day after the wreck markers had been seen. It is possible that the submarine had been salvaged or was badly damaged and was on its way back to Wilhelmshaven. A Distinguished Flying Cross was gazetted for Delap on the same day that Gunning's award was announced. In approving both these awards, the Commander-in-Chief stressed the *'qualities of skill and determination which are required to carry out these flights which were pressed right into the estuaries where the enemy defences are very strong and very alert'*.

By mid-April, 107 Squadron had deployed to Lossiemouth in Scotland to support the military operations in Norway. In particular 107 Squadron was to mount daily attacks against Stavanger the major airfield in southern Norway; their fearless commander would almost always be at the head of his Squadron. In addition to being a dynamic leader, Basil Embry also studied in great detail the most appropriate tactics for delivering co-ordinated attacks and reviewed the methods of collective defence against enemy fighter attacks.

On 17 April, all twelve Squadron aircraft took off, Gunning and his crew flying P 4925 in the second section led by the Flight Commander, Squadron Leader 'Tubby' Clayton. Embry decided to mount a co-ordinated attack with his formation bombing from 18,000 feet, while Clayton led his flight in to attack from 200 feet. Just short of the target Me 110 fighters were observed climbing to attack the high formation, but the bombing attack was completed before any engagements. As the bombs from the high-level formation hit the runways, Gunning and his colleagues dived to low level to release their bombs. Almost immediately, the enemy fighters attacked the higher aircraft and two of the Blenheims failed to return, while a third came home with fifty-three strikes on the aircraft. The low-level formation broke up after their attack and headed for cloud; three aircraft were engaged but all returned to base. Following this raid, Embry produced a detailed report of the engagements and recommended increasing the Blenheim's armament to six Brownings if the aircraft was to be successful as a daylight bomber. With the exception of an ineffectual rearwards-firing 'chin' turret, the Blenheim was to continue flying some of the most murderous operations of the air war with no increase to its defensive armament!

Lack of cloud cover on the 19th and severe icing on the 27th thwarted Gunning's next two attempts to attack Stavanger, but on 1 May he made a successful attack. Six aircraft took off at 1410 hours but two soon returned with mechanical faults. The remaining four departed in formation at 16,000 feet and each aircraft dropped 2 x 250 and 12 x 40 lb General Purpose (GP) bombs which were observed to fall on the runways. The Blenheims departed leaving a pall of black smoke. A number of large aircraft were seen dispersed around the airfield and photographs were taken. The following day Dickie Gunning and his crew made another successful attack against the airfield but it was to be the last raid over Norway by 107 Squadron before it returned to Wattisham to help counter the increasing German threat to Holland.

At dawn on 10 May the Germans launched their Blitzkrieg in the West and the following day Gunning carried out a reconnaissance of the Dutch airfields. As the German advance gathered momentum, the bridges over the River Meuse were attacked and Gunning was piloting one of the twelve 107 Squadron Blenheims to attack the bridgehead at Sedan where moderate anti-aircraft fire was met. Losses were heavy and, after the attack, the Squadron had no service-able aircraft. Within a week the military situation on the ground had become critical and 107 Squadron spent the next ten days attacking the roads being used by the enemy. Troop concentrations, crossroads and railway lines were also bombed in an attempt to stem the advance.

From 20 May, a maximum effort was called for and 107 endeavoured to mount two raids of twelve aircraft each day. Dickie Gunning flew no less than seventeen bombing sorties over a twenty-two day period during which many of his colleagues were lost. A signal received at Wattisham on 21 May highlights how desparate the situation had become. It read:

'The four sections at stand-by from 0900 hours are to take off as soon as possible. Attack everything on road Frevent – Abbeville. This is a real crisis.'

The German Panzer Divisions had made astonishing progress and Gunning flew two sorties on the 21st and again on the 22nd, all led by Basil Embry. The anti-aircraft defences continued to take their toll of the slow Blenheims but the need for a fighter escort had at last been recognised and most raids were now accompanied by Hurricanes. After attacking enemy columns on the roads around Marck on 24 May, Gunning and his crew responded the following day to another urgent request contained in a signal from Headquarters 2 Group.

'Target for 107 Squadron. Pontoon bridges across river Lys between Menin and Courtrai. At request of General Georges who is 'in a hell of a hole'.

This request prompted an attack by twenty-four Blenheims, including twelve from 107 Squadron with Gunning flying L 9306. Photographs confirmed that these raids caused considerable damage, but the German advance had so much momentum that the plight of the British Expeditionary Force remained perilous.

On 27 May, Gunning and his crew had their first rest for many days. They watched twelve Squadron aircraft take off to attack enemy troops around St Omer. The formation encountered very heavy flak and amongst the losses was the Squadron's greatly admired leader Basil Embry, who had 'led from the front' since the day he assumed command of 107. Fortunately, he baled out of his stricken aircraft and returned to Wattisham ten weeks later after an epic escape which is recounted in his own book *Mission Completed*. His navigator survived but, sadly, his gallant gunner was killed.

On the day that the Dunkirk evacuation reached its climax Gunning was bombing enemy transports near Ypres when intense flak and attacks by fighters were encountered. The Hurricane fighter escort drove the fighters off but not before they had inflicted damage on the poorly armed Blenheims. Two days later 107 attacked the heavy guns firing on Allied shipping off Gravelines. The flak was such that three Squadron aircraft were so badly damaged that they were forced to crash-land on their return to Wattisham. Gunning's aircraft (N 6237) was so severely damaged that he had to attempt a landing with no undercar-raige or flaps and the aircraft overturned on landing. Fortunately, the three crew members suffered only minor injuries and they were back on operations five days later.

Following the evacuation from Dunkirk the fighting was far from over, as more than 100,000 British troops remained in France engaging the German forces, with the Blenheim squadrons continuing to provide bomber support. On 7 June, 107 Squadron was tasked to carry out a low-level reconnaissance of the Somme river crossings in the Abbeville-Hesdin area. Three aircraft took off, including Dickie Gunning flying R 3688. All three were subjected to heavy ground fire as they flew at 100 feet before being attacked by three Me 109 fighters. One aircraft was lost and a second, flown by the new Squadron Commander, Wing Commander L. R. Stokes, fought a running battle with the fighters for fifteen minutes before returning safely, having shot down one of the enemy aircraft. Gunning escaped by flying at tree-top height and he brought back his damaged aircraft and valuable information on enemy movements.

Over the next few days the Blenheim squadrons were flying at maximum effort in support of the retreating British forces. On 9 June, three of Gunning's formation were shot down by intense flak as twelve aircraft bombed enemy transports near Poix. With the 51st Highland Division retreating towards Le Havre, the Blenheims attacked the enemy guns near St Valery and Gunning flew two sorties attacking enemy troop positions in the area when the anti-aircraft fire was again intense. The end of the gallant resistance of the British Expeditionary Force occurred on 14 June and during the evening Gunning took part in a raid against the airfield at Merville.

By the end of June, his arduous tour was coming to an end. He flew two sorties in the new bombing campaign against selected targets in Germany and on 3 July, he took off in Blenheim R 3606 to bomb the marshalling yards at Hamm. It was his thirtieth and final operational sortie with 107 Squadron. Only a handful of crews remained from those who had been on the Squadron at the outbreak of war. The casualties in 2 Group had been grievous and Dickie Gunning's crew had survived some of the Second World War's most dangerous air operations.

Gunning was posted as a pilot instructor to 17 Operational Training Unit (OTU) based at Upwood where it was his job to convert new crews to the Blenheim. Shortly after his arrival he was commissioned. He remained in this post for two years, becoming a Flight Commander before returning to more low-level operations in 2 Group. On 3 July, 1942, he was posted to Attlebridge in Norfolk to join 88 Squadron as a Flight Commander. The Squadron was flying the American-built Boston III light bombers. He arranged for his navigator throughout his tour on 107 Squadron, Bill Brinn DFM, to join him.

Boston III - Z 2230 - of 88 Squadron. Gunning flew this aircraft on the St Malo attack of 31 July, 41, and two other bombing sorties. (Author's collection)

Much had changed in 2 Group since the early war years with Blenheims, with more potent aircraft entering service – Bostons, Venturas, Mosquitos and Mitchells. The majority of operations took place in daylight but fighter escorts were much more common. The Group retained its tactical role, with attacks against ports and transportation lines of communication, but it also regularly attacked key industrial targets in Northern France and Holland, thus complementing the heavy bomber force which attacked deep into Germany. These 'Circus' operations became the daily routine for the 2 Group bomber squadrons.

Gunning's first operational sortie on his second tour was a night low-level attack in Boston III Z 2230 against the airfield at De Kooy in Holland dropping his bombs from 900 feet. Daylight 'Circus' operations against the docks at St Malo, the wharves at Ostend and the power station at Mazingbore quickly followed.

Operating from their new base at Oulton, 88 Squadron spent much of November flying on major exercises practising large-formation attacks at low level. This was a prelude to what became the most ambitious and famous low-level bombing operation of the war, the destruction of the Philips radio and valve factory situated in a heavily built-up area of Eindhoven. The need for precision was self-evident and this precluded the use of the heavy bomber force. The Philips factory was a major producer of radio valves and specialist electrical equipment, with an output amounting to a third of the German requirements.

The main bombing force consisted of thirty-six Bostons, forty-seven Venturas and ten Mosquitos, the latter led by Wing Commander Hughie Edwards VC.

Fighter escort was available only as far as the Dutch coast. The raid, Operation Oyster, was led by Wing Commander J. Pelly-Fry, the commander of 88 Squadron, and Dickie Gunning was appointed the Deputy Leader. At 1115 hours on 6 December, a grey, damp Sunday morning, the Bostons took off to form overhead. Gunning, flying AL 289, was third to take off in the first section and he tucked in on the starboard side of his Squadron Commander. At other East Anglian airfields the Venturas and the Mosquitos were taking off to meet their rendezvous. The success of the operation depended on every crew adhering to precise heights, timings and navigation.

The large formation crossed the North Sea at less than one hundred feet and made a pinpoint landfall on the Dutch coast. This stirred the wild geese and a number of aircraft were badly damaged by birdstrikes. Enemy defences were soon alerted and heavy ground fire was directed at the low-flying bombers and, as the large formation approached the target area, FW 190 and Me 109 fighters engaged the bombers. The leader's navigation and timing were faultless as they approached Eindhoven. The first two aircraft bombed from very low level with eleven-second delay-fused 250 lb bombs as Gunning led the remainder in a climb to bomb from 1,500 feet. He attacked the large primary target and saw his leader's bombs strike the key valve factory. With all the defences alerted, a speedy withdrawal to the fighter escort waiting at the Dutch coast was essential and Gunning routed north of Rotterdam to make the rendezvous. He landed back at Oulton two-and-a-half hours after taking off.

The raid proceeded with almost clockwork precision and the factory was so

Low-level attack against the Philips Radio Factory at Eindhoven on 6 December, 1942. (Author's collection)

Bostons depart the severely damaged Philips factory. (MOD)

severely damaged that it took six months for it to resume full production. The price was high, with the loss of fourteen crews, including one of the Ventura Squadron Commanders . However, this single raid made a significant contribu- tiion to the Allied bombing effort and the Dutch Resistance acknowledged that it had given a great boost to the morale of the gallant Dutch people. For his outstanding leadership and skill in bringing back his severely damaged Boston, the leader of the raid, Wing Commander Pelly-Fry, was awarded the Distinguished Service Order and his navigator, Jock Cairns, received one of the eight Distinguished Flying Crosses awarded.

Towards the end of December the newly promoted Squadron Leader Gunning led six Bostons to Exeter where they positioned for an attack the following day on the lock gates at the entrance to the inner harbour of St Malo. Each aircraft carried four 500 lb GP bombs and they bombed from 10,000 feet with many bursts in the target area. A few weeks later Gunning led a similar attack by six Bostons operating from a forward base at Hurn against a 12,000 ton ship in the dry dock at Cherbourg. He returned with flak damage. This was followed on 13 February, 1943, by a further attack on the St Malo lock gates when Gunning led twelve aircraft from Exeter. This was the last major attack by the Squadron for a few months.

In March, 88 Squadron moved to Swanton Morley and was declared non- operational until it had received sufficient of their new aircraft, the Boston IIIA. In the meantime, they were kept busy on numerous exercises including many

Bostons of 88 Squadron cross the North Sea at low level en-route to a target in Holland.
(Author's collection)

smoke-laying demonstrations to Army Commands. In early July, sixteen Bostons put down a smoke screen for a major Army exercise, with Dickie Gunning leading one of the sections which dropped 100 lb phosphorus bombs and 4 lb smoke bombs. At the time few realised that the techniques practised would be employed by the Bostons twelve months later in support of the D-Day landings.

Early in August the Squadron resumed low-level operations against major targets. The tactics employed had the clear stamp of the new Air Officer Commanding 2 Group, Dickie Gunning's old Squadron Commander, Air Vice Marshal Basil Embry. Typically, although there was no requirement for him to take part on operations, he continued to fly with the squadrons on operational sorties, describing himself as 'Wing Commander Smith'. On 8 August, Gunning and his crew in Boston BZ 242 led a flight against the Naval Stores Depot at Rennes which provided crucial supplies for the German U-boats operating from the Biscay ports. This was a major raid by three Boston squadrons, led by 107 Squadron with 88 and 342 (Lorraine) following. This large force flew in sixes line abreast at 250 feet with each aircraft carrying 500 lb Medium Capacity (MC) bombs. The target was attacked from low level by the first formation which dropped time-delay bombs as Gunning's flight climbed to 1,500 feet for their attack. Despite considerable flak, the Naval Stores 'were well and truly plastered' as the photographic evidence later proved.

A week later, on 16 August, an almost identical attack was mounted against the Denain Steel Works in Northern France. Gunning led the twelve aircraft of 88 Squadron and they rendezvoued with the other two Boston squadrons. Again flying in loose formation six abreast, the force headed for the French coast with their Typhoon escort. The attack went according to plan and considerable damage was caused, but as the aircraft left the target area serious trouble was encountered. The sortie had been mounted in the late afternoon and visibility from all the aircraft was severely affected by the countless small flies that had stuck to the windscreen. This was compounded by the need to leave the target pointing directly into sun. The bombers had to spread out to avoid collisions and the intense flak around Arras was able to engage individual aircraft just as the enemy fighters arrived. Within minutes, four Bostons of 88 Squadron were lost. One was Boston BZ 242 flown by Squadron Leader Dickie Gunning with his three crew members.

Other crews had seen Gunning's aircraft, with the starboard propeller feathered, dropping behind the formation as they turned for home having released their bombs on the target. Nothing further was heard for a month when a telegram arrived at the Squadron on 12 September reporting that Bill Brinn,

Bostons of 88 Squadron at Swanton Morley. (Author's collection)

Low-level attack on the Denain Steel Works led by Gunning on 16 August, 1943. (Author's collection)

the navigator in Gunning's crew, had arrived safely in Gibraltar. This raised hopes for the rest of the crew and two days later the Red Cross reported that Gunning and his gunner were prisoners of war. Sadly, the wireless operator, Flying Officer J. Ledgard, had failed to escape from the doomed Boston and had been killed. Dickie Gunning was to spend the rest of the war at the infamous *Stalag Luft 3* at Sagan as Prisoner of War 2267.

Little is known of his 'career' as a prisoner but a colleague indicated that 'there was never a dull moment when he was around' and went on to describe him as 'a model of the tough, intelligent and belligerent regular who was always

Bostons leave the damaged works. Shortly after this picture was taken, Gunning's aircraft was shot down. (Author's collection)

the ring-leader at off-duty times.' It is difficult to imagine that Dickie Gunning made life easy for his captors.

Two months after his capture it was announced that Squadron Leader Gunning had been awarded the Distinguished Flying Cross for '*displaying outstanding determination and faultless leadership having set a splendid example of courage and determination*'. His Station Commander described him as 'the *most outstanding junior officer I have ever known*' and commented on his '*natural leadership, determination and courage of the highest order.*' Air Vice-Marshal Basil Embry, his former commander on 107 Squadron, added some significant comments to the recommendation which was submitted for the approval of the Commander in Chief, Air Marshal Leigh-Mallory. He wrote, '*I have known Squadron Leader Gunning since the beginning of the war and can vouch for all his outstanding merit, as he served in a Squadron I commanded for nearly a year. In his second tour of operations he has set a most courageous example as a leader and has been chiefly responsible for the success of his squadron. In low level attacks, he has shown brilliant leadership, great courage and high skill. He richly deserves the award of the D.F.C.*' Citations for more prestigious awards are rarely written in such glowing terms.

After repatriation in May 1945, Gunning remained in the Royal Air Force, reverting to the rank of Flight Lieutenant. A photograph taken at the time clearly shows that he merely removed the inner rank braid leaving a conspicuous gap in anticipation! He attended No 100 Flying Instructors' Course at the Central Flying School in April, 1947, and shortly afterwards was able to restore his original rank braid when he was promoted to Squadron Leader. He spent the next three years as a pilot instructor on Prentice aircraft at 3 Flying Training School (FTS) at Feltwell in Norfolk where he was re-categorised as an A 2 instructor in April 1949. This was followed by two years as the Chief Ground Instructor at 7 FTS based at Cottesmore and responsible for training Royal Navy pilots using the Harvard and Prentice training aircraft. In July 1951, he departed for the Middle East and a three-year tour as the Senior Administrative Officer at Amman in Jordan. Shortly after his return he converted to jet aircraft at Weston Zoyland and served as a Squadron Commander at 201 Advanced Flying School before retiring from the Royal Air Force at the end of 1954.

After fighting a long illness with the courage and cheerfulness that had epitomised his distinguished wartime career as a determined and gallant low-level bomber pilot, Dickie Gunning died in early 1988.

Dickie Gunning (centre) with his navigator Bill Brinn DFM and gunner Jack Ledgard who was killed on the Denain raid. (J Pelly-Fry)

CHAPTER SEVEN

Bismarck Hunter – Percy Hatfield

The crew of Catalina 'O' of 210 Squadron had been airborne for almost twelve hours when the aircraft broke cloud just before midnight on the night of 26 May, 1941. Below them was a major German naval force which immediately gave the Catalina a very hot reception with tracer ripping into the fuselage of the flying-boat. The pilot, Percy Hatfield, took immediate evasive action by diving to sea level before taking up a shadowing position outside the range of the enemy guns, whilst a sighting report was made to Coastal Command and to the pursuing naval forces. The crew of Catalina 'O' had regained contact with the German battleship Bismarck. Some ten hours later the mighty ship was sunk by the Royal Navy.

Like so many other aircrew of his generation, Percy Hatfield started his long and distinguished RAF service as a Halton 'Brat' joining 27 Entry on 10 January, 1933, to train as a fitter. Over the next three years he distinguished himself and at the end of his training he was one of four apprentices to be awarded a Cadetship to the Royal Air Force College at Cranwell. In addition to excelling at his professional studies, he was recognised as an outstanding sportsman. His achievements at boxing and rugby culminated in a very successful season as captain of the RAF Apprentices rugby side. Those graduating with him included the future Air Marshal Sir John Lapsley who gained the major prize and a cadetship to Cranwell, where Hatfield continued to enhance his reputation as a sportsman gaining his Blue at boxing and rugby. He was awarded his pilot's wings on 30 April, 1937, and graduated six months later as a Pilot Officer.

Percy Hatfield's medals are Distinguished Flying Cross, Air Force Cross, 1939-45 Star, Atlantic Star, Africa Star, Defence Medal, War Medal, General Service Medal (Malaya clasp).

Hatfield continued his training at the School of Air Navigation, Manston and the School of General Reconnaissance at Thorney Island before starting flying-boat training at Calshot. On 3 December, 1938, he joined 202 Squadron based at Kalafrana, Malta, and equipped with London flying-boats. When war broke out, the Squadron had six London IIs on strength and on 9 September it received orders to move to Gibraltar, a naval base of great importance since it guarded the entrance to the Mediterranean. Operating from Algeciras Bay, 202 Squadron's Londons were required to patrol the approaches and the narrow Straits. Operations began immediately and Hatfield flew his first wartime anti-submarine sweep on 17 September when he completed a six-hour patrol in London K 9683.

During the first few months of the war a major requirement was the location and identification of German merchant ships. This involved regular photographic reconnaissance sorties, including a constant watch on the Spanish ports, in addition to the routine convoy protection and anti-submarine patrols. Throughout the winter patrols were maintained despite a shortage of spare parts, and the limited engineering facilities at Gibraltar made it necessary for maintenance to be carried out in Malta, giving the crews some respite from the long and monotonous patrolling.

When Italy entered the war in June, 1940, the situation at Gibraltar changed dramatically. Although there was little threat from Italy, the defeat of France

Hatfield joined A Squadron as a Flight Cadet at the Royal Air Force College, Cranwell in January 1936. (RAF College Cranwell)

A London II flying boat - K 9682 - of 202 Squadron. (202 Squadron)

and the establishment of Vichy forces in North Africa created increased requirements for reconnaissance. At the end of June, Hatfield carried out a detailed recce of the Vichy port of Oran where he confirmed the presence of the French fleet. The new Vichy government refused an order to surrender the French fleet to a British port and Hatfield carried out two more sorties to identify the units, which included two battleships, two cruisers and a number of destroyers and submarines. Two days later, on 3 July, a force of British ships bombarded the port and destroyed a battleship and damaged other ships.

Throughout July and August Hatfield flew many anti-submarine patrols and convoy escort sorties. An attempt to capture Dakar by the Free French in September required the Londons to keep a close watch for Vichy vessels operating from Casablanca. On consecutive days in mid-September Hatfield, flying K 5908, carried out two patrols and reported 'much activity'. On 12 September, he was attacked by Vichy Curtis fighters, but evaded them; the following day

A London II - K 9684 - of 202 Squadron. (via Peter Green)

he reported 'much flak and fighters'. With no other aircraft in the region, it fell to the obsolete bi-plane flying-boats to carry out these important reconnaissance sorties and it was no surprise when London K 9682 failed to return on 14 September. Two weeks later Hatfield flew Admiral Tovey to Plymouth, transiting the Bay of Biscay at night on a flight that took the lumbering London sixteen hours to complete. During September Hatfield had achieved no less than 114 flying hours.

After many months of fruitless searching for enemy submarines, 202 Squadron's luck changed in mid-October. On 18 October, Hatfield was flying K 5913 near the island of Alboran east of Gibraltar, when he sighted air bubbles and a small oil slick. Together with a second London, he attacked the spot with bombs and called up the two Royal Navy destroyers HMS *Firedrake* and HMS *Wrestler*. They sighted a large area of oil and soon obtained an asdic contact. With the two Londons in attendance, the destroyers set up a series of attack patterns with depth charges. With damage to the air supply and a build-up of chlorine gas, the Italian submarine *Durbo* surfaced some ninety minutes later and surrendered. The crew were captured and a party from the destroyers boarded the damaged submarine. Before a tow could be established, the submarine settled by the stern and sank. This action was to be the only success against an enemy submarine of the London flying-boat.

Three days later Hatfield was airborne when British destroyers made contact with another Italian submarine in an area close to the sinking of the *Durbo*. He remained in contact throughout the ninety-minute engagement by the three destroyers. After a full pattern of depth charges, the *Lafole* surfaced but showed no signs of surrender. HMS *Hotspur* increased speed to ram, to prevent the possibility of escape, and struck the stern of the submarine. The *Lafole* sank quickly with the loss of all but ten of its crew.

After this period of excitement it was back to routine patrolling for Hatfield and his crew. For the remainder of 1940 the Londons of 202 Squadron continued with anti-submarine patrols and convoy escorts. In the new year increased numbers of U-boats operating against convoys in the Western Approaches led to more effort from Gibraltar being directed to the Atlantic and Hatfield flew in support of Force H and the aircraft carrier HMS *Ark Royal*. On 21 March, 1941, he flew to Oran for a weather recce. Based on his report of satisfactory weather, *Ark Royal* launched its Blackburn Skua aircraft which completed a successful dive-bombing operation against the harbour. Ten days

Catalina I - W 8406 - of 210 Squadron at Oban. (N Owen)

later Percy Hatfield flew his 150th and final patrol with 202 Squadron. Since the outbreak of war he had flown just over 1000 hours in his antiquated bi-plane flying-boat on very unglamorous but vitally important sorties.

On his return to the United Kingdom Percy Hatfield joined 210 Squadron based at Oban in the north-west of Scotland. The Squadron had just started to re-equip with Catalina flying boats and, after a handful of conversion sorties, Hatfield flew his first convoy escort patrol on 27 April at the controls of AH 531. Two days later, with an experienced Catalina pilot, Flight Lieutenant Guy van der Kiste, as captain, he flew to Sullom Voe in the Shetlands to refuel before departing for a reconnaissance of the coastline between the ports of Hammerfest and Harstad in the extreme north of Norway. The sortie was flown at very low level and, despite heavy anti-aircraft fire, a successful recce was completed. After a nineteen-hour flight, the Catalina alighted at Sullom Voe before continuing to Oban. For this and other daring reconnaissance flights, Guy van der Kiste was awarded the Distinguished Service Order.

The chase and subsequent sinking of the battleship *Bismarck* is one of the great epics of naval warfare. Germany's most powerful warship, together with the battle-cruiser *Prinz Eugen,* had left the Baltic on 18 May for a raiding cruise against the convoys of merchant ships crossing the Atlantic. The Royal Navy had been anticipating such a move and two powerful forces had been despatched to intercept. On 24 May, the battleship HMS *Hood* intercepted the *Bismarck* between Greenland and Iceland. After a brief engagement the *Hood* blew up, leaving just three survivors, and *Bismarck* sailed on looking for more prey. The Royal Navy maintained contact but the German Admiral Lutjens' tactics to shake off the shadowers finally succeeded in the early hours of 25 May. In order to assist re-location, a long-range sweep by Catalinas was organised. 210 Squadron were tasked to provide an aircraft and Percy Hatfield and his crew were called to readiness at the Squadron operations room in Dungallan House, Oban.

A Catalina from 209 Squadron sighted the *Bismarck* at 1030 hours on the morning of 26 May and, two hours later, Hatfield lifted Catalina 'O' (W 8416) off the water at Oban and set heading for the battleship's last reported position. Sitting alongside him acting as co-pilot was Ensign Carl Rinehart, a US Navy Special Observer. Based on the Catalina report, Swordfish aircraft from *Ark Royal* delivered a torpedo attack which was unsuccessful. This was fortunate because the Navy aircraft had attacked the British cruiser HMS *Sheffield* by mistake. Another torpedo strike was ordered which damaged the *Bismarck's* steering gear, causing her to reduce speed.

After twelve hours in the air, and accurate plotting by navigator Frank Cadman, the crew of Catalina 'O' spotted the *Bismarck* and reported its position just before midnight. Hatfield sought some cloud cover and took

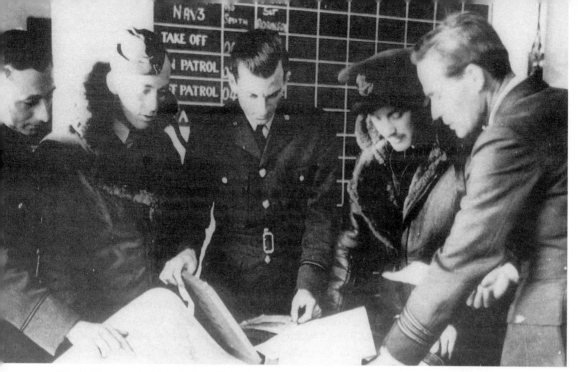

Hatfield, second right, 'de-briefs' the Bismark *sortie in a posed shot for the benefit of the press.*
(N Owen)

the Catalina in for a closer look. On breaking cloud he was directly above the battleship and was immediately engaged by a dense barrage of multi-coloured tracer. Violent evasive action was taken which threw LAC Roy Davis, the aircraft's fitter, from his rest bunk seconds before bullet holes appeared across the full length of the bunk. Further hits were sustained to the wing and aerial. Hatfield managed to get clear and took up a shadowing position as they waited to see the gunflashes which heralded the start of the historic and final duel between the *Bismarck* and the Royal Navy ships. Soon afterwards Cadman took an astro fix over the German battleship under fire and at 0300 hours Hatfield turned his damaged Catalina for Oban, but not before he had tried to engage an enemy Blohm and Voss aircraft which had arrived on the scene.

By the time Catalina 'O' alighted at Oban, the *Bismarck* was history. Hatfield and his crew also carved a small piece of history by being airborne on patrol for almost twenty-seven hours, an endurance record for the Catalina. The following day Hatfield and his crew re-enacted the de-brief at Dungallan House for the benefit of the *Illustrated London News*. Surprisingly, there were no awards for Hatfield and his crew.

Further long patrols were to follow and sixteen to eighteen-hour flights were routine. On 27 July, Hatfield took off in Catalina AH 550 to provide escort for an outbound convoy to Gibraltar which was 300 miles south west of Land's End. The convoy had recently been attacked by a U-boat and, in poor visibility and low cloud, Hatfield spotted a surface craft leaving 'a creamy wake and bow wave with a dark object in the centre'. The identity was suspected and the Catalina challenged but received no reply. A flare was dropped and the wake, which had been very visible on the black surface, was gradually disappearing. Hatfield dropped a flame float, followed by two 450 lb depth charges, from 200 feet on the estimated position. Unfortunately, there were no conclusive results and Hatfield resumed his patrol, eventually alighting at Oban after a twenty-five hour flight.

More long flights followed when Hatfield transported three VIPs to Archangel and returned with a Polish General. Over the following few days he completed two more convoy patrols in excess of twenty hours. During August, 1941, he completed no less than 122 hours of flying. Bearing in mind the primitive nature of the Catalina's rest facilities and the noise levels from the engines situated just above the aircraft's cabin, this was a prodigious feat of endurance and too little has been made of the outstanding contribution of Coastal Command's long-range anti-submarine force and the gallant crews who spent so many long and tedious hours keeping open the vital sea lanes across the Atlantic.

Hatfield recorded another 135 hours in October and November and then it was time for a rest tour. He was posted as a test pilot to the Maritime Experimental Aircraft Establishment based at Helensburgh! His only reward after his arduous and successful tour was promotion to Squadron Leader.

During his fourteen-month period as a test pilot, Hatfield flew sixteen types of flying-boats and float-planes on a wide variety of trials. These included the

The Spitfire Vb floatplane - W 3760 - flown by Hatfield during his time at the Maritime Experimental Aircraft Establishment at Helensburgh. (via Peter Green)

dropping of many types of bombs, depth charges, flares and flame floats. Many trials were flown in Catalinas, Sunderlands, Walrus and Stranraer flying-boats, but flights in Shark, Seafox and Scion float-planes were also frequent. Parachute dive-brake trials in Sunderlands and Catalinas provided some excitement and Hatfield was to carry out much of the flying during these trials. Just before returning to operational flying he flew two sorties in a Spitfire V (W 3760) equipped with floats. Assessed as an above average flying-boat test pilot, he was promoted to Wing Commander and posted to Bathurst in West Africa to assume command of 95 Squadron equipped with Sunderland III flying-boats.

There are many who believe that the battle against the U-boat was restricted to the North Atlantic and the Bay of Biscay, but the menace ranged over a much wider area, including the South Atlantic and along the supply routes rounding the Cape of Good Hope. These routes were crucial during the period that shipping had to avoid the Mediterranean. There was little protection for the convoys on these long routes and the U-boats were able to operate with relative ease; losses of merchant ships reached alarming proportions in 1941 and 1942. The deployment to West Africa of a number of maritime patrol squadrons started to redress the balance and sinkings became less frequent.

It was March 1943 when Percy Hatfield arrived at Bathurst in the Gambia, known in earlier years as 'the white man's grave'. With such large areas to patrol, detachments were established along the West African coast at Port Etienne, Freetown and Jui. Within a few weeks of arriving, Hatfield had 'acquired' an unserviceable Walrus which his engineers soon made fit for flying. This aircraft proved to be a valuable taxi, allowing the Squadron Commander to keep in touch with his widespread unit.

Hatfield flew his first patrol on 1 April, 1943, and over the next few months he completed another twenty convoy escorts and anti-submarine sweeps. On 12 August, he was flying Sunderland III 'S' on an anti-submarine patrol when he was diverted to search for survivors from a 200 Squadron Liberator which had reported that it was under fire from a U-boat. Hatfield arrived at the scene some time after a Sunderland, captained by Flight Sergeant C. H. Watkinson of 204 Squadron, had located the lifeboat and dropped a Lindholme survival gear. Hatfield dropped further supplies to the survivors while reporting their position. On returning to base, he learnt that the men were the only surviving members of *U 468*, a 500 ton submarine commanded by *Oberleutnant zur See* Clemens Schamong which had been attacked and sunk by Flying Officer L. Trigg and his crew. They had caught the U-boat on the surface and imme-

A Sunderland III of 95 Squadron at Bathurst in 1944. (Author's collection)

Sunderland - JM 671 - at Cape Verde Islands just after Hatfield landed on 22 January 1944 with vaccine for the military unit ashore. (via Andy Thomas)

diately came under intense and accurate anti-aircraft fire which set the Liberator on fire. Trigg continued to attack and his depth charges were dropped accurately as his aircraft plunged into the Atlantic with the loss of all his crew. Among the few German survivors was the U-boat Captain and his First Lieutenant and they spoke very highly of the courage of the tenacious New Zealand Liberator pilot. On the basis of their evidence, Trigg was posthumously awarded the Victoria Cross, the only occasion on which a citation was based solely on the evidence of the enemy.

Percy Hatfield's apprentice training as a fitter and his experiences as a test pilot gave him a very innovative approach to flying and he spent much time modifying the gun turrets of his Sunderland by fitting twin .5 inch cannons which he tested at every opportunity. Patrols continued and on 22 January, 1944, he flew Sunderland DM 671 on a reconnaissance to the Cape Verde Islands. He landed with supplies of yellow fever vaccine to counter an epidemic among the small military detachment. After a series of visits flying his Walrus to his various detachments, Hatfield left 95 Squadron at the end of May after just over one year in command. His wartime career was over, after flying 1850 hours on 240 operational sorties. Shortly after, it was announced that he had been awarded the Distinguished Flying Cross for his *'outstanding record as a pilot and for his excellent leadership.'*

At the end of the war Hatfield was a student at the RAF Staff College and this was followed by a ground tour at the Headquarters of Technical Training Command. He was not content to 'fly a desk' and managed to maintain his flying currency on Proctors, Austers and Hurricanes. In May, 1947, he was posted to Seletar, on Singapore Island, as the Commanding Officer of 209 Squadron. The Squadron was equipped with Sunderland V flying-boats and was employed mainly in the transport support role. This included a weekly

Borneo Courier Service and Hatfield flew many VIPs to Sarawak, Brunei and Sabah. Later, regular flights were flown to Hong Kong via Manila.

Always keen to fly new aircraft, Hatfield accepted an open invitation to fly the first jet to visit Singapore, a Meteor IV. He was one of twenty pilots to participate in the 'trial' and on 21 August, 1947, experienced jet flying for the first time. When the trial was reported in an edition of *Flight* magazine, he took umbrage at the comment, 'twenty pilots ranging from the 'Spit' fighter boys to a pilot of the ponderous Sunderlands', and he wrote an amusing retort in reply.

Flights to Christmas Island, to Tokyo and an Australian Cruise to Brisbane added variety to the routine of carrying Government passengers on official business on the Borneo Courier Service, but in February, 1949, Hatfield was required to perform a more urgent task.

Burma had become an independent Republic the previous month and was facing an uncertain future. Plans had been formulated to evacuate any British nationals whose lives might be in danger should there be any violence during the transition period. In the early hours of 22 February, a message was received at Seletar seeking immediate assistance. Within three hours a scratch ground-crew had prepared a Sunderland and Hatfield took off with the minimum briefing and just two flares to mark the flarepath. The flight encountered appalling weather and once he entered Burmese airspace he was told that flying over Burma was forbidden. Hatfield pressed on, however, and eventually obtained permission to land on the river at Chauk in the middle of the Burma oilfields. His landing was described as 'brilliant' as he manoeuvred between native craft and long fishing nets spread across the river.

Only the British families in the immediate vicinity could be organised in time for Hatfield to make a daylight take-off. However, it was late afternoon before everything was ready. With a ban on night flying in Rangoon, it was decided to stay overnight and, with rebel forces near, a nervous night was spent guarding the aircraft. At dawn the next morning the evacuees, consisting of nineteen women, fifteen children and six men, were taken on board and Hatfield made a safe take off for Rangoon. On return to Singapore, he received a signal from the Commander-in-Chief which complimented him and his crew for an operation that ' reflected great credit on you and your squadron, amply demonstrating to all the efficiency of the Royal Air Force and which has earned the sincere thanks of the British community in Burma.'

Four months later the Royal Air Force handed over responsibility for the Borneo Courier Service to Malayan Airlines and Hatfield flew the last sortie, taking the Air Officer Commanding on a farewell visit. On return, he received another letter of congratulation, this time from the Commissioner General on behalf of the Governments of Sarawak and North Borneo.

During July 1949, 209 Squadron started training for operations against the

Communist guerrilla forces operating in Malaya. The Sunderland's role was bombing with 20 lb bombs, followed by low-level strafing of the area. The average bomb load on these operations was 288 bombs and 4000 rounds of .303 and .5 ammunition. Hatfield flew the Squadron's first Operation 'Firedog' sortie on 7 July.

Within a month there was more excitement for Hatfield when he was scrambled to assist the US ship *Pecos* in the South China Sea with a dangerously ill seaman aboard who needed immediate medical attention. Hatfield took off with a Royal Air Force doctor and a nursing sister aboard his Sunderland and headed for a rendezvous at Mangkai Island, 150 miles north-east of Singapore. The ship had been delayed and had not reached the island so Hatfield had to make an open sea landing and the heavy under-swell caused damage to the fabric of the tailplane as the aircraft landed. Hatfield taxied alongside *Pecos* and stopped engines before a boat took the surgeon and nursing sister on board. He then took off without further damage and returned to Seletar.

Within a month, Hatfield's tour at Seletar came to an end. This coincided with the need to ferry a Sunderland (NJ 272) back to England for major servicing and Hatfield captained a crew made up of men returning at the end of their tours of duty. The aircraft left Seletar on 23 September and five days later alighted at Calshot. A short time later it was announced that Wing Commander Percy Hatfield had been awarded the Air Force Cross for his valuable services in command of 209 Squadron.

Over the next few years he attended a number of flying courses and completed a tour as the weapons officer at HQ Coastal Command before he undertook a short tour in Hong Kong where he managed to fly fifty hours in a Meteor VII. His final tour was spent in the Ministry of Defence and on 5 February, 1958, he made his last flight in a service aircraft when he flew Chipmunk WK 533. During his twenty-year flying career with the RAF Percy Hatfield had accumulated 5070 hours, flying almost every type of flying-boat,

Sunderland V - VB 888 - of 209 Squadron at Seletar. (via Peter Green)

in addition to Spitfires, Hurricanes and the early jets.

Throughout his Royal Air Force career Hatfield had taken every opportunity to fly any aircraft available. It was no surprise, therefore, that within a month of his last service flight he was airborne again, having started a crop-spraying company flying a Tiger Moth (G-ANRX) from Boxted near Colchester. When he began these operations, crop spraying was in its infancy and he became a recognised expert, frequently giving lectures and addressing seminars. During 1959 he hit the headlines again when the *Daily Mail* reported his 'bombing' of the Roman city of Colchester with thousands of leaflets publicising a competition organised by a local radio firm offering TV sets as prizes. One landed at the feet of a patrolling policeman and the ex-Cranwell cadet ended in court charged with 'depositing litter' and causing a breach of the Air Navigation Order. After being fined £34, Hatfield chuckled that 'it was great fun aiming off for wind and flying this new operation'. Unfortunately, the fine was more than the fee he received for the flight.

Hatfield became the aviation director of Airspray (Colchester) Ltd operating from Boxted airfield, and obtained a major contract for spraying the cotton crops in Sudan. Following a coup, he flew to Khartoum to rescue the three Jackaroo aircraft and two of his pilots. The trio flew the aircraft back to Boxted, a flying adventure that deserves its own story.

On 27 July, 1965, he was flying a Bellanca Citabria high-wing monoplane on a crop-spraying sortie near Chelmsford when he crashed while turning to line up for a further run. The aircraft burst into flames and 49 year old Percy Hatfield died in the wreckage, a tragic loss of a dedicated and courageous airman who had served his country throughout the war flying many hazardous operational sorties and test flights.

Wing Commander P Hatfield, OC 209 Squadron poses with his Squadron at Seletar in 1949.
(Author's collection)

CHAPTER EIGHT

From Greek Tragedy to Night Intruder – Len Page

Standing in the late afternoon sunlight of Easter Sunday, 13 April, 1941, Len Page and his colleagues of 211 Squadron stood watching as the six Blenheims of their depleted Squadron took off in a final attempt to stem the on-rushing German advance into Greece. A few hours later they gathered again on the airfield at Paramythia to form a welcoming party, but their wait was in vain. None of the aircraft returned. Without fighter escort, the formation had been attacked by Me109Es of 6/JG 27 and all six aircraft had been shot down near the Albanian border. 211 Squadron had ceased to exist as an operational squadron and Len Page's war in Greece was over, but he would fight on until victory four years later.

Ipswich-born Leonard Robert Page had joined the Royal Air Force as an aircraft hand/mate in July, 1935, qualifying as a flight rigger some twelve months later. Initially he was posted to 206 (GR) Squadron where he soon

Len Page's medals are Distinguished Flying Medal and Bar, General Service Medal (Palestine clasp) *1939-45 Star, Africa Star, France and Germany Star, Defence Medal, War Medal with Mention in Despatch.*

volunteered for duties as a part-time air gunner which qualified him for 'crew pay'. In June, 1937, he joined 211 (B) Squadron, equipped with the Hind, at Grantham . Within a year the squadron moved to the Middle East and Len Page had remustered as a Flight Rigger/Air Gunner, known throughout the Royal Air Force as 'tradesmen aircrew' and entitled to wear the 'winged bullet' on the right sleeve of their uniform. Len Page was soon in action. Following disturbances between the Arabs and Jews, the Squadron moved to Ramleh in Palestine and for his services he received the General Service Medal with the clasp for Palestine.

After three months the Squadron returned to Helwan in Egypt and started intensive training as tension in Europe increased. A move to Ismailia in January, 1939, coincided with the arrival of Blenheim Is to replace the Hinds. The Squadron took a more operational posture as it moved forward to El Daba in the Western Desert where it remained until Italy declared war on 10 June, 1940.

Initially there was sporadic air activity only and it was to be four weeks before Page flew his first operational sortie. With Pilot Officer Ken Dundas at the controls, Blenheim I (L 1482) took off as part of a twelve-aircraft formation to bomb a petrol dump and magazine at Tobruk. With no formal training, Page flew as the observer, a role he was to fill on many occasions over the next few years.

Activity started to increase during September in support of Wavell's offensive tactics, with raids against transport and troop concentrations and further attacks against Tobruk. The Squadron lost its Commanding Officer on one of these raids and the Flight Commander assumed command. Squadron Leader J. R. Gordon-Finlayson, known throughout the Middle East as 'the Bish', was to achieve legendary status as a fearless leader, always leading his squadron from the front.

By the end of October Page had flown ten operational sorties as the four Blenheim squadrons of 202 Group continued to harass the slow Italian advance which, at one point, reached Sidi Barrani, fifty miles into Egypt, before it came to a halt. On 28 October, as the Blenheims prepared to support Wavell's counter-attack, Italy invaded Greece, and, together with 84 Squadron, 211 was withdrawn to Ismailia where it prepared to re-deploy to Greece.

The need to support our Greek allies created many dilemmas for the British Government. With the Battle of Britain at its height and invasion threatening, reinforcements and support could only come from the Middle East, an area which itself had been starved of additional forces. With Wavell preparing for his counter-attack, this call for squadrons to go to Greece came at a critical time and was to have a major bearing on the future conduct of the desert war.

The aircraft of 211 Squadron left for Menidi, near Athens, to join 84 Squadron on 23 November as Gladiators of 80 Squadron flew into Trikkala, the first fighter squadron to arrive in Greece. The Blenheim squadrons were to support the Greek army which was heavily engaged in the mountains in the north of their country. They were also to carry out strategic attacks against the well-equipped Albanian ports of Durazzo and Valona, the main ports for the disembarkation of the invading Italians.

The Squadron was in action the day after its arrival when nine aircraft, led by the Squadron Commander, took off to bomb Durazzo. Len Page was observer to Ken Dundas in L 1539. Anti-aircraft fire over the target was intense but successful attacks were pressed home. Three aircraft were hit, including the Squadron Commander and Len Page's aircraft. With the hydraulic system and the tail trimming gear damaged, Ken Dundas had to make a wheels-up landing. 'The Bish' was not so fortunate and failed to return. Just as the Squadron started to mourn the loss of its commander, news came through that his aircraft had made a successful crash landing on a beach in Corfu. The pattern for 211 Squadron's air war over Greece had been established.

During December the crews soon became aware of the acute dangers posed by the weather. Numerous attacks were mounted against the docks at Valona but many of the raids had to be aborted because of the extreme weather encountered as the aircraft tried to cross the mountains. The lack of navigation aids added to the problems. On 7 December, nine aircraft took off for a bombing raid, but only three reached the target, the remainder returning with severe icing problems. Two aircraft crashed in the mountains with all six crew

A 211 Squadron Blenheim I prepares to taxi at a Greek airfield in early 1941. (MOD)

Blenheim I - L 6670 - of 211 Squadron lands at Paramythia, Greece after a bombing sortie over Albania in March 1941. (J Dunnett)

members losing their lives. On the 17th, Page and his crew turned back for the third consecutive time when severe weather prevented them from carrying out a photographic reconnaissance of Durazzo harbour.

During the final week of December, Page and his colleagues achieved two successful sorties against Valona when their sticks of bombs were seen to fall amongst dockside buildings and the cargo being unloaded. For good measure, and perhaps to vent some frustration, they followed up one of their bombing attacks with a series of low-level runs, machine-gunning aircraft on the nearby airfield. The Italian aircraft had been very active against the Blenheim formations and any opportunity to strike back was taken. So ended 1940 which had provided two months of intense activity against a spirited enemy and conducted in some dreadful weather.

The start of 1941 brought no respite from the weather. With the strategic campaign against the Albanian ports continuing, routes avoiding the mountains had to be found. A coastal route along the Gulf of Corinth and past Corfu was used. This brought an additional hazard as raids were frequently intercepted by Italian fighters and the CR 42s and G 50s claimed a number of Blenheims. On 20 January, Page and his crew were attacked by three CR 42s as they completed their bombing run against the military stores and jetties at Valona. With help from others in the formation the enemy fighters were driven off.

Early February saw the Squadron moving to Northern Greece to a forward base at Paramythia situated in a high valley in the mountains and known as the 'Valley of Fairy Tales'. The move allowed the Squadron to react quickly in support of the hard-pressed but successful Greek Army. Accompanying them were 80 Squadron, who with their Gladiators and fighter escort, were to be a regular and welcome feature. At the same time, Len Page was allocated to a new pilot when he crewed with Pilot Officer John Hooper, one of two

Rhodesian brothers who had joined the Royal Air Force and trained together and had now joined the same squadron. Flying alongside each other, they were to remain together for over a year.

On their first sortie the Hooper crew in L 1542 was attacked by fighters but little damage was inflicted. To support a new Greek Army offensive, bombing sorties against enemy camps, dumps and roads became the feature and the presence of a fighter escort, often led by the South African ace Pat Pattle, helped reduce losses. Hurricanes replaced the Gladiators and on 24 February, they escorted 211 as they attacked military buildings and motor transport near the eastern bridgehead on the Tepelene to Kelcyre road. Page saw his bombs hit the target causing a large fire and dense smoke.

March brought increased activity and Len Page and his crew were to complete twelve close-support sorties in their Blenheim L 1496. On 4 March, led by 'the Bish', they flew as the number 2 as nine Squadron aircraft and six from 84 Squadron took off with a fighter escort to attack an Italian cruiser and escorts which were shelling the coastal road near the Albanian – Greek border. Several near misses were noted and the fighter escort had many successful engagements with enemy fighters. On 15 March, the Blenheims bombed Valona airfield at night as part of a diversionary raid for Fleet Air Arm Swordfish aircraft attacking shipping in the harbour. For the rest of the month it was back to attacking targets in direct support of the Army. It was the last raid for 'the Bish' as he was promoted and awarded the Distinguished Service Order. Few gallantry awards were more popular or richly deserved.

The situation in Greece changed dramatically when the Germans invaded from Bulgaria on 10 April. Within three days the Squadron suffered the tragic loss of the whole formation of six aircraft shot down by Me109Es and 211 ceased to exist as an operational unit; they had flown their last raid in Greece.

The few remaining Blenheims were used to evacuate the Squadron personnel, first from Paramythia to Agrinon, and within a few days they were carrying nine groundcrew in each aircraft as they withdrew to Eleusis. By 21 April, few Blenheims remained serviceable and a shuttle to Crete was set up; finally the Squadron straggled back to Egypt. By the end of April, the few survivors assembled at Lydda in Palestine to re-equip and rebuild.

Len Page was one of the few to fly throughout the Greek campaign, taking part in some of the most dangerous missions and seeing the loss of most of his long-standing friends.

During May the Squadron re-equipped with Blenheim IVs. With their regular gunner, Sergeant Curly Kearns, John Hooper and Len Page took off in N 3581 on 26 May for the Squadron's first bombing sortie against the Vichy French in Syria. Together with another Squadron aircraft they bombed the airfield at Palmyra and Page saw the four 250 lbs bomb score direct hits on the hangars.

Len Page on left with his pilot, Pilot Officer John Hooper and 'Curly' Kearns the Wireless Operator/Air Gunner at Menidi, Greece in April 1941. (Jack Hooper)

Two days later they carried out a five-hour offensive reconnaissance of Syria machine-gunning aircraft at Palmyra and scoring hits at Rayak with bombs. On 30 May, they flew their third sortie over Syria with a five-and-a-half-hour recce of the pipeline in East Syria.

In early June, the few remaining operational crews of 211 were transferred to 11 Squadron at the nearby base of Aqir. Over the next four weeks Page flew a further fourteen bombing sorties with John Hooper and Curly Kearns, attacking targets with 250 lb bombs and incendiaries. After attacks against the airfields at Aleppo and Rayak, Page scored a direct hit on the bow of a merchant ship off Beirut. A few days later heavy light flak and machine-gun fire was encountered while attacking a destroyer in Beirut harbour and a petrol and explosives depot at Telkalakh was severely damaged. After successful attacks on camps and storage areas at Talia and Rayak, Page took off in V 5953 for a strategic reconnaissance of shipping at Beirut, Tripoli and Lattiqui. It was his fifty-fifth operational sortie and he had been on continuous operations for just over a year. Shortly afterwards, the *London Gazette* announced that he had been awarded the Distinguished Flying Medal, the recommendation stating that '*he has taken part in 50 raids and has always shown himself to be a very determined and courageous man. In times of action he always remained cool and collected and proved himself an exceptionally fine navigator.*'

In late July 11, Squadron was withdrawn from the front line and spent the next three months in the relative quiet of Iraq. October, 1941, saw the Squadron back in action when it moved to Landing Ground (LG) 104 in the Western Desert and Page and his regular crew took part in the first raid, an attack against military workshops at Bardia. Caught by searchlights and engaged by night fighters, they still managed to carry out a successful attack and return safely to base. After one more sortie Pilot Officer John Hooper and his brother Jack, together with their crews, were posted to the Strategic Reconnaissance Unit equipped with Marylands.

After a short conversion course of two weeks, during which time Sergeant Hall joined the crew, Len Page and his colleagues took off from LG 122 in Maryland AH 346 for a photographic reconnaissance of Sidi Rezegh and Capuzzo at 25,000 feet. Over the next few weeks six similar sorties were flown with particular attention being paid to the enemy's airfields and landing grounds. These included Maturba, Derna, Bir Hacheim and Gazala, all to change hands on numerous occasions over the coming months.

On 6 December, John Hooper lifted off from Fuka in Maryland AH 370 for a reconnaissance of Benina and Benghazi harbour. At 23,000 feet he steadied his aircraft for the run over Benghazi. Over the harbour the aircraft was hit by anti-aircraft fire and Hooper was badly wounded in the neck by a piece of shrapnel. Seeing that his pilot was paralysed and unable to speak, Len Page immediately took control of the aircraft and turned for base. Approaching the airfield two hours later, he offered Kearns and Hall the option to bale out while he attempted to land the aircraft. They both chose to stay and assist. Hooper regained consciousness and gesticulated that he would attempt a landing. With Page assisting at the controls and talking him down through a sandstorm and in high winds, a safe landing was made.

Three weeks later it was announced that Len Page had been given the immediate award of a Bar to his Distinguished Flying Medal for his '*outstanding courage*', the award of a Bar being one of only sixty to be awarded in the Second World War. His pilot, John Hooper, was awarded an immediate Distinguished Flying Cross. He eventually made a good recovery after a long spell in hospital

A Maryland I - AH 371 photographic reconnaissance aircraft at an airfield in Egypt. Page flew a similar aircraft back to Fuka after his pilot had been severely wounded. (via Andy Thomas)

An extract from John Hooper's log book giving details of the Maryland reconnaissance sorties in December 1941. (Jack Hooper)

AIRCRAFT		PILOT, OR	2ND PILOT, PUPIL	DUTY	SINGLE-ENGINE AIRCRAFT				MULTI-ENGINE AIRCRAFT	
					DAY		NIGHT		DAY	
Type	No.	1ST PILOT	OR PASSENGER	(INCLUDING RESULTS AND REMARKS)	DUAL (1)	PILOT (2)	DUAL (4)	PILOT (4)	DUAL (5)	1ST PILOT (6)
—	—	—	—	— TOTALS BROUGHT FORWARD	66.40	97.35	2.40	1.45	4.55	243.45
SUMMARY OF FLYING FOR NOVEMBER, 1941.		J.R. Hooper. P/O	1 MARYLAND.							27.25
										OFFIC
MARYLAND.	1640.	SELF.	SGT. PAGE. D.F.M. SGT. KEARNS. SGT. HALL.	PHOTO RECCO. FUKA - L.G.122 (LANDED) - GADD-EL-AHMAR. -MARTUBA MAIN & WEST - DERNA (VISUAL) - TIMIMI - ROAD W. OF GAZALA - BIR HACHEIM - RETURN L.G.122 (LANDED) & TO FUKA. FIRED ON BY OWN A.A. SE. EL GOBI. 18 BURSTS — ACCURATE.						4.45
MARYLAND.	A.H.370	SELF.	SGT. PAGE. D.F.M. SGT. KEARNS. SGT. HALL. (HEIGHT. 23,000)	PHOTO. RECCO- FUKA- L.G.122.- BENINA-BERKA L.G. BENGHASI HARBOUR SELF HIT OVER HARBOUR BY PIECE OF A/A IN THROAT. SGT. PAGE FLEW BACK TO FUKA. J LANDED.						5.20
BOMBAY			12 PASS.	FUKA TO. HELIO. HOSPITAL.						
GRAND TOTAL [Cols. (1) to (10)] 439 Hrs. 50 Mins.				TOTALS CARRIED FORWARD	66.40 (1)	97.35 (2)	2.40 (3)	1.45 (4)	4.55 (5)	253.50 (6)

and returned to Europe to complete a tour on Mosquitos. For Len Page it was the end of his operational flying for the time being.

On return to Britain, Page spent a year as an instructor at 4 Air Observer School at West Freugh during which time he was commissioned. For twelve months from May, 1943, he served with the Telecommunications Research Establishment at Defford where he was involved in the development of airborne radar equipments. After his well-earned rest he returned to operations. With his extensive knowledge and experience of air-interception radars gained during his test and evaluation flying at Defford, he was given a posting to a nightfighter squadron. Before joining 605 (County of Warwick) Squadron at Manston, he completed the Mosquito conversion course at Harwell and the Intruder Course at High Ercall.

Arriving at Manston in May, 1944, he crewed with Flight Lieutenant L. Welch DFC and they were to fly together throughout their tour, becoming one of the most effective crews on the Squadron. 605 Squadron had developed an excellent reputation as a night-intruder squadron seeking out *Luftwaffe* aircraft over their own airfields. Flying a Mosquito VI, Len Page and his pilot took off on 10 May for their first sortie, an 'ops training sortie' over the *Luftwaffe* base at Creil in France. A few nights later they were on patrol over a very busy Venlo airfield where they engaged an enemy night fighter but were unable to observe the results.

On 28 May they took off early in the morning in company with the Flight

A Mosquito FB VI of 605 Squadron. (MOD)

Commander heading for the Heligoland area. Between Wangerooge Island and Heligoland they encountered three Ju 52 aircraft flying low over the sea on an anti-mining operation. These aircraft were fitted with the ring for exploding mines but within minutes all three had fallen to the guns of the two Mosquitos, Page and his pilot being credited with one destroyed. Sir Roderic Hill, C-in-C Fighter Command, signalled his congratulations to the two crews 'for their excellent show in shooting down the 'ringed' Ju 52s'.

In support of the Normandy landings on D-Day 605 were out in force keeping the German night fighters firmly grounded. Welch and Page patrolled over the airfields of St Dizier, Metz and Nancy in Eastern France. For the remainder of June and all of July the Squadron was heavily engaged on patrols against the new menace of the V-1 rockets. Flying mainly at night, the Mosquito crews would set up a patrol line outside the area designated as a gun-belt and hope to gain visual contact with the bright exhaust flame emitted by the V-1. The Mosquito would dive down to gain speed and aim to close on the target. The crew would then position the aircraft astern and just below before shooting the flying-bomb down with cannon fire. This was a hazardous operation as the 'bomb' was always likely to explode just ahead of the pursuing nightfighter and there were numerous occasions when the fabric-covered Mosquitos were forced

A formation of Mosquito FB VI aircraft of 605 Squadron. (MOD)

to fly through the debris. While flying with Manston's Station Commander, Wing Commander G. Raphael DSO DFC, on 3 July, a number of divers were attacked, two being shot down. During the month the Squadron destroyed twenty-nine of the 'doodlebugs' and another signal of congratulation arrived from the Commander-in-Chief.

In early August, the night intruders were armed with bombs and Welch and Page took off on the 8th on a 'Freelance' sortie during which they damaged two trains at Altenburg. A few days later two barges were shot up on the River Rhine and two 250 lb bombs were left on the railway bridge which crossed the Rhine at Rees.

During August Bomber Command had re-commenced its major offensive against the German cities and the *Luftwaffe* nightfighters were taking a heavy toll of the heavy bombers. The night intruder sorties by the Mosquitos were designed to cause maximum disruption to these nightfighter operations. With the Allies firmly established on the continent, the Mosquitos could stage through French airfields and extend their range considerably. Despite intense and accurate light flak, Page attacked the dispersals at Kitzingham and Illesheim airfields deep into Germany, using the Mosquito's high speed and manoeuvrability to return safely at low level. Next they turned their attention to the airfields in North Germany and Denmark. On 18 September, they bombed the airfields at Jagel and Husum and, two nights later, they found activity at the *Luftwaffe* nightfighter airfield at Ahlhorn where they were fired on by the light flak batteries.

Early on the morning of 7 October, Page and his pilot flew to St Dizier in Eastern France, accompanied by Flight Lieutenant A. J. Craven in a second Mosquito. After refuelling and briefing, the two Mosquitos took off in good weather on what proved to be one of the outstanding day-intruder flights of the war. Flying at tree-top level, Len Page navigated the pair to Fischamend-Markt airfield just outside Vienna which had just suffered a heavy bombing attack. At the airfield they found mainly Ju 52 transport aircraft and the Mosquitos went straight into a low-level attack with cannons. On this first pass they set two aircraft on fire before heading for the airfield at Munchendorf which 'was simply littered with aircraft'. On arrival they strafed the numerous aircraft, including Ju 88s, Ju 52s and He 111, claiming ten destroyed and six damaged between them. Welch and Page caught a Me 108 as it was landing and a burst from the cannons sent the enemy aircraft careering across the airfield on fire. After a second diving attack, both Mosquitos were damaged by the intense flak and the air speed indicator of Page's aircraft was put out of action. With defences alerted, the two Mosquitos escaped at very low level and arrived back at St Dizier after spending almost six hours over enemy territory. Returning to Manston later in the evening they were feted by their colleagues. Two days later they were invited to London and appeared with the famous wartime newsreader Frank Philips on BBC radio immediately after the nine o'clock news when 'they thrilled millions of listeners' with their experiences.

After two more uneventful 'Flower' sorties, Len Page and his pilot were rested after an outstanding tour of thirty-six operations which earned Welch a Bar to his DFC and a Mention in Despatches for Page. Flying together in the ultimate two-seater aircraft, where crew co-operation was so fundamental for success, many must wonder how a distinction could be drawn between the two crew members who had shared every sortie and danger together.

Flying in two of the most demanding roles, daylight bombing in Greece and North Africa and night intruding over Germany, Len Page had completed no less than 101 operational sorties. After a period as the training officer on 151 Squadron and a spell at Headquarters Fighter Command, he left the service as a Flight Lieutenant in October, 1945.

So ended an action-packed ten years in the RAF, and a record of service to be proud of, by a very gallant air gunner, observer, bomb aimer, radar operator and navigator who had to turn his hand to piloting in order to save his captain's life.

CHAPTER NINE

Air Gunner – Kenneth Edingborough

Just after midnight on 12 April, 1941, Ken Edingborough and his fellow crew members approached the darkened dispersal at RAF Newton where their Wellington Ic bomber was bombed-up and ready for action. Edingborough made his way to the rear turret, his lonely and cold outpost for the next six hours. He was about to embark on his first operational war sortie, a bombing raid on the port of Brest. Incredibly, he had just forty flying hours recorded in his log-book and this was the very first time he had ever flown at night.

Kenneth Edingborough, a quiet, modest North Londoner, joined the Royal Air Force in August, 1938 as an aircraft hand/driver petrol. After completing his training at the end of October, 1939, he joined the recently formed 613 (City of Manchester) Squadron equipped with Hectors and Lysanders. The Squadron operated in the Army Co-operation role and the ground crew were kept very busy as the aircraft flew from Hawkinge in support of the British Expeditionary Force and the evacuation from Dunkirk. As the Battle of Britain raged, the Squadron moved to Martlesham Heath in Suffolk and gave valuable service searching for aircrew shot down into the sea and guiding the RAF's air-sea rescue launches.

During May Edingborough had volunteered for aircrew duties and was

Kenneth Edingborough's medals are the Distinguished Flying Medal, 1939-45 Star, Aircrew Europe Star, Defence Medal, War medal.

Ken Edinborough wearing the ribbons of the DFM and 1939-45 Star. (Author's collection)

selected for air gunner duties but he had to wait until the end of August before travelling to Manby in Lincolnshire to start his training. After one week learning the theory, he took off on 31 August in a Demon (K 8181) for his first flight. Four more training flights followed on his first day of flying during which he fired 310 rounds. The hectic pace of flying training continued and within three weeks he had completed his *ab-initio* gunnery course, having flown twenty-eight sorties, fired 2,500 rounds, all achieved in just eleven hours flying.

Selected for fighters, Edingborough moved to Aston Down to join 55 Operational Training Unit (OTU) for his advanced gunnery training where he completed twenty hours in the Blenheim Mk I. He finished this phase of his training just as the Battle of Britain came to an end and the need for gunners in Fighter Command receded. He found himself posted to bombers and joined the Wellington-equipped 150 Squadron at Newton, but he had to wait a few months before he could join an advanced gunnery course. In the meantime, there was the opportunity for the occasional training flight and air-test. This continued until 12 April, 1941, when he was detailed to fly on operations with Flying Officer Savage, whose regular gunner was sick. Wellington Ic (R 1347) was part of a force of sixty-six bombers sent to attack Brest in poor weather conditions. The sortie was uneventful but one wonders what the thoughts were of the partially trained Ken Edingborough as he looked down at the bomb-bursts on his first night flight.

Within a week he started a detachment to the 3 Group Training Flight where he was trained to operate both the front and rear turrets of the Wellington. On completion of his course, on which he flew twenty-three hours, he was posted on 9 May to Feltwell to join 57 Squadron. Four nights later he took off with his Flight Commander to bomb Cologne. After this initial sortie he joined the crew of Sergeant Fryer and they were allocated Wellington Ic R 1799, the aircraft that would take them on the majority of their operational sorties. After a further bombing raid on Cologne, Bomber Command was tasked to support Coastal Command in the search for the German cruiser *Prinz Eugen*, following the sinking of the *Bismarck*. Edingborough's crew joined fifty-two Wellingtons and twelve Stirlings to search the South-West Approaches but nothing was seen and the ship escaped eventually to dock at Brest.

On four occasions during June Ken Edingborough flew to targets in the Ruhr and there was a return visit to Brest where low cloud hindered bomb-aiming. A mixture of 1,000 and 500 lb bombs were carried on most sorties and they were dropped from 10,000 -14,000 feet. With virtually no navigation or bombing aids, and the advent of the Pathfinder force still some months away, bombing accuracy was often very poor. If the target was obscured, crews had to resort to dropping their bombs on timed runs or on approximate positions and sometimes on dead reckoning positions. It is little wonder that some bombs fell miles from their intended targets.

Early in July a new directive arrived at Headquarters Bomber Command which highlighted that the main bombing effort was to be directed at 'dislocating the German transportation system and to destroying the morale of the civil population as a whole and of the industrial workers in particular'. The major effort was to be directed against the towns and cities of the Ruhr and the Rhine, but, when the weather there was unfavourable, more distant targets were to be attacked.

Throughout July the priority targets were attacked and Edingborough flew nine sorties to the Ruhr towns of Essen, Munster and Duisburg, in addition to longer-range sorties to Mannheim, Bremen and Kiel. The most successful was the attack against Munster on the night of 7 July when the marshalling yards were identified and bombed by the Wellingtons of 57 and 75(NZ) Squadrons. These were the two resident squadrons at Feltwell and it was for an action on this raid that a young New Zealand second pilot, Sergeant J Ward of 75 Squadron, was awarded a Victoria Cross for climbing on to the wing of his aircraft to extinguish a fire.

With the exception of the attack against Munster, results continued to be disappointing. On numerous sorties the Squadron Record Book records that crews reported 'bombing on timed run', others reported 'no fires seen, bomb blind' and some crews simply recorded 'bomb district.' Although bomb tonnages were increasing, this lack of accuracy severely limited the effectiveness of the bombing effort. Following a raid by forty-four bombers on 21 July, the authorities in Mannheim reported just four high-explosive bombs and seventeen incendiaries falling on the city and photographs taken by reconnaissnace Spitfires failed to show any damage. Adding to the difficulties for the bomber crews was the increasing effectiveness of the German night fighter force, *die Nachtjagd*, under the skilful leadership of *Oberst* Joseph Kammhuber.

During June and July concern over bombing accuracy became a major issue. As the availability of long-range photographic reconnaissance Spitfires improved and more bombers were equipped with night cameras, it became apparent that very few of the bombers were finding their targets. Mr D. M. Butt of the War Cabinet Secretariat was invited to conduct a review and his findings highlighted that just one-third of the attacking aircraft came within five miles of the target. The difficulties faced by the ill-equipped bomber crews were recognised, but the Butt Report came as a great shock to the senior Commanders of the Royal Air Force. It prompted an urgent review of Bomber

Wellington Ic of 57 Squadron at Feltwell. (Author's collection)

Command's operations and highlighted the need for better navigation and bomb-aiming aids. Eventually, it led to the appointment of a new Commander-in-Chief, the introduction of new navigation aids and the formation of the Pathfinder Force.

At the beginning of August Ken Edingborough joined the crew of Flight Lieutenant E. G. Warfield, the new Flight Commander. Their first sortie together was on the night of 17 August to Duisburg in one of the Squadron's new Wellington IIs (W 5445). For the first time a 4,000lb 'cookie' was carried, but the weather was bad and results poor.

During September Bomber Command began bombing targets at longer range and on 8 September, Edingborough took part in the first large-scale attack against Kassel. As his aircraft left the target area, he was able to report large fires. The town suffered considerable damage. After sorties to Kiel and Brest, 57 Squadron attempted to go to Italy for the first time but all the aircraft were recalled after a warning of fog. Two nights later a further attempt was made and thirty-nine Wellingtons set out to bomb Genoa. On this flight Edingborough spent almost eleven hours in the cold, cramped rear turret of his Wellington. The fortitude and dedication of such men can only generate the greatest admiration. His ordeal was not over when the aircraft arrived back at base. The crew of Wellington Z 8789 encountered very poor weather on their return to Feltwell and, with the aircraft running out of fuel, the pilot had to make a crash landing close to the airfield. The aircraft immediately caught fire and burnt out, fortunately with only slight injuries to the crew.

Two weeks after this ordeal the recently promoted Flight Sergeant Ken Edingborough flew the last two sorties of his tour. First he went to Cologne for the sixth time and, two nights later, on 12 October, he took off on his thirtieth and final sortie. The target was Nuremberg. One hundred and fifty-two bombers attacked the city but many crews expressed doubt about the accuracy of the raid. Subsequent analysis showed that few bombs fell on Nuremberg but two villages over sixty miles away were devastated! Sadly, one has to conclude that such results were typical of many of the raids mounted by Bomber Command during 1941. Such a conclusion does scant justice to the gallantry and determination of the men flying their ill-equipped and out-dated bombers.

By the end of his first tour Ken Edingborough had flown thirty night bombing sorties to most of the major German cities. As a veteran with just 300 hours, of which almost 200 had been flown at night, he was posted as a gunnery instructor to 27 OTU based at Lichfield.

For the next six months Edingborough continued his 'rest tour' at Lichfield as an instructor with B Flight. Meanwhile, significant developments were occurring in Bomber Command. A new Commander-in-Chief, Air Marshal Arthur Harris, arrived in February, 1942, to prosecute the new Directive which concentrated on 'area bombing'. New navigation aids were coming into service and the four-engined bomber force began to expand rapidly. Notwithstanding this progress, the future of Bomber Command was still in doubt and Harris was determined to mount a spectacular riposte to the critics. He conceived the audacious plan to mount a thousand-bomber raid against a major German city. With just four hundred front-line bombers, he had to seek reinforcements from other Commands if the figure of 1,000 was to be achieved. In the event, the bulk of the reinforcements came from his own second-line training units, in particular the Operational Training Units.

During the afternoon of 25 May, all the instructor crews at 27 OTU were placed on standby and training was temporarily suspended. The following day Edingborough formed part of a scratch crew with Flying Officer Chown as the captain. The crew were allocated an old Wellington Ic (P 9259) and, together with three other aircraft crewed by instructors, they departed for Feltwell to be attached to 75 (NZ) Squadron and briefed for Operation Millennium the first of the thousand-bomber raids. The weather remained unsuitable over Germany for a number of days and, with no improvement forecast for the north of Germany, Harris had to abandon his first choice to attack Hamburg. During the afternoon of 30 May, he gave the order to attack Cologne.

Edingborough and his crew had completed a thorough air-test of their venerable Wellington before attending the final briefing. The long and anxious wait finally came to an end for the crews as they made their way to the bombers dispersed around the airfield at Feltwell. To accommodate the maximum effort, a second flare-path had been laid and the forty-seven Wellingtons taxied to the take-off point. Twenty minutes before midnight Flying Officer Chown opened the throttles of his heavily laden bomber and took off to join the huge stream of bombers heading for Germany. The bomb load consisted of a 4,000lb bomb and two 1,000lb bombs. To achieve the greatest concentration of bombers, and to saturate the enemy defences, Harris employed a 'bomber stream' with all the aircraft flying the same route and adhering to precise height bands and timing. This raid was to be the forerunner of future bombing tactics.

Edingborough and his crew had been one of the last to take off from Feltwell and they had a grandstand view of the massive bomber stream. By the time they

A Wellington of 27 OTU where Edingborough served as an instructor and flew on the first 1,000 bomber raid. (via Andy Thomas)

arrived over the target there were many fires in all parts of the city of Cologne. They bombed successfully and returned to Feltwell, landing after a five-hour flight to report an uneventful sortie and to observe that the enemy anti-aircraft fire was very erratic. Two nights later Harris launched his second thousand-bomber raid and this time the target was Essen. Edingborough and his colleagues remained at Feltwell and took part in this follow-up raid carrying a similar bomb load. The attack on Cologne was a great success but less was achieved on the raid to Essen, where the weather was less favourable and the bombing was much more scattered.

Many would argue that the thousand-bomber raids marked the turning point in the night bomber offensive and Bomber Command never looked back. Ken Edingborough and his instructor colleagues could justly claim to have been involved in the making of aviation history. However, after this exciting interlude for the 27 OTU crews, it was back to the mundane but crucially important instructional duties at Lichfield.

The end of June heralded the completion of Edingborough's 'rest tour' and he returned to operations with 21 Squadron which had recently re-equipped with the Lockheed Ventura light bomber and was flying from Methwold. The Ventura was equipped with a dorsal turret and the air gunners were all required to attend a short course at 1482 Flight at West Raynham, where they spent two weeks on air firing exercises flying in the Defiant, which had a similar turret mounted in the rear cockpit of this out-dated single-engine aircraft.

The introduction into service of the Ventura was protracted and the Squadron was not ready for operations until November when small formations attacked targets in Holland, approaching at very low level. On 7 November, it was Edingborough's turn to fly his first operation on Venturas. Flying in AE 852 with his Flight Commander, Squadron Leader Ray Chance, they attacked a large ship in the Scheldt Estuary, return fire wounding the wireless operator.

Throughout November Headquarters 2 Group staff had been planning the most ambitious low-level raid of the war, the destruction of the Philips radio and valve works at Eindhoven in Holland. The great majority of Germany's requirements for radio equipment was met by the Philips factory and its destruction was seen as a top priority. With the works situated in a heavily built-up area, precision was paramount and this dictated a daylight attack. The heavy bombers could not be risked in daylight so the task was passed to 2 Group.

Ninety-six light bombers were assigned to the task including forty-seven Venturas, each armed with three 250 lb thirty-minute delay bombs and four containers of 30 lb incendiary bombs. Due to their slower speed and poorer manoeuvrability, the Venturas were to bomb from very low level and to follow the initial attack made by the Bostons of 88 Squadron. The target for the seventeen Venturas of 21 Squadron was the lamp and valve factory a mile to the south

A Ventura I - *AE 660 of 21 Squadron at Methwold in March 1943. It has special markings for* Exercise Spartan. (via Andy Thomas)

of the main plant.

After a final briefing during the morning of 6 December, Headquarters 2 Group gave the order to execute Operation Oyster. Ken Edingborough and his crew, captained by Flight Lieutenant D. Dennis DFC, were assigned Ventura 'J' (AE 699) and after start-up they joined the long line of aircraft at the marshalling point. They were the fourth aircraft airborne, taking off at 1126 hours, and soon joined up with the rest of the force. With the formation complete, all forty-seven Venturas flew low over Methwold as they set course for Southwold on the Suffolk coast. A stirring sight for the groundcrew no doubt. Once over the sea the formation descended to 'zero feet' to avoid detection by enemy radar and headed for the entry point on the Dutch coast. The earlier Bostons had alerted the enemy defences and the Venturas received a hostile reception as they coasted in. However, there was an even more serious hazard as large flocks of ducks were encountered over the mud-flats and many aircraft were damaged.

The Venturas arrived over the target six minutes after the Bostons at 1236 hours, to find the factory engulfed in smoke. The time-delay bombs were dropped from 150 feet with heavy flak engaging the bombers. Alongside Edingborough's aircraft, a blazing Ventura continued to the target before crashing just after releasing its bombs. Over the target visibility was nil as the pilots tried to avoid chimneys and power lines before making their escape to the north. The gallant Ventura crews struggled back to the coast where they were met by their Spitfire escort which shepherded back the bombers, almost all of which had been damaged. Two of the Squadron aircraft failed to return and a third ditched off the Suffolk coast. Only three aircraft escaped flak damage and they had all suffered from bird strike damage.

Shortly after the Venturas left the target area, a reconnaissance Mosquito

A photograph taken by a 21 Squadron Ventura as it completes its attack against the Philips Radio Factory at Eindhoven on 6 December 1942. (Author's collection)

flown by Flight Lieutenant Charles Patterson DFC flew over the target and obtained some spectacular cine-film which highlighted the extensive damage to the Philips factory. The Germans acknowledged the considerable damage and the raid gave a great boost to the Dutch people and to the aircrews. But the price for success had been high. Fourteen aircraft had been lost which included nine Venturas.

A month after the raid on Eindhoven Edingborough had been teamed up with the new Flight Commander, Squadron Leader J. Westcott, and they flew together on all future operations. Ventura medium-level 'Circuses' began in the New Year and Edingborough flew on the first operation on 9 January which was an attack on the Royal Dutch Steel Works at Ijmuiden with long-range Spitfires

A Ventura leaves Eindhoven at very low level. (MOD)

providing escort. Photographs were taken during the attack which confirmed the success of the operation. Four days later the dispersals at Abbeville airfield were attacked from 7,000 feet.

In mid-February the Squadron returned to attack the Ijmuiden steel works. Flying in AE 852, Edingborough took part in two raids on 13 February. The morning raid achieved poor results and the Squadron returned in the afternoon. Enemy fighters were ready for the slow and vulnerable Venturas, and Focke-Wulf 190s mounted a head-on attack. Fortunately, the bombers had an escort of Spitfires from 118 Squadron which drove the enemy fighters away. The Ventura was the most vulnerable and least effective of the quartet of 2 Group light bombers and, without the fighter escort, they would undoubtedly have suffered unacceptable losses. Three months later, on a low-level raid on Amsterdam, a complete force of eleven Venturas from 487 (NZ) Squadron was lost with the leader, Squadron Leader Len Trent, being the last to be shot down. He and his crew baled out and he was subsequently awarded the Victoria Cross.

'Circus' operations continued throughout March and on 4 April Edingborough's crew led a twelve aircraft formation to attack the railway sheds at St Brieuc. The aircraft deployed to Exeter and fighters of 10 Group provided the escort. A successful attack was made from 10,000 feet and all the aircraft returned safely. Sadly, on the following day four Squadron aircraft failed to return from a low-level attack on Brest. Three weeks later twelve aircraft attacked the marshalling yards at Abbeville. As they approached the target they were engaged in a fierce attack with fifteen Focke-Wulf 190s and Ken Edingborough was kept very busy in his turret as he strove to beat off the fighters. He returned safely, but three aircraft were lost. In the period since he had joined the Squadron six months earlier over half the original crews had been lost.

At 1130 hours on the morning of 11 June, Edingborough and his crew took off in a Mark II Ventura (AJ 163) to join eleven other Squadron aircraft to attack the coke ovens at Zeebrugge; a strong fighter escort was provided. Edingborough's bomb-aimer saw his bombs fall across buildings on the western side of the target area. Two hours later the Venturas returned to base and Edingborough was informed that he had been awarded the Distinguished Flying Medal: '*He has always displayed the greatest keenness to take part in oper-*

A Ventura over the Ijmuiden Steel works attacked by Edingborough and his crew on 13 February 1943. (MOD)

Photograph taken from a Ventura of 21 Squadron as bombs strike the Zeebrugge coke ovens. Edingborough flew on this raid on 11 June, 1943. (Author's collection)

ations and his excellent example has helped to maintain the fighting efficiency of the Squadron.' Eight days later he was commissioned as a Pilot Officer.

After his crew had led twelve aircraft to attack the power station at Yainville on 24 June, operations for 21 Squadron were reduced. Edingborough flew a sortie to the airfield at Poix during August before embarking on his final two sorties. On 8 September, he attacked the railway yards at Abbeville and the following day 21 Squadron mounted its last raids before replacing its Venturas with Mosquitos. At 1400 hours twelve Venturas took off for the last time on a 2 Group operation. With Squadron Leader Westcott at the controls of AJ 452, Edingborough surveyed the familiar scene of his colleagues in close formation, with two squadrons of Spitfires providing fighter cover. After bombing the airfield at Merville, the Venturas returned to base for the last time and the quiet and efficient air gunner recorded his fifty-second and final bombing sortie against the enemy.

After a short spell as an instructor at 13 OTU at Bicester, Ken Edingborough volunteered for further operations. However, having completed two full tours in Bomber Command, he was 'screened from operations'. Undaunted, he managed to join 275 Squadron operating Ansons and Walrus aircraft in the air-sea rescue role from Valley on Anglesey. After a quiet two months he transferred to 278 Squadron at Coltishall and on 9 February, he took off in Anson EG 558 with Warrant Officer Peskett at the controls to search an area north-east of Cromer. Three weeks later he was on patrol off Cromer to cover the return of a large bomber force. The following day he attended an Investiture at Buckingham Palace where he received his Distinguished Flying Medal from His Majesty The King.

Throughout March he carried out further searches and patrols east of Yarmouth to support the returning bombers. It must have been a great comfort to those returning in damaged aircraft to know that a force of air-sea rescue aircraft and launches was on constant and immediate alert to offer assistance. As a bomber veteran himself, perhaps Ken Edingborough felt he was still making a contribution to the bombing campaign and was repaying those who had supported his efforts. With the re-equipment of 278 Squadron with long-range Warwicks, he was finally grounded to spend the remainder of the war in ground appointments in Rhodesia and Iraq.

Ken Edingborough was released from the RAF as a Flight Lieutenant in January 1946. He had completed two hazardous tours in Bomber Command and participated in some of the most significant raids of the war. The thousand-bomber raids had a profound impact on the future conduct of the strategic bomber offensive and the raid against the Philips factory in Eindhoven must rank as one of the most spectacular and courageous daylight attacks of the war. Ken Edingborough certainly made a significant contribution to the bomber war.

Anson I - LT 592 - of 278 Air-Sea Rescue Squadron, Edingborough's last operational unit.
(via Andy Thomas)

CHAPTER TEN

Desert Fighter Pilot – Tom Morris

After increasing tension and much flexing of muscles, Italy declared war on the Allies on 10 June, 1940. At first light the following morning the Royal Air Force mounted its first war sorties in Egypt when three Gladiator fighters of No 80 Squadron took off from the RAF airfield at Amriya to set up a patrol fifteen miles to the west of Alexandria. Flying as number two to the leader, Flight Lieutenant E. Gordon-Jones, was Flight Sergeant Tom Morris in Gladiator K 8009. The patrol was uneventful but it marked the first of many operational sorties flown by the ex-Halton 'brat' who had turned fighter pilot.

Thomas Charles Morris was born in Eastbourne on 25 October, 1911, and enlisted into the Royal Air Force as an aircraft apprentice at Halton on 28 August, 1928, joining 18 Entry. He was trained at the Electrical and Wireless School at Flowerdown but after one year the school was closed down on re-location to Cranwell where Morris qualified as an electrician two years later. After a short time at Upper Heyford, he left for India and a two-and-a-half-year

Tom Morris's medals, Distinguished Flying Cross, General Service Medal (Palestine Clasp), 1939-45 Star, Africa Star, Defence Medal, War Medal.

Line up of 80 Squadron Gladiators in peacetime markings at Ismailia in late 1938 (Author's collection)

posting to the Aircraft Depot in Karachi. Apart from a brief spell in 1937, he was to spend almost ten years away from the United Kingdom.

In June 1935, Tom Morris re-mustered as a pilot and began his training at 4 Flying Training School, stationed at Abu Sueir. With Flight Lieutenant MacDonald as his instructor, he took off on 15 October, 1935, in Avro Tutor K 3335 for his first training flight. Three weeks later, with eleven hours dual flying, he completed his first solo flight and after a further sixty hours, he progressed to the advanced training phase on the Hart and Audax aircraft. In July, 1936, he was authorised to wear the pilot's flying badge. With 120 hours in his log book, and an assessment of 'Average' from a future Chief of Air Staff, Flight Lieutenant T. G. Pike, his Flight Commander, he was posted to 29 (F) Squadron flying Demons and Gordons from Amriya.

In October, 1936, the Squadron returned to England to be based at North Weald where it received the Demon with power-operated turrets. The following February Tom Morris moved across the airfield to join the recently reformed 151 Squadron flying the Gauntlet II. With the rapid expansion of the Royal Air Force in the late thirties numerous fighter squadrons were re-formed and each received a nucleus of experienced pilots. Hence, after a year with 151, Morris found himself joining fourteen other pilots as 80 Squadron was brought up to full establishment in March, 1938, in preparation for departure to Egypt. Equipped with Gladiators, the Squadron completed its work-up to operational status at Debden and in May it was settling into its new home at Ismailia.

Within a few weeks of his arrival in Egypt trouble broke out in Palestine and a detachment of the Squadron moved to Ramleh to support the ground forces in operations against the Arab rebels. Tom Morris was one of four pilots involved; the others included the great South African pilot 'Pat' Pattle and the then Pilot Officer P. Wykeham-Barnes, who was to become one of the RAF's

80 Squadron SNCOs at Heliopolis, Egypt in 1939. Morris is seated second from right.
(80 Squadron Association)

top fighter pilots and later reach Air rank and be knighted. In the two-week period this small detachment flew seventy-two hours in support of the Army, inflicting about sixty casualties. They were subsequently awarded the General Service Medal with the Palestine clasp.

Following the outbreak of war in Europe, the Squadron stepped up security and continued with training and air defence exercises. The Squadron had moved to Helwan but maintained a Flight at Amriya for the defence of Alexandria and it was during this period that Tom Morris's hidden talent was discovered. Gathering a number of other enthusiasts together, he produced a variety show which was a huge success, with Morris's own brand of humour prominent. Such was the success of this venture that monthly shows became a feature and they are still recalled with much pleasure by surviving members of the Squadron.

Tension increased in May, 1940, with the occasional Italian bomber being escorted through Egyptian airspace en route to Abyssinia. The Squadron prepared for war with constant practice alarms, scrambles and interceptions, until Mussolini finally declared war on the Allies on 10 June, 1940.

After his first operational sortie, Tom Morris flew four more interception sorties in the Gladiator during the first week of hostilities. Although sighting enemy aircraft on each of these sorties, his old Gladiator was too slow to close with them for an interception. However, the first Hurricanes had just started to arrive in the Middle East and these were allocated to 80 Sqn and, with seven

Gladiator - K 7882 - of 80 Squadron in wartime camouflage at Ismailia in September 1940.
(Andy Thomas)

on strength, A Flight was converted to the aircraft. The new Squadron Commander, Squadron Leader 'Paddy' Dunn, chose to fly with the Hurricane Flight. The composition of this eight-man Flight must have been unique in Air Force history. It included three future Air Marshals, all of whom would be knighted (Paddy Dunn, Peter Wykeham-Barnes and John Lapsley), together with 'Pat' Pattle and Pilot Officer 'Imshi' Mason, the top-scoring desert pilot in the First Libyan Campaign. Tom Morris and two Sergeant Pilots completed this impressive line up.

During late June and July the Squadron operated detachments of aircraft from Sidi Barrani near the Libyan/Egyptian border in support of Wavell's initial aggressive patrols into Libya. Contact was soon made with Fiat CR 42 fighters and the Savoia-Marchetti SM 79 bombers, and the Squadron quickly achieved its first successes, with Pat Pattle prominent. Within a few weeks, the Squadron had claimed a number of 'kills'. For Tom Morris and his fellow pilots in the Hurricane Flight there was only frustration as they remained at Amriya to provide protection for Alexandria and the Mediterranean Fleet.

With the arrival of more Hurricanes in the Middle East it was decided in August to form a new all Hurricane unit at Amriya, with Squadron Leader Paddy Dunn as the CO. He took with him the Hurricane Flight of 80 Squadron and, with the addition of some pilots from 33 Squadron, the new 274 Squadron was made up to wartime strength. After a short period of training, the Squadron began operations.

With the Italians massing near Sidi Barrani there was a general withdrawal to safeguard the major British military installations in Egypt. There were, however, a number of engagements, the most notable being when John Lapsley shot down two SM 79 bombers, making him the first British pilot to shoot down five aircraft in the Middle East. For Tom Morris it was to be standing patrols over Alexandria harbour and over Mersa Matruh. These sorties assumed even greater importance as a number of squadrons were transferred to support the Greek campaign following the unexpected Italian invasion of Greece and Albania at the end of October.

Notwithstanding the loss of squadrons to Greece and the build-up of Italian forces in Western Egypt, the British Commander-in-Chief, General Wavell, decided to mount an offensive in early December. 274 Squadron moved forward to Sidi Heneish to support Operation Compass which began a few days later at dawn on 9 December.

At 1145 hours on the morning of the 9th Tom Morris, flying Hurricane V 7300, took off with fifteen other Hurricanes to patrol a line between Sidi Barrani and Sofafi. Just after midday five SM 79s were sighted and the Squadron attacked. One bomber was shot down by Flying Officer Godden, and Morris shared with four other Squadron pilots in the destruction of two more, with two others damaged. On an afternoon patrol the Squadron claimed a further five victories; this time the victims were CR 42 fighters.

General Wavell's 'limited' offensive made rapid progress and he decided to push forward towards Tobruk. The Middle East's only fully operational Hurricane squadron was in great demand and soon found itself generating forty or more sorties a day. Early on 12 December, twelve Hurricanes took off to refuel at LG 70 before heading for Sollum to attack Italian troops and trans-

274 Squadron personnel and camp followers at Bardia in the Western Desert late 1940. Tom Morris is standing in the centre of the second row with his arms folded. Three future Air Marshals are seated in the front row (Jones, Wykeham-Barnes and Lapsley). *'Imshi' Mason is seated far left with the dog.* (Author's collection)

Hurricane I aircraft of 274 Squadron lined up at Amriyah, Egypt in early 1941. (Author's collecton)

port as their withdrawal gathered momentum. Tom Morris failed to return from this attack, but news was received later in the day that he had force-landed thirty miles west of Matruh and was safe. Even better news followed when it was confirmed that he had shot down two SM 79 bombers.

As the armies advanced, ground support and strafing missions were called for daily. The Italian Air Force tried to harass the advance and 274 Squadron continued to take its toll of the enemy as John Lapsley, 'Imshi' Mason, Peter Wykeham-Barnes and others added to their scores.

Tom Morris had to wait until 4 January, 1941, for his next success. The Squadron was ordered to maintain a constant patrol over Great Gambut with aircraft taking off at fifteen-minute intervals. Taking off at 1015 hours in V 7293 he intercepted some CR 42s and in the ensuing fight he shot one down but his aircraft was hit in the radiator and he was forced to land in the desert a few miles west of Capuzzo. He was picked up by an advance Army patrol and

Hurricane I of 274 Squadron over the Western Desert. (MOD)

arrived back on the Squadron in the early evening. Also missing from the morning patrols was Sergeant Hulbert; Morris was able to confirm that he had last seen his aircraft going down in a vertical dive with five CR 42s on its tail.

The Squadron continued to patrol over the landing grounds at Gambut and, as the Australian troops converged on Tobruk, protective patrols were set up. After the capture of Tobruk, the Allied advance gathered pace and 274 resumed attacks on the retreating Italians. Early February saw Tom Morris flying offensive patrols from advanced landing grounds. On 4 February, six aircraft attacked an Italian convoy of lorries, inflicting severe damage. While returning, Tom Morris had a fuel leak and found himself making his third desert force-landing within a few weeks. Both he and his aircraft (V 7770) were recovered later in the day.

With the Italians cleared out of Cyrenaica, Wavell's spectacular victory was complete and 274 returned to Amriya in the Delta to rest after their own magnificent effort. However, the war in North Africa was soon to enter a new phase. Rommel and his German Panzers had arrived, and it was not long before they started to push the Allies back eastwards; by the time 274 rejoined the fray in mid-April German forces had reached the Egyptian border.

On 15 April, the Squadron moved back to the Western Desert and took up residence at Gerawla. Immediately they were back in action, mounting offensive patrols to the west of Tobruk. On 19 April, Tom Morris flew five patrols as a pair with the Battle of Britain veteran, Flying Officer N. Agazarian. Two days later he flew a four-hour tactical reconnaissance sortie in the Gambut-Sidi Omar area. With the deployment to Greece of 208 Squadron, the only specialist tactical reconnaissance squadron, 274 found itself increasingly tasked in this demanding role and Morris was to fly a number of long-range sorties over the next few weeks gathering vital information on activities behind enemy lines. Flown without support and deep into enemy territory, this form of flying operation has always been, and still is, one of the most demanding for a single-seat pilot.

Throughout the remainder of April and through May the Squadron flew at intensive rates against an increasingly tough enemy, not least because the CR 42s had been replaced by Me 109s. During this period the Squadron lost Flying Officer T. L. Patterson, who had scored seven victories, and, with further squadron losses, the quality of the opposition had been established.

As Wavell launched a short-lived counter-attack in mid May, Tom Morris was airborne daily on long-range Tac Recce and ground strafing missions. He attacked an ammunition lorry on the 15th, twenty lorries on the 16th and a convoy of 100 lorries the following day. Sadly, on the 16th, he lost his colleague Flying Officer Agazarian. Four days later he was attacking two staff cars. The end of May saw the Squadron displaying its flexibility as it provided support for the withdrawal from Crete and Morris found himself flying cover for the Fleet as it fought its way under constant air attack from the evacuation beaches to Egypt.

After a very brief respite, Tom Morris was back flying ground strafing sorties against motor transports in the Gazala-Bardia area as General Wavell launched his Operation Battleaxe and flying operations were conducted at maximum pitch. On 15 June, his section was attacking motor convoys and tanks when it was intercepted by Me 109s. Three pilots of 274 failed to return and a fourth crash landed, but returned to the Squadron a few days later.

Within a few days it was clear that Operation Battleaxe had failed and the Allied armies had been driven back to the start line at the Libyan-Egyptian border. With a lull in the ground fighting it was back to bomber escorts and Royal Navy protective patrols. On 22 August, it was announced that Warrant Officer Tom Morris had been awarded the Distinguished Flying Cross for gallantry and devotion to duty. The recommendation concluded; '*He has displayed great courage and initiative whilst taking part in over 30 ground strafing operations of enemy aerodromes and transport and he has destroyed at least 3 enemy aircraft in the air. He has also carried out several reconnaissances which have been of great value to the Army. At all times his keeness and skill have set an excellent example to the less experienced pilots.*'

Three weeks later Tom Morris flew his one hundreth and final operational

Tom Morris at readiness in the cockpit of his Hurricane in the Western desert 1941. (MOD)

sortie on 274 Squadron. Added to his earlier sorties with 80 Squadron, this was an achievement that few could have surpassed in such a relatively short time.

For his 'rest' tour, Morris was posted at the end of September to 71 OTU which had recently moved from Ismailia to Gordon's Tree near Khartoum. This unit was equipped with a mixture of singe-seat aircraft, providing fighter and army co-operation training, including tactical reconnaissance. Here Morris met up with his old Squadron Commander, Wing Commander Paddy Dunn, who commanded the OTU. He had recently reported to higher authorities his opinion of Gordon's Tree. He signalled. 'As a location for a training unit, Gordon's College stands out as being very nearly entirely unsuitable.' He went on to say, 'A pupil must arrive at his first unit bubbling with energy, not partially tired out as he will do coming from the Sudan.' Sadly, this perceptive and experienced officer's views were ignored and many young pilots would find their training almost as great an ordeal as fighting the enemy.

Shortly after arriving in the Sudan Tom Morris was commissioned. After six months working and flying in the trying conditions of Khartoum, he finally returned to England where, for the next twelve months, he was a pilot instructor at various Flying Schools. On 23 April, 1943, he made the long journey to the Moray Firth to join No 8 Air Gunnery School based at Evanton.

At Evanton Morris flew the Martinet, the first aircraft to be designed specifically for target-towing duties. Based on the Master trainer, it had a longer nose to compensate for the extra weight of the towing gear which altered the centre of gravity. During 1943 there was a significant requirement for trained air gunners and Morris found himself flying two or three times each day. By the end of August his tour was almost over and he could have expected to return to operational flying.

On the morning of 26 August, he took off in Martinet HN 939 for a low-level air gunnery exercise. Shortly after the start of the exercise the engine failed. Too low to bale out he made an emergency wheels-up landing in the only available field. Unfortunately it was too short and the aircraft crashed into a low wall on

Martinet target towing aircraft at a snowy Evanton. (via J Hughes)

Proncy Farm, near Dornoch, and caught fire. The winch operator, Corporal Sommerville, died in the crash, but Tom Morris was rescued suffering from multiple injuries and serious burns. He was transferred to Golspie Hospital but died from secondary shock twenty-four hours later. A few days later he was buried in Portsmouth Milton Cemetry near the home of his parents .

Tom Morris was a member of that unique breed who had dedicated his life to service in the Royal Air Force while still a boy, and subsequently he answered every call made on him during peace and in war. The Halton 'Brats' produced some remarkable men and Tom Morris can stand proud among their ranks. The last assessment before his death should be his epitaph: 'Exceptional Fighter Pilot'.

CHAPTER ELEVEN

Gallant Wing Walker – Surtees Elliott

As night fell on the evening of 12 June, 1940, Leading Aircraftman Surtees Elliott climbed into the air gunner's position of Vincent (K 4681) for his first wartime sortie. Italy had entered the Second World War just forty-eight hours earlier. Taking off in the obsolescent bi-plane from the airfield at Khormaksar in the Aden Protectorate, he and his pilot set off alone to drop some of the Royal Air Force's first bombs of the often forgotten air war of East Africa. Their dive-bombing sortie was more reminiscent of those of the Great War which had finished over twenty years earlier. It was as if the progress in aviation made in the previous few years had by-passed this outpost of the British Empire. Yet, within three years, Elliott would be hunting U-boats with all the latest sophisticated scientific aids.

Surtees Elliott, known to his family and friends as 'Stan', was born in Tynemouth. Aged sixteen, he joined 29 Entry at the School of Technical Training at RAF Halton to train as a Fitter/Rigger. During his three years as an

Surtees Elliott's medals, Air Force Medal, 1939-45 Star, Africa Star, Defence Medal, War Medal.

Surtees Elliott. (Mrs L Elliott)

apprentice, he distinguished himself as an outstanding athlete. He won many awards for sprinting and he was a member of the winning relay team at the Amateur Athletics Association Junior Championships held at the White City stadium in July, 1936. The correspondent of *The Times* newspaper reported that 'the feature of the relay race was the splendid teamwork of the RAF Halton four.' On graduation from Halton a few months later, Elliott was awarded the Barrington-Kennett medal, an honour reserved for outstanding sportsmen.

Elliott spent the first eighteen months of his adult service as a fitter with 102 Squadron based first at Finningley and then Honington before being posted to Aden in June, 1938, where he joined 8 Squadron equipped with Vincent general purpose aircraft. Within a year he had volunteered for flying duties and was trained to operate the Lewis gun mounted in the rear cockpit.

The Vincent had entered service with the Royal Air Force in 1934 and was employed exclusively in the Middle East as a general purpose aircraft. It became a key aircraft in Aden where its rugged construction and surprisingly long range (1,250 miles with an external fuel tank) made it well suited for the control and policing role that had been entrusted to the Royal Air Force during the late 1920s. The aircraft had replaced the Fairey IIIFs on 8 Squadron in 1935.

The Barrington-Kennett medal awarded to Surtees Elliott as an Aircraft Apprentice at the School of Technical Training, RAF Halton for outstanding success in athletics

Since its arrival in Aden in 1927, 8 Squadron had regularly been in action against dissident tribesmen throughout the Protectorate. Leaflets had been the main 'weapon', but any failure to heed warnings soon brought a 'demonstration' with bombs and machine guns. In addition, the RAF had been heavily involved in the development of internal communications between the myriad small villages, and numerous temporary landing grounds had been established throughout the British-protected areas. With the outbreak of war in Europe in 1939, there was little change in the routine of Aden's only resident squadron.

Throughout the latter part of 1939, Elliott continued to mix his duties as a fitter with those of aircrew and he flew on many liaison and re-supply sorties to the outlying villages. With Mussolini firmly established across the Red Sea in Abyssinia and Eritrea, a new requirement to escort convoys arose from early 1940 and Elliott flew his first 'war' sortie on 9 February, 1940, in Vincent K 4149. Although still on the squadron establishment as a fitter, he was authorised to draw air gunner pay and, from early 1940 and for the remainder of his time on 8 Squadron, he was employed predominantly as an air gunner. During March and April he flew from a detachment landing ground at Fuwa on many

A Vickers Vincent - K 4149 - of 8 Squadron in Aden December 1939. Elliott flew five dive-bombing sorties over Eritrea in this aircraft during July 1940. (via Andy Thomas)

dive-bombing sorties against local dissident tribes. These attacks often attracted concentrated ground fire which was suppressed with bombs, the forward firing-machine gun and Elliott's Lewis gun.

Following the fall of France in June, 1940, the Italians had started to reinforce their units in East Africa including a bomber force with the capability to attack British interests in the Middle East, with Aden well within range. The Allied Air Forces in the region could best be described as modest and 8 Squadron remained the only RAF squadron based in Aden.

On the evening of 10 June, the Italians declared war on the United Kingdom and France. 8 Squadron increased its state of readiness and, within 48 hours, the Italians had made their first attack against Aden. On 12 June, the Blenheim Flight of 8 Squadron mounted an attack against the Italian airfield of Macaaca at Assab in Eritrea. That evening it was the turn of the Vincent Flight, and five aircraft led by Wing Commander Barrett took off at thirty-minute intervals to attack the same airfield. With Flying Officer Winning as his pilot, Elliott took off in good weather in K 4681 and two hours later arrived over the enemy airfield. A dive-bombing attack was made and the bombs were released against some small fires which had been started by an earlier raid. After a four-hour flight, all five aircraft returned safely. This first bombing effort was summarised in the Squadron Operations Record Book as 'Several small fires observed. Actual results unknown.' Quite a contrast to the scale of bombing achieved over the forthcoming five years. Nevertheless, it still required courage to fly into the unknown at night in obsolescent aircraft against a superior force.

The Blenheim Flight was frequently in action over the next month, but it was not until the night of 13 July that the Vincents carried out another bombing raid. Two aircraft took off to bomb Assab, but one was forced to return. Surtees Elliott and his pilot, Sergeant Elshaw, pressed on and carried out a dive-bombing sortie against the airfield at Macaaca. Four nights later Elliott took off in K 4149 to dive-bomb a supply dump south of Assab. Three searchlights tried to illuminate the Vincent and three fighters were seen, but none engaged. Before the end of July, Elliott flew three more night dive-bombing sorties over Eritrea, the last with the newly promoted Group Captain Barrett. They were briefed to attack the wireless station, but, not surprisingly, they failed to identify this pinpoint target in the dark and so they released their bombs over the naval barracks at Assab. By the end of July the Vincents had effectively been withdrawn from night bombing sorties and they concentrated on reconnaissance operations.

Over the next few months Elliott and his colleagues in the Vincent Flight returned to their more familiar role of air-policing over the Protectorate with occasional reconnaissance sorties over the Red Sea. With the Battle of Britain at its height, it is difficult to visualise the nature of the war over East Africa where Gladiators, Hartebeestes, Vincents and Battles were more numerous than the 'modern' Blenheim Is and the sprinkling of Hurricanes.

During October, 1940, the Vincents were heavily involved in more disturbances by dissidents in the interior of Aden. Elliott flew twenty dive-bombing and strafing sorties during the month. 250 lb bombs and incendiaries were

A Vincent - K 4140 - of 8 Squadron. This picture illustrates clearly the difficulites faced by Elliott when he left his rear turret to climb on to the starboard wing. (via Andy Thomas)

dropped to destroy strongholds in the villages of Urkub, Sauda and Habib when crops were set on fire and cattle were killed. Opposition was described as 'Natives firing rifles from cave; but silenced by machine gun.' Elliott flew his last operational Vincent sortie on 15 November with Flight Lieutenant Powles in K 4664 when they dive-bombed the village of Rafsa. Within a week the Vincents had been transferred to the newly formed General Purpose Flight at Khormaksar to carry out re-supply and liaison duties.

On 15 January, 1941, Elliott was detailed to fly as the crewman in Vincent K 4716 on a routine flight carrying spares to a detached flight in the Hadhramout region of the Aden Protectorate. Lashed to the starboard wing was a spare wheel being delivered to an Army unit. The air was very turbulent, the lashing on the wheel worked loose and the tyre was forced up by the slipstream against the hot exhaust of the aircraft. The tyre was set alight and molten rubber was blown against the fabric fuselage sides and the wing. Elliott immediately saw the danger and attempted to climb on to the wing. He was hindered by his parachute which he was forced to remove. Once on the wing he pulled the wheel clear of the exhaust and attempted to re-secure it to the wing strut. With a very precarious hold, this difficult operation took him over thirty minutes. The severe turbulence merely compounded the problem. Eventually he managed to lash the wheel down and return to the safety of his cockpit before the pilot made an emergency landing.

Some weeks later it was announced that Leading Aircraftman Surtees Elliott had been awarded the Air Force Medal for his gallantry. The citation recorded that: '*On his own initiative and without hesitation he climbed on to the wing to secure the wheel. He undoubtedly saved the aircraft from catching fire and the crew from serious injury.*'

The Air Officer Commanding-in-Chief, Middle East Command, had recommended the award of the George Medal but the RAF Awards Committee, sitting in their comfortable London office, considered that Elliott's deed merited the Air Force Medal. Whilst the latter is a most prestigious and rarely awarded medal (just 259 during the Second World War), there are undoubtedly many who believe that the higher award was entirely justified. On his return to the United Kingdom in August, 1941, the medal was presented to Elliott by His Majesty The King at an Investiture held at Buckingham Palace.

After three years in the oppressive climate of Aden where living and recreational facilities were basic at best, Elliott returned to England to join 44 Squadron at Waddington in his old trade of Fitter. Notwithstanding his considerable flying experience, he was not recommended for aircrew training until early 1942 and it was a further seven months before he re-mustered as a Flight Engineer/Air Gunner and began a short refresher training course at 10 Air Gunnery School. On completion, he moved to 131 Operational Training Unit based at Killadaes in Northern Ireland to train on Catalina flying boats. It was normal practice on flying boat squadrons for the Flight Engineers and Wireless Operators to be dual-trained as Air Gunners.

On completion of the five-month course at Killadaes he and his crew were posted to Oban to continue their training with 302 Ferry Training Unit, prior to joining a Catalina Squadron in the Indian Ocean. The trainee crews carried out long-range navigational exercises and ASV radar training. Occasionally they were required to fly air-sea rescue sorties.

On 4 November, 1943, Elliott and his crew were ordered to carry out an air sea rescue patrol in Catalina IIA (VA 728). They returned to Oban just after darkness and prepared to land on the Seaplane Alighting Area on the Forth of Lorne. The flare path, consisting of three flares approximately 300 yards apart, had been laid into wind with the control boat at the windward end. The visibility was good and there was a slightly choppy sea, but no swell. The pilot carried out a standard approach, but he was still thirty feet above the sea as he passed the second flare. He touched down fifty yards after passing the final flare and bounced twice. The control boat crew heard the pilot open the throttles but it was too late to prevent the aircraft from crashing beyond the flare path. The Catalina broke up and started to sink as the control boat arrived on the scene. Ignoring orders not to jump into the freezing waters, Corporal Fred Sykes dived from the control boat and was able to release three survivors from the sinking flying-boat before failing strength and the cold forced him to give

A course photograph taken at 302 Ferry Training Unit of Elliott and his crew. Six members of the crew were killed when their Catalina crashed on landing at Oban on 4 November, 1943. Elliott was one of four survivors. (Mrs I Elliott)

4 COURSE ~ 4 CREW.

GT. ELLIOTT. SGT. MIDDLETON. SGT. WHYTE. SGT. FRITH.

LEY. SGT. MACKAY. F/O. CREAMER. SGT. ALLEN. SGT. CUMMINGS.

up his rescue attempt. Six of the ten crew members of the aircraft were lost. One of those rescued was Surtees Elliott, who was suffering from severe shock and exposure. For his outstanding gallantry Corporal Styles was awarded the British Empire Medal.

After this tragic accident Elliott joined a crew captained by Flying Officer 'Jock' Lough, a tough Scotsman recognised by his colleagues as a 'born leader.' In early December, 1943, Lough and his crew set off in a Catalina for the long flight to East Africa to join 265 Squadron at Diego Suarez on the northern tip of Madagascar. They arrived at this spartan base on Christmas Eve just in time to celebrate Surtees Elliott's promotion to Flight Sergeant.

With the Mediterranean closed for much of the war, the sea-routes around the Cape of Good Hope became crucial for the ships re-supplying Britain. The Germans recognised Britain's vital need for these routes and an increasing number of U-boats and support vessels were sent to attack Allied shipping in the Indian Ocean and off the coast of East Africa. A number of Catalina squadrons were sent to the area in early 1943 to combat the submarine threat. 265 Squadron was placed under the operational control of 246 Wing with head-quarters at Mombasa in Kenya. Although the Squadron Headquarters were at Diego Suarez many of its operations were mounted from a number of widely dispersed bases including the Seychelles, Mauritius and the Comoro Islands.

Elliott and his crew carried out their first patrol in early March, 1944. They were allocated Catalina Ib 'H' (FP 104) and most of their long-range patrols were carried out in this aircraft. The patrol areas for the three Catalina squadrons of 246 Wing were enormous. To allow the greatest possible area to be covered, many of the long patrols originated at one base and terminated at another of the detachment locations. On most of these sorties fitters and engineers from the Squadron's ground staff would fly as supplementary crew and carry out basic maintenance at the remote landing areas.

The routine sorties included convoy patrols and anti-submarine sweeps. Throughout March, Elliott and his crew flew four eighteen-hour patrols alighting at a different location on each occasion. April heralded a change and the crew of H/265 set off for a two-month detachment to Durban where they reinforced the South African Air Force maritime patrols. Towards the end of the detachment period a naval appreciation indicated the possibility that three German *U-boats* could be moving north through the Mozambique Channel. With four important convoys due the authorities increased the number of anti-submarine patrols and the crew of H/265 flew a number of sweeps from Durban

Catalina IB - FP 263 - of 265 Squadron at Diego Suarez, Madagascar. (Peter Green)

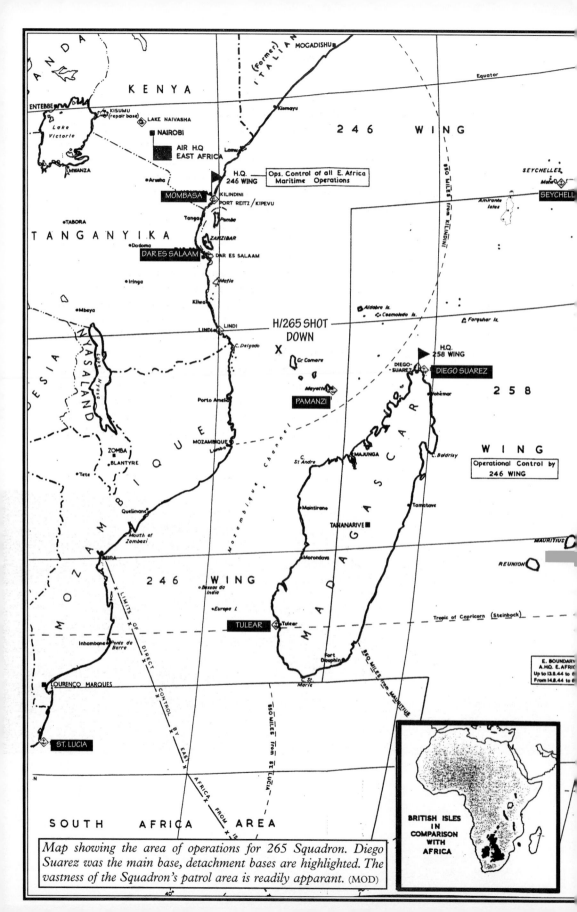

Map showing the area of operations for 265 Squadron. Diego Suarez was the main base, detachment bases are highlighted. The vastness of the Squadron's patrol area is readily apparant. (MOD)

without making contact with the enemy.

Following the safe passage of the convoy Elliott's crew returned to Diego Suarez during early July just as another Catalina caught an enemy submarine *(U.859)* on the surface south-east of Durban. Despite a determined attack by the anti-submarine aircraft the *U-boat* escaped. Within 24 hours a South African Ventura caught a second surfaced U-boat *(U.198)* which immediately dived. A depth-charge attack was mounted and oil, air bubbles and life-rafts were seen on the surface shortly afterwards. Later events showed that this was a ruse. These sightings created a fervour of activity and Elliott's crew flew to Mauritius to carry out anti-submarine patrols. More eighteen-hour patrols were flown but the situation remained quiet until early August.

At midnight on 5 August, an SOS was received from the SS *Empire City* indicating the presence of enemy submarines in the Mozambique Channel. 265 Squadron immediately sent reinforcements, including H/265, to Pamanzi in the Comoro Islands. Within hours the *Empire City* had been sunk and twenty-four hours later her sister ship the SS *Empire Day* was torpedoed a hundred miles to the north. Both had been sunk by *U.198*. Over the next few days the net closed in on the U-boat as Catalinas established stopper patrols and Naval Force 66 followed up bearings obtained from the U-boat's transmissions. The Catalinas trailed the U-boat for seven days and Elliott and his crew flew four of these patrols, the first from Pamanzi and three from Mombasa, as the submarine tracked north. On each occasion they were airborne for over eighteen hours.

Catalina IB - FB 263 - 265 Squadron on patrol over the Indian Ocean. (Peter Green)

On 10 August, the U-boat was sighted on the surface 600 miles east of Mombasa and the naval force closed for the attack. The Catalinas continued to patrol the area and obtain contacts and the joint operation continued for a further forty-eight hours before the frigate HMS *Findhorn* delivered the final and fatal attack at 1400 hours on 12 August. The following day Elliott and his crew returned to Diego Suarez.

In the meantime, unknown to the Allies, two more U-boats had entered the southern Mozambique Channel. *(U.861* and *U.862)*. *U.862* sank four ships in quick succession in mid-August as *U.861* headed for the Indian Ocean. In response, 265 Squadron launched two Catalinas on 16 August, including Elliott and his crew who took off for their seventeenth anti-submarine patrol. Nothing was seen and the U-boat effectively disappeared for the next few days.

Every day from the 20th to the 25th, Catalinas from Pamanzi, Diego Suarez, Tulear, Dar-es-Salaam and Mombasa swept wide areas in the North Mozambique Channel, but no contacts with the enemy submarine were established over this period.

Elliott, standing second from right, and his 265 Squadron crew. The captain, 'Jock' Lough, is seated second from right. All were killed on 20 August, 1944. (A Banks)

During the early morning of 20 August, 'Jock' Lough lifted Catalina 'H' off the water at Diego Suarez and headed out into the Mozambique Channel. Two other aircraft took off shortly after. All three were due to land at Pamanzi on completion of their patrol where they would be joined by other Squadron aircraft as the forces built up to intensify the search for the elusive U-boat. Hence, in addition to the normal nine-man crew, on board there were four members of the Squadron's ground crew who would bolster the under-strength detachment at Pamanzi.

Routine radio reports were heard from H/265 until 1613 hours when a submarine attack report (SSS) was received, followed by complete silence. Nothing further was heard from the Catalina. Other Squadron aircraft were diverted to the area and the search was continued for a further four days. Hopes rose on 24 August when a continuous note on 520 Kc/s was picked up, but the signal was too weak for the searching aircraft to attempt a homing. Shortly afterwards the Squadron finally accepted that Surtees Elliott and his colleagues had been lost at sea. The search for *U.862* continued but it soon became apparent that it had escaped.

Following the end of the war in the Far East, the full story of Surtees Elliott's final flight became known. *U.862* eventually sailed to Penang in Malaya where it was taken over on VE Day by the Japanese Navy. The log of the U-boat's

A dramatic photograph, taken by one of U.862's *crew, as Elliott's Catalina crashes alongside the* U.boat. (via A Banks)

captain, *Korvettenkapitän* Heinrich Timm, gave the full story of the fierce battle fought out by *U.862* and 'Jock' Lough and his crew.

Five days after sinking the SS *Radbury*, the U-boat was in transit on the surface forty miles west of Great Comoro Island when it was surprised by a Catalina diving out of the setting sun at a range of 3,000–4,000 yards. There was insufficient time to dive, so the Captain decided to remain on the surface and engage the diving aircraft. The gunner manning the 3.7 cm gun opened fire on the Catalina, which made a steady approach towards the submarine despite the intense fire from three guns. The bow gunner in the Catalina (quite possibly Elliott) opened fire just as the aircraft received a direct hit in the starboard wing and engine which set the aircraft on fire. 'Jock' Lough never wavered even when the short-range 2 cm flak started to register hits in the cockpit area. The U-boat manoeuvred violently when it appeared that the burning Catalina would ram the submarine. The aircraft just missed the submarine and crashed into the sea a mere fifty yards away, where it exploded. There were no survivors.

So died a very gallant crew whose courageous action only came to light a few years after the end of the war and which went unrecognised. The cheerful ex-Halton apprentice, who had risked his life to save his colleagues a few years earlier, had paid the supreme sacrifice many miles from the Tyneside mining community that was his home. Surtees Elliott was lost at sea and he and his twelve colleagues are commemorated on the Air Forces Memorial at Runnymede.

The crew of U.862 *sail into Penang after a successful cruise.* Korvettenkapitän *Heinrich Timm the captain is marked by the cross on the right. The gunner, A Ridler, is marked on the left.*
(via A Banks)

CHAPTER TWELVE

The Magnificent Seven – Sydney Smith

Just after midnight on the night of 25 September, 1942, Lancaster R 5724 of 61 Squadron was crossing Denmark after a successful mine-laying operation in the Baltic Sea when an anti-aircraft shell smashed into the rear of the bomb bay. Sitting just above the fierce fire which broke out was the mid-upper gunner, Sydney Smith. Over the next four hours, he and his six young colleagues fought to bring their severely damaged bomber home.

Sydney Smith, of Bolton, Lancashire, had enlisted in the Royal Air Force Volunteer Reserve as a Wireless Operator/Air Gunner in late 1940, shortly after his eighteenth birthday . Qualifying as an air gunner in early 1942, he joined 61 Squadron at RAF Syerston on 9 September, after completing his training at 19 Operational Training Unit and 1654 Heavy Conversion Unit. Equipped with the Lancaster Mk I, the Squadron had just returned to bombing operations after a short period operating from St Eval in Cornwall on anti-submarine patrols with Coastal Command. During this period, the aircraft that is central to this story had become the first Bomber Command aircraft to sink a U-boat.

Sydney Smith's medals are the Distinguished Flying Medal, 1939-45 Star, Aircrew Europe Star, Defence Medal, War Medal.

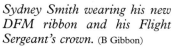

Sydney Smith wearing his new DFM ribbon and his Flight Sergeant's crown. (B Gibbon)

The Lancaster I - R 5724 - of 61 Squadron before the amazing flight of Smith and his colleagues. (M Gunnell)

With five other young Sergeants, who had all joined the Squadron together, Sydney Smith was crewed with Flight Sergeant Paul Campbell, an experienced captain with twenty-two operational sorties already to his credit. On the night of 19 September, they took off for Munich on their first sortie. With the star-board inner engine failing, Campbell decided to jettison his bombs in the North Sea and return to base three hours after take off. Five nights later, with his novice crew of five and Sergeant Mike Gunnell flying as second pilot, Campbell took off at 2100 hours, heading for the Baltic on a 'Gardening' sortie. The 'vegetables' were dropped in the briefed position and the bomber turned for home returning over Denmark. Flying over the town of Viborg at 6,000 feet, the aircraft was engaged by the anti-aircraft batteries and two shells hit R 5724 with devastating effect.

The first shell hit the rear part of the bomb bay starting a major fire as flares and distress signals ignited. Simultaneously, another shell burst in the nose, blowing in all the perspex and the majority of the perspex of the pilot's cupola, with the exception of the front windscreen. The bomb aimer, Sergeant F. Bunclark, was blown back alongside the pilot and Sergeant Gunnell, the second pilot, was knocked to the floor, landing by the navigator's compartment. Both pilots and the bomb aimer, as well as Sergeant E. Corbett the navigator and Sergeant C. Coakley, the wireless operator, received facial burns. The aircraft was full of smoke, preventing the pilot from seeing his instruments, and, as the crew started to assess the situation, two fighters attacked the damaged bomber. Cannon and machine-gun fire struck the aircraft, with cannon fire hitting the rear turret, seriously wounding the gunner, Sergeant S. Thompson. Further hits were registered on the mid-upper turret setting off the ammunition and causing serious burns to Sydney Smith. The aircraft stalled and lost 2,000 feet before the smoke cleared sufficiently for the pilot to regain control. He immediately dived for some cloud just below them in order to escape the fighters and the anti-aircraft fire.

By now there was a big fire in the fuselage and ammunition was exploding in all directions inside the aircraft. The rear gunner had a broken leg and was unable to leave his turret. Sydney Smith left his mid-upper turret and started to beat out the flames with his flying jacket and his hands, at one point attempting to smother the flames by throwing his body on the fire. With the help of the navigator and the bomb aimer, Smith then fought his way through the fire, pulled the rear gunner out of the turret and carried him to the rest chair. The fire was still of considerable proportions and the floor of the fuselage was largely burnt away. Their efforts were then re-directed to getting the fire under control, which they almost achieved before the last of the fire extinguishers was emptied, leaving the fire to smoulder for the rest of the flight.

With the perspex missing from the nose and most of the pilot's cupola, there was a constant gale blowing through the aircraft. All the maps, navigation and wireless logs had been blown out of the aircraft when the shell exploded in the nose. The wireless operator, Sergeant Coakley, immediately set about trying to

The damage caused to the bomb bay by the first shell is readily apparent. The blackened mid-upper turret illustrates the danger faced by Smith. (M Gunnell)

The two pilots faced major problems after the second shell smashed into the nose and cockpit area. (M Gunnell)

raise his home base. He transmitted an SOS over the Danish coast and gained contact. He then obtained a succession of bearings which the pilots steered throughout the long crossing of the North Sea. With no navigation aids, these bearings were to prove vital for the safe return. Throughout the return flight he remained at his post despite considerable burns to his face and hands. His captain was to describe his work as 'absolute wonders, especially as it was his first operational trip'.

The second pilot, Sergeant Gunnell, nursed the engines and the petrol supplies before taking over the controls to give the captain some respite from the

The Lancaster after crash-landing at Wittering. (M Gunnell)

intense cold. He was to remain at the controls for two hours before exhaustion forced him to hand back to the captain just as they crossed the coast at Mablethorpe. The searchlights were waiting for them and they were directed towards the Wash. Despite lowering cloud and bad weather, the Wittering searchlight canopy was identified and Flight Sergeant Campbell decided to attempt a landing.

On arrival, the crew discovered that the hydraulic system had been shot away and, despite using the emergency system, the undercarriage and flaps could not be lowered. With most of the parachutes destroyed by fire, a belly landing was inevitable. The captain ordered crash positions and Sydney Smith immediately placed his wounded body over the seriously injured gunner in a selfless act to protect his comrade. Despite his wounds and fatigue, the captain made a perfect crash landing without further damage to the aircraft or injury to the crew.

The next morning the true extent of the damage to the Lancaster could be seen and reports at the time spoke of a 'miracle landing' and the Wittering ground crew were 'baffled that this aircraft could fly'. A local paper reported that 'it was amazing that any plane could have got home in such a condition'. The aircraft had completed its twenty-fifth and final war sortie and was declared 'beyond economical repair'.

Sydney Smith and the rear gunner were to spend time in Rauceby Hospital recovering from their wounds. The captain compiled his report and of Sydney Smith he wrote, 'He did exceptional and courageous work in getting under control a very serious fire at great personal risk and in getting Sergeant Thompson out of his turret, over the fire and to the rest bunk where he remained to comfort and protect him'.

Within a few days it was announced that the Commander-in-Chief of Bomber Command, Sir Arthur Harris had approved the immediate award of the Distinguished Flying Medal to all seven members of the crew, an almost unprecedented event. In addition, the captain was awarded an immediate field commission. The legendary Group Captain Gus Walker, Station Commander at RAF Syerston, wrote in the recommendation for Smith's DFM that he had

CONFIDENTIAL. **RECOMMENDATION FOR IMMEDIATE AWARD.**

Christian Names: Sydney, Surname: SMITH,

Rank: Sergeant, Official Number: 1128846

Command or Group: No. 5 Group, Bomber Command. Unit: No. 61 Squadron.

Total hours flown on operations: 8.15

Number of sorties: 1

Recognition for which recommended: Immediate D.F.M.

Appointment held: Mid upper gunner.

Particulars of meritorious service for which the recommendation is made, including date and place.

Sgt. Smith was mid upper gunner to F/Sgt. Campbell on the night of 24/25th September, 1942. When the aircraft was hit by A.A. and fighter fire his turret was set on fire and ammmunition was bursting all around him. He immediately went to the scene of the main fire in the fuselage and was the first to attempt to extinguish it. He was considerably burnt about the hands and face and body before he attacked the fire. Nevertheless, he stripped off his flying clothing and fell on top of the fire on his clothing. He then greatly assisted in extracting the rear gunner from the tail turret and played a major part in getting the fire under control. Despite his injuries he returned to his post for the remainder of the trip.

It is considered that Sgt. Smith displayed outstanding gallantry and devotion to duty and contributed greatly to the safe return of the aircraft and crew.

Date...27/9/42.........

GROUP CAPTAIN, COMMANDING,
R.A.F. STATION, SYERSTON.

Remarks by Air or other Officer Commanding. After having inspected this aircraft I strongly support this recommendation. It is almost inconceivable that any crew could have carried on for the four hundred miles to [illegible] & land without further incident.

W A Coryton

Date...30/9/42.......

Air Vice-Marshal,
Commanding No. 5 Group, R.A.F.

The recommendation for Smith's Immediate DFM endorsed personally by Air Officer Commanding No 5 Group displayed *'outstanding gallantry and devotion to duty.'* Most unusually, Air Vice Marshal W. A. Coryton, the Air Officer Commanding 5 Group, added to all seven recommendations a hand-written comment: *'After having inspected this aircraft, I strongly support this recommendation. It is almost inconceivable that any crew could have carried on for the four hundred mile sea crossing and land without further incident.'*

A few months after this incident, it was announced that a new medal had been authorised for gallantry in the air. There can be little doubt that had the Conspicuous Gallantry Medal been available, then the captain and most of his crew would have received this award which is second only to the Victoria Cross for non-commissioned aircrew. On 24 November, 1942, Sergeant Sydney Smith attended Buckingham Palce to receive his medal from His Majesty The King. Tragically, his captain, Flight Sergeant Campbell and Sergeants Bunclark, Coakley and Corbett were not with him. Five days earlier they had been killed attempting a crash landing in Devon while returning from a minelaying operation in the Bay of Biscay in their badly damaged Lancaster.

On 6 December, Sydney Smith returned to operations with 61 Squadron. With Flying Officer Foster as captain of Lancaster W 4236, he took part in the attack on Mannheim. Three nights later he was over Turin. However, it was clear that he had not fully recovered from his injuries and he was rested for six months

A Halifax II - LW 235 - of 78 Squadron. (Author's collection)

during which time he served in a ground appointment with 49 Squadron.

After refresher training and a course at 1652 Heavy Conversion Unit at Marston Moor, he joined 78 Squadron operating the Halifax from the 4 Group station at Breighton in East Yorkshire just as the Battle of Berlin was opening. Flight Sergeant Sydney Smith's first operation was on 31 August, 1943, the second major attack against Berlin, but engine failure forced a turn back over the North Sea. With Sergeant W. H. Scott as captain, he took off in Halifax Mk II, JD 417 ('Q') on 5 September for Mannheim, which was bombed from 18,000 feet. They returned safely, but the Squadron was to lose three of its aircraft on the raid. During this period the casualties among the heavies of Bomber Command was on the increase as the *Luftwaffe* night fighter force developed tactics to combat the increasingly sophisticated aids and deception methods of the bomber force. However, Sydney Smith was to complete three more bombing sorties without incident. On 8 October, Sergeant Scott's all Sergeant crew took off in LW 236 at 2236 hours to join 503 other heavy bombers for an attack on Hanover. After take off, nothing more was heard of the aircraft or its crew.

On the night of 8 October the *Luftwaffe* air defence control system had been badly confused by the RAF's tactic of attacking two major cities (the other being Bremen) on the same night. Among their few successes was Halifax LW 236 which had been shot down near Diepholz as it approached Hanover. The rear gunner, Sergeant L. W. Colman, parachuted to safety and capture, but Sydney Smith and his five comrades died. They rest together in the British Military Cemetery at Hannover-Limmer.

Three days later Sydney Smith's 21-year-old brother Jack was killed as he stormed Monte Cassino in Italy. Courage was no stranger to the Smith brothers. During the First World War, their father had been awarded the Military Medal for bravery in the field. Today, neighbours in Blackburn Road, Bolton still remember the smart, cheerful and gallant Sydney Smith and his brother.

CHAPTER THIRTEEN

Jungle Supply Pilot – Bill Perry

The only reference to break the darkness was the flashing signal lamp which marked the drop zone. Bill Perry gently eased his Dakota (FD 823) lower to fly just above the jungle canopy, barely visible in the moonlight, as he concentrated on bringing his aircraft and its two-ton load of urgently required supplies directly over the jungle clearing. His precious load was destined for an intelligence-gathering patrol deep inside Japanese-held territory in North Burma. It was 18 November, 1943, and Bill Perry was on his sixty-fifth supply dropping sortie since joining 31 Squadron fifteen months earlier. Over the next three months he would almost double that number as the 'Forgotten War' gathered momentum.

Bill Perry, born and educated in Farnham, Surrey, was nineteen when he reported to Cardington in October 1940 to enlist as a trainee pilot. After completing his initial training the following March, he left for Rhodesia to start his flying training, first on the Tiger Moth and then the Harvard. Awarded his pilot's wings at the end of the year, he was posted to India with the majority of his colleagues. He arrived at Lahore to join 31 Squadron just ten days after the

Bill Perry's medals, Distinguished Flying Medal, 1939-45 Star, Burma Star, France and Germany Star, War Medal.

Bill Perry at Initial Training Wing, standing second from left, third row from front. (Mrs B Broomhead)

Japanese started their attack on Burma with a big air-raid directed at Rangoon. Before joining an operational crew, Bill Perry first had to attend a flying course at the Air Landing School in Delhi to qualify as a co-pilot on the Dakota.

31 Squadron had moved to India immediately after forming in 1916 and had introduced the aeroplane to that vast country; hence the Squadron's motto '*In Caelum Indicum Primus*' which translates as 'First in the Indian Skies'. After twenty-six years' service in the rugged terrain of the North West Frontier, no squadron was better equipped to face the rigours of a desperate war under such inhospitable conditions for the next four-and-a-half years. Although the war had only recently reached the Far East by the time that Perry joined 31, the Squadron had already distinguished itself, with detachments of its Valentia and DC 2 transport aircraft to Iraq and the Middle East for troop transporting duties. The detachment arrived back in India at the beginning of February 1942

and moved to Akyab on the coast of Burma to assist in the evacuation of the Air Forces as the Japanese advance gained momentum.

At the time of the Japanese invasion of Burma 31 Squadron was the only transport squadron in India and it would be many months before the increasing burden of air transport would be shared by the formation of a second unit. The ancient Valencias had finally been retired and the Squadron was operating eight very old and worn-out DC 2s and three DC 3 aircraft which had arrived just a few days earlier. Following the fall of Rangoon and the Japanese advance the situation in Central Burma became precarious and Squadron headquarters returned to Lahore. To maintain support for the retreating ground forces, detachments were established in Assam at Tezpur and Dinjan with the Dakotas flying supplies and reinforcements into Schwebo and Mandalay and returning with the wounded.

Having completed his various conversion courses, Bill Perry rejoined the

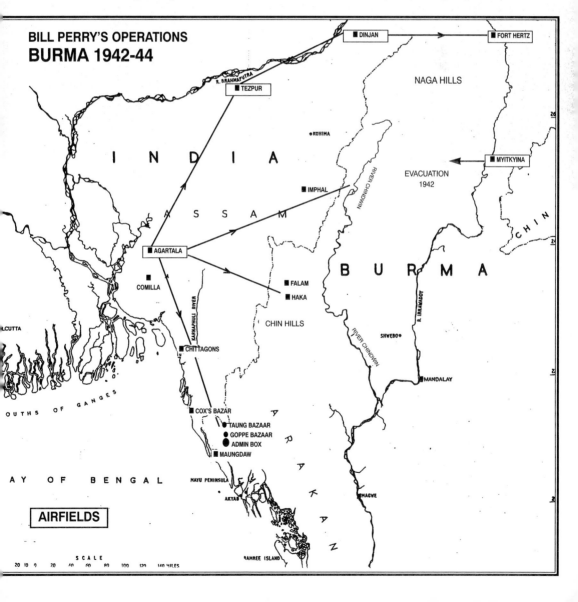

BILL PERRY'S OPERATIONS
BURMA 1942-44

A 31 Squadron Dakota concealed during the day at Fort Hertz, 1942. (George Parkinson)

Squadron in May 1942 and immediately left for the detachment at Dinjan. Within days, the emergency evacuation of Myitkyina began and 31 played a gallant part in the rescue of British families and troops. With the loss of three aircraft to Japanese dive-bombers, the airfield had to be abandoned and 31 flew out the last refugees in its surviving, heavily overloaded aircraft.

Following the withdrawal of the ground forces from Burma across the Indian border, Bill Perry left the detachment at Dinjan for the Squadron's headquarters at Lahore to join a number of other new arrivals where he started to build up his experience, flying the internal mail and passenger runs to Bombay and Calcutta. He was also involved in the collection of the Squadron's new Dakotas from Bombay.

By the end of 1942, Perry had returned to the Squadron detachment at Dinjan and flown his first operational sorties including flights into the remote garrison at Fort Hertz in the north of Burma. This was a very important post and airstrip. Apart from its value for possible operations in northern Burma, it provided a vital emergency strip for the aircraft flying the perilous route between India and China, forever known as 'The Hump.' With no overland route to the west, this isolated post could only be resupplied from India by air. With the highly experienced Flying Officer Mike Vlasto as captain, Perry first flew into Fort Hertz to evacuate twenty Chinese on 17 September. As soon as the aircraft landed, it was marshalled into a small clearing in the trees and Gurkha soldiers and local Kachin tribesmen rushed out with camouflage to prevent Japanese reconnaissance aircraft confirming that the strip was still in use.

A British team was established at the Fort Hertz garrison with the task of training Kachin levies who would mount a successful guerrilla war against the invaders. In addition to making numerous other resupply flights to this remote airstrip over the following weeks, Perry often flew in support of these brave natives who relied exclusively on air support as they carried out their patrols deep into enemy territory

At the beginning of December the British mounted the first Arakan offensive towards the island of Akyab. To support this operation, 31 Squadron moved its Dinjan detachment further south in Assam to Tezpur, where Bill Perry remained for almost four months flying stores to Fort Hertz and carrying out supply air-drops to the Army detachments in the Chin Hills. The names of Tiddim, Falam and Haka figured on the Squadron operations board on a daily basis.

Throughout December, 1942, and January, 1943, Perry continued to fly as a co-pilot and on 9 January, he flew to Fort Hertz with one of the most experienced captains on the Squadron, Pilot Officer David 'Lummie' Lord, who was soon to be awarded a Distinguished Flying Cross. They would fly together on numerous occasions in the future. Lord had a richly deserved reputation as an outstanding pilot and as a most likeable person. He returned to Great Britain later in the year to help establish the RAF's Dakota force in preparation for the invasion of Normandy.

As the Arakan offensive petered out and the Japanese counter-attacked, the demands on Perry and his colleagues mounted; 31 Squadron was still the only transport squadron in the Indian theatre. During February the Squadron

Dakota - MA 929 - of 31 Squadron at Dinjan, January 1943. Perry flew numerous re-supply sorties in this aircraft. (31 Squadron Association)

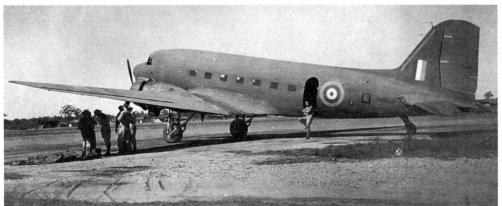

dropped almost 178 tons of supplies. By early March, Perry had accumulated sufficient experience to start a conversion course to qualify as a captain. He returned to the Squadron, now based near the Burmese border at Agartala, at the beginning of May just as the Japanese counter-offensive ended. With the Allied forces back at the Indian border in Assam, General Bill Slim arrived to assume command of the Allied armies in the Arakan.

During the period that Perry was away on his captain's course General Wingate's first Chindit Expedition had been mounted and 31 Squadron had provided all the crucial resupply sorties, attracting high praise from the enigmatic leader who described the supply-dropping operations as a 'brilliant success.'

Perry flew his first sortie as a captain on 3 May when he took off in Dakota FD 781 to air-drop three-and-a-half tons of supplies to the Army detachment at Falam. When the monsoon broke later in the month there was no-let up in the flying effort. Indeed, despite the weather and the formidable difficulties for the ground crews, the number of supply-dropping sorties flown and the tonnage of supplies dropped in July, 1943, reached record figures. The Squadron flew 286 sorties and delivered 784 tons of supplies with just fifteen aircraft available. During August Perry flew eleven air drops to the detachments in the Chin Hills and a further fifteen in September.

On 29 September, he flew no less than three sorties each of three hours' duration with just two hours on the ground. Two days later he repeated this outstanding performance being on duty for over thirteen hours in the oppresive heat and humidity. During October the pressure on the air and ground

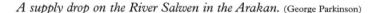

A supply drop on the River Salwen in the Arakan. (George Parkinson)

crews of 31 Squadron became even greater and Perry flew as many as twenty-four three-hour supply-dropping operations during the month. This imposed a great strain on the aircrew. Operating over the mountainous and frightening terrain of Burma during the height of the monsoon created some of the most demanding flying conditions anywhere in the world. In addition they knew that, if they were unfortunate to be shot down, their chances of survival were very slim. It is a sobering thought to recall that most of the aircrew had been pupils at flying training school just eighteen months earlier. Without doubt they were a very special breed of young men. General Giffard, the General Officer Commanding the Eastern Army, commented that without the air supply by 31 Squadron, the Army could not have held on to its positions throughout the monsoon.

With the monsoon over, the new 'campaigning season' opened with the Japanese becoming increasingly active in the Arakan and the Chin Hills. Bill Perry and his colleagues in 31 Squadron continued to bear the brunt of the increasingly intensive routine of supply-dropping. The great success of these operations stemmed largely from air superiority achieved by the fighter squadrons but, whenever there was a risk of encountering Japanese fighters, the Dakotas were escorted by Hurricanes or Spitfires.

The routine of daily supply drops to the Chin Hills was interrupted for Bill Perry and his crew in mid-Novemebr when they embarked on their first 'Phyllis' Op. These night sorties deep into enemy-held territory carried supplies to the small intelligence-gathering patrols of locally-trained natives led by British offi-

Bill Perry, extreme right, and his crew wait for their aircraft to be re-fuelled. George Parkinson, the wireless operator, is third from left. (George Parkinson)

cers who had previously served with the Burma Forestry Commission. The Dakotas were their only lifeline. Late on the night of 16 November, 1943, Bill Perry took off in Dakota FD 803 and headed east beyond the Chindwin River. At the drop zone they failed to make radio contact and the ground signals had not been displayed. After loitering for as long as possible, the crew reluctantly abandoned the sortie.

The following night Perry tried again and this time the sortie was successful. The radio link was established and, to their great surprise, it was a female voice that answered their transmission and, for a brief moment, the aircrew thought they were talking to Tokyo Rose! However, having authenticated the ground signals, Perry began his long low run-in heading for the drop zone and, on his signal, the air despatchers released the two tons of supplies. Perry turned for his second objective which was a leaflet drop on the east bank of the Chindwin near Namalin. This ploy was intended to disguise the real objective of the sortie. After a five-hour flight Perry brought his Dakota in to land at Agartala.

With virtually no overland access to the Army detachments in the Chin Hills and the Arakan, air supply was the lifeline for the troops. The intensity of operations continued to increase and November saw 31 Squadron record its highest number of supply dropping sorties with 261 during which 816 tons of stores were dropped. Over the next few months the totals would continue to rise. Not only is this an enormous tribute to the aircrew, but it is testimony of the wonderful support provided by the ground crew who toiled on in extreme weather, with disease an everyday occurrence, and no permanent living quarters or entertainment. Added to these difficulties was the poor availability of spare parts for the aircraft; improvisation was paramount.

In the last ten days of December Perry flew every day, including a seven-hour

A Dakota of 31 Squadron takes off in the monsoon from an airfield in Assam. (MOD)

Indian troops embark on a 31 Squadron Dakota at Agartala. (31 Squadron Association)

sortie with Hurricane fighters providing escort for some of the route as he took four tons of supplies deep into the Burmese jungle to support a West African Division. January followed a similar pattern and Bill Perry flew twenty-three sorties, almost all in his Dakota FL 537. The long-expected Japanese offensive started in early February and their infiltration to encircle two Indian Divisions was quickly successful. The isolated area soon became well known as the 'Admin Box' and the Indians held out for many months, being supplied entirely from the air.

On 9 February, 1944, seven Dakotas with a fighter escort headed for the Admin Box. As the Dakotas began their runs towards the drop zone, Zero fighters appeared and the unarmed Dakotas were forced to scatter. The Hurricanes engaged the enemy fighters, but some of the transports were attacked. One enemy aircraft closed in on Perry and he started violent evasive action, but this didn't prevent cannon fire damaging his aircraft and putting both airspeed indicators out of action. Undaunted, he carried on to the drop zone for a successful drop before escaping by flying almost in the jungle canopy. Unfortunately, one of the Squadron aircraft was less fortunate and Flight Lieutenant J Walker DFC and his crew failed to return. Bill Perry limped home with a Hurricane providing an escort for his damaged Dakota.

The increased Japanese fighter activity forced the Dakotas to carry out the resupply of the Admin Box at night. Over the next week Bill Perry took off every night heading for the drop zones at Goppe Bazaar and Taung Bazaar to supply the beleaguered Division. On the night of 18 February, Perry landed his Dakota at Agartala having completed his ninety-seventh and final air drop over the Burmese jungle. His arduous tour with 31 Squadron was over.

Although Bill Perry returned home to England, 31 Squadron continued to provide the crucial support needed by the Army for another eighteen months. It is recognised now that the war in Burma provided a striking example of the crucial value of air supply. The Air Commander, Air Chief Marshal Sir Keith Park, commented that 'air supply in Burma made history'. The role of a transport aircraft pilot has never attracted the same degree of attention as that of the bomber or fighter pilot but to fly a defenceless Dakota at night through storms and the mountainous terrain of Burma to bring supplies to troops cut off behind Japanese lines must stand alongside the bravest actions in the air.

Bill Perry and a number of his Squadron aircrew colleagues returned to England in March 1944 expecting a 'rest tour'. However, together with other experienced Dakota air-drop crews from the Middle and Far East, they formed the nucleus of the rapidly expanding transport force being gathered for the forthcomong invasion of Europe. Together with his navigator friend from 31 Squadron, Frank Barritt, Perry joined the newly formed 512 Squadron at the recently-opened airfield at Broadwell near Brize Norton. Close by were the other recently activated airfields of 46 Group at Blakehill Farm and Down Ampney where David Lord was based with 271 Squadron. A number of Perry's 31 Squadron colleagues were posted to the nearby squadrons.

Just after arriving at Broadwell it was announced that Flight Sergeant W Perry had been awarded an immediate Distinguished Flying Medal for his outstanding tour of operations on 31 Squadron during which time he had flown over 700 operational hours. The citation commented on '*the great many supply dropping sorties both by day and night and his utmost keeness and ability*', and drew particular attention to his continuing to the dropping zone despite his aircraft having been hit in many places.

The newly formed squadron equipped with Dakota III aircraft immediately began training in preparation for the D-Day airborne assault. Formation flying, paratroop drops and glider towing quickly became the routine. Bill Perry flew on the first major squadron exercise when fifteen aircraft dropped 230 troops over the Winterbourne drop zone. Other large-scale exercises were flown involving three squadrons flying in stream out over the English Channel before turning in to drop the paratroopers over the Salisbury training areas.

To give experience of cross-Channel operations, each crew flew a 'nickelling' leaflet dropping sortie over France and Perry flew on the first war sortie of the newly formed 512 Squadron. Taking off in Dakota KG 377 on 22 April, his was one of four squadron aircraft to drop leaflets over Angers.

Training intensified as D-Day approached and this included supply dropping and glider towing. Particular emphasis was placed on practising take-offs with all thirty-two of the Squadron's aircraft airborne in the minimum time. To achieve this concentration, meticulous planning on the ground was essential and take-off times had to be met to a matter of seconds, involving perfect

Paratroopers embark on a 512 Squadron Dakota at Broadwell, June 1944. (Author's collection)

marshalling arrangements by the ground crew.

With all personnel confined to the airfield, the air and ground crews made their final preparations for the airborne invasion of Europe. Just before midnight on 5 June, Operation Tonga was under way and the Squadron Commander, Wing Commander Coventry, rolled down the runway at Broadwell to be followed by the remainder of the Squadron. Bill Perry was one of the last airborne in his Dakota 'A' (KG 324), his five-man crew including Frank Barritt as his navigator. All thirty-two aircraft were airborne in eleven minutes and they formed up in vics of three aircraft flying at thirty-second intervals before joining two other squadrons (271 and 48). After leaving the beacon positioned at Worthing, the formation set course for Cap d'Antifer on the French coast where they began the final run in for Drop Zone V three miles south-east of Merville.

As the Dakotas approached the French coast the crews could see a force of 100 Lancasters bombing the coastal batteries that would be the objective of the 9th Battalion of the Parachue Regiment being carried by Perry and his fellow 512 Squadron pilots. A small amount of light flak greeted the Dakotas but fell too short to interfere with the formation keeping.

Subsequent events showed that Drop Zone V was a poor choice due to the waterlogged ground, and the Parachute Brigade Pathfinders had a very difficult time setting up the necessary homing aids for the incoming fleet of Dakotas. This caused some congestion; most crews completed the drop on the first run but a number had to make a second approach. Altogether 512 Squadron dropped 568 troops.

Two nights later Operation Rob Roy was mounted and five aircraft took off at 2230 hours to resupply the 6th Airborne Division with ammunition onto Drop Zone N. Bill Perry and his crew were second away in their aircraft 'A' and formated on the leader. After routeing via the Littlehampton Eureka beacon, the formation switched off the formation lights and descended to 800 feet. While running up to the coast, a considerable amount of light flak was encountered. When only a mile or two offshore, and homing to the Drop Zone beacon, the formation was caught in a heavy concentration of crossfire from naval vessels either side of track. The formation broke to take immediate evasive action, while all fired the identification colours of the day. It was not until another series of flares had been fired that the Navy's fire ceased and the run could be completed. In taking evasive action, Perry had to jettison his load over the sea. Tragically, two other aircraft in the formation were shot down and their crews were lost. Other squadrons suffered losses in the same incident.

Once the Invasion forces had established themselves in Northern France, the Dakotas started to fly in supplies to the hastily constructed airstrips. On 19 June, fifteen crews flew to Hurn to collect supplies before proceeding with a Spitfire fighter escort to the landing ground at B 6. Perry was flying KG 570. The following day a second operation was mounted to deliver supplies and return with casualties. As the formation approached the coast, the cloud base was down to 300 feet and the Squadron went into line astern with Bill Perry bringing up the rear. All aircraft landed safely and disembarked 269 passengers and fifteen tons of freight before bringing out seventy-four casualties.

Throughout July and August the Dakotas continued their shuttle service to the French airstrips returning with casualties whenever possible. Throughout this period Perry and his crew flew all their operations in Dakota 'A' KG 324. On 19 August, he took elements of the 1st Battalion SAS and their jeep transports to Rennes and a few days later he was joining the major food relief operation into Orleans. The Dakotas flew hard on the heels of the advancing armies, taking fuel supplies in jerry-cans to airfields within hours of their capture from the retreating German Army.

By early September the ground armies had made rapid progress to the Belgian border and Brussels became a regular terminus for the resupply flights. Over the three-day period 10 to 12 September Bill Perry flew four sorties as part of a thirty-two aircraft operation on supply runs to the Belgian capital. Two days later, the Squadron was withdrawn to prepare for another major airborne operation codenamed Market.

The aim of Operation Market was to position the 2nd Army in the Nijmegen-Arnhem area. The objective of the 1st British Airborne Division, with the 1st Polish Brigade Group, was to capture the bridges at Arnhem and the force was to be dropped by the RAF transport force of 38 and 46 Groups.

Bill Perry did not fly on the first day when the opposition was relatively light but he was at the controls of his Dakota for the second lift on 18 September. Twenty-four aircraft from 512 Squadron took part in the reinforcement Operation Market 2, each towing a Horsa glider. Although there was more flak than on the previous day, Perry released his glider successfully to a drop zone 8 miles north-west of Arnhem. The operation was completed with the loss of one Squadron aircraft. By the following day the situation on the ground had become extremely serious and the day was devoted to resupply. 512 Squadron mounted fourteen sorties and, again, Bill Perry released his load over the drop zone.

By this third day, the flak had increased considerably in intensity and casualties among the resupply aircraft were high. Among the Dakota crews lost on the 19th was Bill Perry and Frank Barritt's old friend from their days on 31 Squadron, David 'Lummie' Lord. Lord's gallantry over Arnhem was witnessed in awe by the ground forces of both sides as he repeatedly brought his burning Dakota through the heavy flak to complete his drop. As the aircraft dived to the ground just one crew member escaped and Lord was killed. Shortly after, he was posthumously awarded the nation's highest award for gallantry, the Victoria Cross, and the only such award to an aircrew of the air transport forces.

On 20 September some of the drop zones had fallen into enemy hands, but

RAF Dakotas over the Arnhem drop-zone during Operation Market, *September 1944.* (MOD)

the deteriorating situation on the ground dictated that a resupply drop had to be attempted and new zones nearer to the town were identified. Fifteen Squadron aircraft were prepared and Bill Perry and his crew boarded their Dakota 'A' at 1430 hours for their third Arnhem operation. The force of 122 transport aircraft flew the southern route over friendly territory but as they approached the drop zone they faced the heaviest barrage of flak yet encountered since Market had begun.

Perry began his supply dropping run at 1720 hours on the newly established drop zone two miles west of Arnhem. He dropped his panniers successfully from 800 feet, but as he turned away his aircraft was immediately engaged by heavy and medium flak. Hits were sustained in the port and starboard wings and the fuel supply line to the port engine caught fire. As Perry started a climb the flames spread quickly and efforts to extinguish the fire failed. Within minutes the flames had spread and the Dakota was streaming ten-foot-long flames. At 1,200 feet Perry ordered the crew to bale out while he tried to keep control of the aircraft. The wireless operator and three of the despatchers left immediately but Frank Barritt had to 'assist' the fourth despatcher out. He turned to look at the cockpit and noticed that Perry had donned his parachute but was still struggling to control the aircraft. He then jumped from a low level just before the flame-engulfed Dakota hit the ground with the gallant Bill Perry and his co-pilot still on board.

The aircraft came down close to the Dutch village of Schaijk near Nijmegen and the local people buried the two pilots in the local churchyard. Frank Barritt landed on the roof of a bungalow; the villagers gave him shelter and he was able to evade capture. Two days later he was walking into a transit camp in Brussels when he was hailed by his wireless operator who had also been assisted by the brave Dutch villagers. Within four days they returned to the Squadron with the full story of Bill Perry's final sacrifice.

After the war Bill Perry and his co-pilot, Warrant Officer Ivan Gilbert, were re-interred alongside each other in the Uden War Cemetery. Just ten yards away rests David Lord VC. For four years the two pilots had flown their unarmed aircraft over some of the most inhospitable terrain in the world, through appalling weather and against formidable enemy fire in order to take urgently-needed supplies to their comrades, who depended on them to get through whatever the difficulties. In the end the two friends paid the ultimate sacrifice delivering those supplies and remaining at the controls of their stricken aircraft so that their crews could escape. Theirs was a very special kind of gallantry.

Bill Perry's grave at Uden War Cemetery, Holland. (Frank Barritt)

CHAPTER FOURTEEN

Night Fighter Navigator 'Ace' Nat Addison

On the night that Rudolph Hess, deputy Führer of Germany, flew a Messerschmitt 110 to Scotland and baled out over Glasgow, the Luftwaffe *mounted its final major night-bombing blitz on London. It was late on the night of 10 May, 1941, that Bill Addison and his Canadian pilot, Gordon Raphael, scrambled from their base at Hunsdon in their Havoc night fighter to intercept the incoming raiders. Two hours later they landed, having destroyed the first enemy aircraft that would help establish them as an 'Ace' night fighter crew.*

Manchester-born William Nathan 'Nat' Addison had joined the Royal Air Force in September, 1938, as an electrician, having served with the Royal Artillery (TA) for seven months. After training at Henlow, he was posted to Martlesham Heath and then served briefly on two fighter squadrons in Yorkshire where he volunteered for duties as an air gunner. At the height of the

'Nat' Addison's medals are Distinguished Flying Cross, Distinguished Flying Medal, 1939-45 Star with Battle of Britain Clasp, Aircrew Europe Star with France and Germany Clasp, Defence Medal, War Medal.

A photograph of 'Nat' Addison taken in 1945 showing him wearing his DFC and DFM ribbons. (MOD)

A Blenheim I night fighter of 23 Squadron at Wittering 1940. Addison flew ten patrols during the Battle of Britain. (Andy Thomas)

Battle of Britain he was posted to 23 Squadron equipped with the Blenheim 1F night fighter, at Wittering. On the night of 16 September, with Flight Lieutenant Knight at the controls, he took off in Blenheim YP-D on his first patrol. By the end of October he had flown a further nine night patrols and his service in Fighter Command up to this period qualified him for the rare 'Battle of Britain' clasp attached to his 1939-45 Star. Before leaving 23 Squadron he completed fifteen night patrols without ever encountering the enemy.

By the end of 1940 Addison had qualified as a radio operator (air); the name given to those who operated the early Airborne Interception radars (AI); and he was posted to 85 Squadron based at Debden. This famous fighter squadron had enjoyed considerable success during the Battle of Britain under its dynamic Commanding Officer, Squadron Leader Peter Townsend DFC, and had recently converted to the night fighter role equipped initially with Hurricanes. This superb single-seat day fighter was unsuited to the night fighter task and, with the *Luftwaffe* concentrating on night bombing operations against Great Britain, the need for a fighter to be equipped with an AI radar became a priority. By mid-February 1941, 85 Squadron began to re-equip with the night fighter version of the Douglas Havoc Mk 1 which carried the AI Mk IV radar. The Havoc was a modified version of the Boston bomber and was fitted with eight Browning .303 ins machine guns in the nose. The overall matt black finish gave the aircraft an appropriately sinister appearance.

The key to successful night fighting was teamwork. The two-man crew of pilot and radio observer (RO) were the key elements, but the work of the controllers at the Ground Control Interception (GCI) radar stations was crucial. The early AI sets had very limited range, sometimes as little as two to three miles, and it was the job of the ground controller to vector the night fighter to the right position and height to allow the RO in the fighter to pick up the contact on his AI radar. The RO then gave instructions to his pilot to bring the aircraft just below and behind the contact until the pilot achieved a visual sighting. The pilot then manoeuvred his aircraft into position before opening fire.

Shortly after arriving on 85 Squadron, Nat Addison was crewed with Flight Lieutenant Gordon Raphael who had already been awarded a Distinguished Flying Cross for his work as a Whitley bomber pilot. Throughout the next two years Addison flew every one of his operational sorties with this Canadian pilot. It was to prove an ideal team and the Raphael/Addison combination was to become one of the most successful night fighter crews in the Royal Air Force. After an initial period for familiarisation with their new aircraft, the Squadron was declared operational in early April and moved to Hunsdon in the North Weald Sector.

On 7 May, 1941, Nat Addison took off on his first patrol in a Havoc I (VY-F) and just three nights later he vectored Raphael on to a contact and they achieved their first confirmed victory. The night of 10/11 May marked the end of the

A Havoc I night fighter - BJ 461 - of 85 Squadron 1941. Addison and his pilot Gordon Raphael were the highest scoring Havoc night fighter crew. (via Peter Green)

German blitz and saw the *Luftwaffe* mounting its heaviest night bombing effort against London; the RAF's night fighter crews were soon in action. Addison took off just before midnight and within thirty minutes GCI took control of Havoc 'V' and vectored the aircraft onto a contact just north of London. Levelling at 14,000 feet, Addison obtained a blip on his radar at maximum range and started giving instructions to his pilot. After four or five corrections, Raphael obtained a visual contact at 600 yards slightly above and dead ahead. He closed to 100 yards and identified the enemy aircraft as a Heinkel 111. He fired one burst of four seconds at the starboard engine and the bomber immediately burst into flames and went into a left-hand spiral dive. At about 8,000 feet it came out of the spiral but continued diving and exploded just before it crashed near Chelmsford.

Raphael and Addison had destroyed a Heinkel 111 (1T+HH) of *I/KG 28* piloted by *Leutnant* D Kruger who lost his life with his crew. During this heavy raid, over 1,400 people were killed in London and one-third of the streets in Greater London were rendered impassable. About 2,000 fires were started and the House of Commons, Westminster Hall and St Clement Danes Church (now the Royal Air Force Church) were severely damaged. The night fighters brought down twenty-nine of the raiders and a further four were shot down by the Anti-Aircraft defences.

Within a few days the *Luftwaffe* withdrew many of its bomber units from France and the Low Countries as it prepared for operations in the Balkans and the invasion of Russia. The enemy bombers would continue to appear in the skies of Britain, but 'tip and run' raids would, to a large extent, replace the large formations attacking the country's major cities.

On the night of 13/14 June, Raphael and Addison, who still held the lowly

A Havoc night intruder at readiness. (MOD)

rank of Aircraftman 1, achieved further success on what proved to be a busy night for them. Under the GCI control of Waldringfield, Addison vectored his pilot onto a contact which was visually identified as a Heinkel 111. The rear gunner of the bomber immediately engaged the Havoc, but Raphael had too much overtake speed and he was unable to engage and the contact was lost.

While orbiting over Shoeburyness at 10,000 feet, Addison picked up an enemy aircraft at maximum range on his AI radar (4,000 yards). Closing on the contact, another Heinkel 111 was identified. The aircraft was weaving from side to side and Raphael fired a five-second burst from 100 yards which provoked an immediate response from the top gunner. The Havoc's bullets were seen to strike the forward fuselage of the Heinkel in a shower of sparks. The enemy dived with the Havoc in pursuit and appeared to be out of control at 7,000 feet over Gravesend. Raphael claimed a probable. Post-war analysis shows that this Heinkel 111 (5J+KS) of *III/KG 4* ditched in the North Sea and the crew were saved. However, a Junkers 88 saw the crew in the sea and set up an orbit. Shortly afterwards, it dug a wing in the sea and crashed.

After this engagement the Havoc crew were instructed by North Weald to continue patrolling in the Gravesend area. At 12,000 feet Addison soon picked up a blip at random and closed on a manoeuvring target which proved difficult to intercept. Eventually Addison put Raphael in a good position astern and he fired a long burst into the fuselage and starboard engine of another Heinkel 111. The enemy pilot appeared to lose control as the enemy aircraft dived away to port with the top gunner firing. Shortly afterwards the Havoc crew and ground personnel at Hunsdon saw the Heinkel explode in a great orange flash and the aircraft crashed on the Isle of Grain. Although Raphael claimed the destruction of the aircraft, post-war analysis shows that this aircraft was almost certainly destroyed by Pilot Officer R H Stevens whose 151 Squadron Hurricane was severely burnt as it flew through the fire-ball of the exploding Heinkel.

Ten days after this engagement on the night of 23 June, the Raphael/Addison team were once again in action. Taking off just after midnight, they were vectored by Waldringfield GCI towards an enemy aircraft approaching the coast just south of the Naze. Although Addison picked up the contact on his 'gadget', the enemy dived hard to port and was lost. Shortly afterwards another contact was picked up by GCI on the same approach as the first, but the Havoc crew had similar problems and lost the enemy in the ground returns on Addison's radar. The Havoc was again vectored out to sea on to a third enemy aircraft approaching on the same track as the previous two. This time a successful interception was made and Raphael closed to 100 yards before opening fire on a Junkers 88 which was hit and immediately started to slow. As the Havoc overshot it was hit repeatedly by intense fire from the rear gunner. One bullet passed through Addison's clothing and scorched his thigh. Despite this he stayed at his radar and re-directed his pilot for a second attack, during which the rear gunner was silenced. After a third attack, the engines of the Junkers appeared to stop and the German bomber began to glide towards the sea. Raphael lost sight of it at 6,000 feet.

Shortly after this attack a Junkers 88 of *2/KFG 106* crashed into the sea off Harwich. This maritime version of the Junkers 88 was almost certainly part of a minelaying operation aimed to disrupt the East Coast convoy traffic. Twenty-seven holes were found in the Havoc (VY-R), the majority in the starboard engine. During the attacks Raphael fired 3,440 rounds. He considered that, equipped with cannon, one attack would have achieved the same results as his five attacks with machine guns. He was not the first, and certainly not the last, to make the case for cannon.

Following this third success, it was announced that Aircraftman 1st Class W. N. Addison had been awarded the Distinguished Flying Medal for '*displaying excellent skill having taken part in the destruction of three enemy aircraft at night.*' His pilot Flight Lieutenant G Raphael was awarded a Bar to his Distinguished Flying Cross. This brought to twenty-three the number of decorations awarded to members of 85 Squadron since the outbreak of the war.

June, 1941, brought Nat Addison long overdue promotion to Sergeant and he was re-categorised as an Observer (Radio). 85 Squadron started conversion to the Havoc II, powered by two 1,600 HP Wright Double-Cyclone engines and equipped with no less than twelve Brownings in the nose. However, it was while flying one of the last Mk 1s that Addison and Raphael achieved their next success, one which required all Addison's exceptional skill and the great team-work he had established with his outstanding Canadian pilot.

Taking off in the early hours of 14 July, 'Rainbow 23' was taken over by Waldringfield GCI east of Aldeburgh. After an abortive attempt at an interception, Addison finally obtained a contact at maximum range on his radar. He gave frequent corrections to Raphael as the contact made numerous hard turns, and eventually the Havoc closed to 200 yards when visual contact was made with a Junkers 88. Raphael held his fire until he was just below the enemy at 50 yards, when he fired short bursts into the starboard engine. Return fire was experienced but the Havoc was not hit and Raphael continued firing further bursts into the fuselage of the enemy raider. The Junkers caught fire and soon started to dive away steeply before striking the sea in flames. Like their previous victim, the Junkers 88 was from *2/KFG 106*.

During September Raphael was promoted to Squadron Leader and appointed as a Flight Commander. A few nights later he and Addison suffered a rare 'defeat' when they closed three times to visual range on a Junkers 88, but the enemy pilot skilfully evaded the Havoc on each occasion, finally outrunning the slower fighter. However, further success was just two nights away.

85 Squadron crews with Wing Commander Gordon Raphael DSO, DFC standing with hands in pocket and 'Nat' Addison in front row on extreme right. (Andrew Brookes)

Taking off in their Havoc II (VY-T) from Hunsdon at 2200 hours on 16 September, 'Rainbow 23' was immediately vectored by the North Weald controller, Squadron Leader Stammers, on to a 'Bandit' at 10,000 feet and Addison obtained a contact at maximum range. He had difficulty holding the contact but he regained it after further assistance from ground control. A fifteen-minute chase ensued during which the Havoc was twice illuminated by searchlights which allowed the enemy gunner to engage the chasing night fighter. The enemy took violent evasive action, but Addison held on to the radar contact tenaciously and finally brought Raphael into visual range at 300 yards. The Havoc closed to under 100 yards and the pilot fired a two-second burst which set the enemy on fire and it plunged into the sea off Clacton. As it fell in flames the enemy aircraft was illuminated by searchlights and identified as a Junkers 88.

The Junkers 88c 4 (R4+NH) belonged to *I/NJG 2* and was on an intruder mission from its base at Gilze Rijen in Holland. Three of the crew escaped by parachute; *Oberfeldwebels* E Veil and H Welker and *Unteroffizier* E Wegener were captured and taken to Clacton police station.

There was to be a brief respite from operations for Addison when he was summoned to Buckingham Palace on 28 October to receive his Distinguished

FORM F.

Date	(C)	XXXXXXX 16-9-41.
Flight, Squadron.	(D)	"B" Flight No. 85 Squadron
Number of E/A.	(E)	One
Type of E/A.	(F)	Ju 88
Time attack was delivered.	(G)	2220
Place attack was delivered.	(H)	Clacton on Sea
Height of enemy.	(J)	9,000 ft.
Enemy casualties.	(K)	One Ju 88 Destroyed
Our casualties.(Aircraft).	(L)	Nil
Our casualties (Personnel).	(M)	Nil

Searchlights. Did they illuminate enemy, if not, were they in front of, or behind, target. (N)(i)

Did not illuminate E/A

Anti-Aircraft guns. Did shell bursts assist pilot in intercepting enemy. (N)(ii)

No

General Report. (R)   One Havoc Mk 11 (Twelve m/g) with S/Ldr. Raphael as pilot and Sgt. Addison as A.I. Operator took off Hunsdon at 2125 hours on 16-9-41 and landed Hunsdon 2245 hours.   Havoc was controlled by North Weald throughout, the controller being S/Ldr. Stammers.

The pilot's report is as follows   .-   " After taking off, the Havoc was put on to a Bandit at 10,000 ft and a blip was obtained at maximum range, hard to starboard and slightly below.   The time was approximately 2145 hours.   The blip was lost but regained after two more vectors from Sector Control, and after a chase of about fifteen minutes during which we were twice illuminated by searchlights, E/A fired at us each time, but his fire was well above us.   The E/A also took violent evasive action but finally the Havoc was able to close without being illuminated and a visual of the E/A's exhausts was obtained at 300 yds.

The Havoc closed to under 100 yds and fired a $1\frac{1}{2}$ second burst which caused the E/A to catch fire and plunge into the sea just off Clacton."

As it fell in flames the E/A was illuminated by searchlights and identified as a Ju 88.   Three members of the crew baled out and were held at Clacton.

Total number of rounds fired -330.   A.P. 110   De Wilde 220

Stoppages.   No 9 gun fired 20 rounds, stopped due to a blow back of round in feed through overheating of gun compartment.
No 4 gun fired 10 rounds, stopped due to weak ejection of empty case.

Weather   Visibility good, 10 miles.   No cloud.   No moon.

Pilot's Signature   . . . .

Sqdn Intelligence Officer.

The combat report submitted by Gordon Raphael after he and Addison had shot down a Ju 88 on the night of 16 September, 1941.

Flying Medal from His Majesty the King.

With many *Luftwaffe* bomber units re-deployed to Eastern Europe, targets for the night fighter force were becoming difficult to find. In addition, the increasing effectiveness of the Royal Air Force's night fighter force, working in close co-operation with the early warning radar stations, made the skies of Britain a perilous place for night raiders. Although flying eight or nine night patrols each month, Addison and his pilot had a long period of chasing elusive contacts with very few converted to interceptions. Indeed, they had to wait until 31 July, 1942, before achieving their next success. By this time Gordon Raphael had been promoted to Wing Commander and command of 85 Squadron, and Nat Addison had become a Warrant Officer.

On the night of 31 July, Raphael and Addison took off in their Havoc II (VY-V) as 85 Squadron launched ten aircraft on operational patrols. Flight Lieutenant Neilson, the controller at GCI Easthill, gave the Havoc crew several vectors to intercept a bandit at 9,000 feet. Addison gained the contact on his AI radar and the aircraft closed to minimum range before Raphael picked up a faint light from the ventral turret of the enemy aircraft which he visually identified as a Junkers 88. He closed in to fifty yards and fired two bursts of two seconds on the enemy, which had taken no evasive action. Strikes were seen round the turret before the aircraft dived vertically from 8,000 feet and crashed north of Cambridge. After the claim had been investigated, it was awarded to the Oakington Light Anti-Aircraft Battery and Raphael and Addison had to be content with a damaged.

Two days after this engagement Nat Addison attended a two-week navigation course and his friend Reg Bray took his place as Raphael's radar observer. Late the following night the Squadron Commander and Bray shot down a Junkers 88 off the east coast, the only occasion that Wing Commander Raphael achieved a kill without Addison. There was much friendly banter between the two friends and Addison vowed never to leave the Squadron again if operations were likely.

The day of Addison's return from his course coincided with the arrival of the Squadron's first Mosquito II. Deliveries were slow but Raphael exercised the traditional Squadron Commander's privilege and allocated the aircraft to himself and his dedicated observer. The following day they flew their first operational patrol in a Mosquito under the control of GCI Foulness. By mid-September all the Squadron's Havocs had been replaced by Mosquitos fitted with the AI Mk 5 and there followed a few weeks of training and searchlight co-operation sorties during which attempts were made to resolve the 'teething' troubles being experienced with the new AI radar.

At 2000 hours on the night of 17 January, 1943, Raphael and Addison took off in their Mosquito (VY-V) for a routine patrol under the control of GCI Foulness. As a reprisal for the bombing of Berlin, the *Luftwaffe* had chosen this

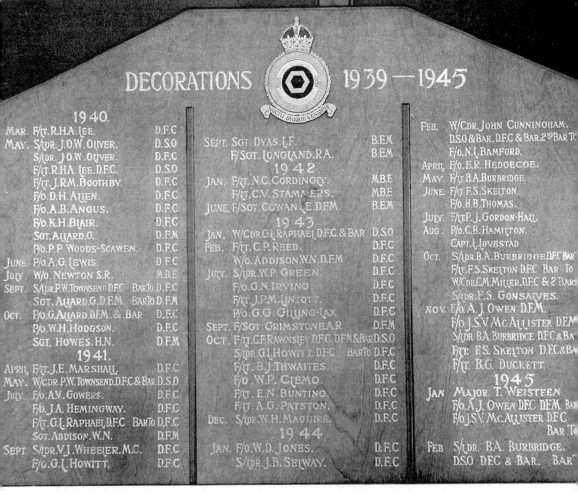

DECORATIONS 1939—1945

1940.
MAR.	F/LT. R.H.A. LEE.	D.F.C
MAY.	S/LDR. J.O.W. OLIVER.	D.S.O
	S/LDR. J.O.W. OLIVER.	D.F.C
	F/LT. R.H.A. LEE. D.F.C	D.S.O
	F/LT. J.R.M. BOOTHBY.	D.F.C
	F/O. D.H. ALLEN.	D.F.C
	F/O. A.B. ANGUS.	D.F.C
	F/O. K.H. BLAIR.	D.F.C
	SGT. ALLARD.G.	D.F.M
	P/O. P.P. WOODS-SCAWEN.	D.F.C
JUNE.	P/O. A.G. LEWIS.	D.F.C
JULY.	W/O. NEWTON S.R.	M.B.E
SEPT.	S/LDR. P.W. TOWNSEND DFC BAR To	D.F.C
	SGT. ALLARD.G. D.F.M BAR To	D.F.M
OCT.	P/O. G. ALLARD. D.F.M. & BAR	D.F.C
	P/O. W.H. HODGSON.	D.F.C
	SGT. HOWES. H.N.	D.F.M

1941.
APRIL.	F/LT. J.E. MARSHALL.	D.F.C
MAY.	W/CDR. P.W. TOWNSEND. D.F.C & BAR.	D.S.O
JULY.	F/O. A.V. GOWERS.	D.F.C
	F/O. J.A. HEMINGWAY.	D.F.C
	F/LT. G.L. RAPHAEL. D.F.C BAR To	D.F.C
	SGT. ADDISON. W.N.	D.F.M
SEPT.	S/LDR. V.J. WHEELER. M.C.	D.F.C
	F/O. G.L. HOWITT.	D.F.C

SEPT.	SGT. DYAS. L.F.	B.E.M
	F/SGT. LONGLAND. R.A.	B.E.M

1942
JAN.	F/LT. N.C. CORDINGLY.	M.B.E
	F/LT. C.V. STAMMERS.	M.B.E
JUNE.	F/SGT. COWAN.C.E. D.F.M.	B.E.M

1943
JAN.	W/CDR. G.L. RAPHAEL. D.F.C. & BAR	D.S.O
FEB.	F/LT. C.P. REED.	D.F.C
	W/O. ADDISON. W.N. D.F.M	D.F.C
JULY.	S/LDR. W.P. GREEN.	D.F.C
	F/O. G.N. IRVING	D.F.C
	F/LT. J.P.M. LINTOTT.	D.F.C
	P/O. G.G. GILLING-LAX	D.F.C
SEPT.	F/SGT. GRIMSTONE.A.R	D.F.M
OCT.	F/LT. C.F. RAWNSLEY. D.F.C. DFM & BAR	D.S.O
	S/LDR. G.L. HOWITT. D.F.C BAR To	D.F.C
	F/LT. B.J. THWAITES.	D.F.C
	F/O. W.P. CLEMO.	D.F.C
	F/LT. E.N. BUNTING.	D.F.C
	F/LT. A.G. PATSTON.	D.F.C
DEC.	S/LDR. W.H. MAGUIRE.	D.F.C

1944
JAN.	F/O. W.D. JONES.	D.F.C
	S/LDR. J.B. SELWAY.	D.F.C

FEB.	W/CDR. JOHN CUNNINGHAM.	
	D.S.O & BAR. D.F.C & BAR. 2ND BAR To	
	F/O. N.L. BAMFORD.	
APRIL.	F/O. E.R. HEDGECOE.	
MAY.	F/LT. B.A. BURBRIDGE.	
JUNE.	F/LT. F.S. SKELTON.	
	F/O. H.B. THOMAS.	
JULY.	F/LT. P.J. GORDON-HALL.	
AUG.	P/O. C.B. HAMILTON.	
	CAPT. L. LOVESTAD	
OCT.	S/LDR. B.A. BURBRIDGE DFC BAR	
	F/LT. F.S. SKELTON DFC BAR To	
	W/CDR. C.M. MILLER. DFC & 2 BAR	
	S/LDR. F.S. GONSALVES.	
NOV.	F/O. A.J. OWEN D.F.M	
	F/O. J.S.V. McALLISTER DFM	
	S/LDR. B.A. BURBRIDGE. D.F.C & BA	
	F/LT. F.S. SKELTON D.F.C & BA	
	F/LT. B.G. DUCKETT.	

1945
JAN	MAJOR. T. WEISTEEN	
	F/O. A.J. OWEN DFC DFM BAI	
	F/O. J.S.V. McALLISTER DFC	
		BAR To
FEB	S/LDR. B.A. BURBRIDGE.	
	D.S.O DFC & BAR. BAR	

The 85 Squadron decorations board showing Raphael and Addison's awards. Other famous names appear. (Andrew Brookes)

night to mount their biggest attack on London since the great blitz of May 1941, the night of Raphael and Addison's first success. The controller, Squadron Leader Anson, soon directed the Mosquito crew to a 'bogey' flying at 6,000 feet. Raphael descended and Addison soon gained radar contact and controlled his pilot to a position behind the enemy aircraft which was visually identified at 200 yards as a Junkers 88. At 100 yards Raphael opened fire with his four 20 mm cannons as the Junkers weaved and jinked, but the first burst caused a big explosion near the port engine and, as pieces of the airframe fell away, the enemy bomber dived away steeply with the Mosquito firing further bursts into the fuselage. Raphael pulled out of his dive at 300 feet as the Junkers entered a bank of sea-fog. Ground observers at the Bradwell Beacon saw the burning aircraft crash into the sea and were able to confirm Raphael and Addison's sixth and final success as a crew. This engagement provided a graphic example of the effectiveness and advantages of the cannon over the Browning machine guns.

The following night Raphael and Addison took off on their 115th and last operational patrol together when they intercepted a raid on Dover, but were unable to make an interception. Together they were the highest scoring Havoc night fighter crew of the war. Within a few days of their last sortie, Wing Commander Raphael handed over command of 85 Squadron to the legendary Wing Commander John Cunningham DSO, DFC before departing to be Station Commander at Castle Camps. A few weeks later Nat Addison joined his staff just in time to celebrate the award of the Distinguished Service Order to his former pilot and his own award of the Distinguished Flying Cross for '*his unflagging devotion to duty in participating in the destruction of 3 enemy aircraft at night since the award of the Distinguished Flying Medal.*'

Over the next twelve months Nat Addison served as an instructor at night fighter OTUs before returning to operations with 488 (NZ) Squadron equipped with the Mosquito NF XIII. Based at Colerne in Wiltshire, he teamed up with the New Zealander, Flying Officer Doug Robinson, who had already achieved three confirmed kills. Within three weeks this highly experienced crew had added to their scores.

A Mosquito NF XII - HK 197 - of 488 (NZ) Squadron over Bradwell Bay in October 1943. Addison gained his last 'kill' with 488 Squadron. (Andy Thomas)

On the evening of 9 August, 1944, Addison took off with Robinson in Mosquito MM 439 to patrol south of the French city of Caen which had recently been subjected to intense bombing by the Allies. Radox Control gave the Mosquito crew vectors to a bogey to the east of the city. Addison gained contact on his AI Mk VI radar set and brought his pilot into visual range at 300 yards. The target was evading and deploying 'window' in an attempt to disrupt the night fighter's radar. The pilot identified a Junkers 188 which Addison was able to confirm with his night glasses. After three or four bursts with the 20 mm cannon, the port engine caught fire and the enemy bomber banked steeply and dived vertically into the ground, exploding with the bombs still on board.

After converting to the Mosquito NF XXX, 488 Squadron deployed to the continent as part of the 2nd Tactical Air Force and operated from Amiens, later moving to Gilze Rijen in Holland. Addison flew another twenty-six patrols but opportunities for further interceptions became rare as the Allied armies pushed east and the petrol-starved *Luftwaffe* concentrated on fighter operations in defence of their besieged country. Shortly after the end of the war Nat Addison was discharged from the RAF.

Warrant Officer Nat Addison DFC, DFM is remembered as one half of an outstanding and very successful night fighting partnership with Wing Commander Gordon Raphael DSO, DFC and Bar. Tragically, his pilot was lost in a mid-air collision just before the end of the war. To his wartime friends, Addison is remembered as a very popular and lively colleague who was ever ready to befriend and help the new, inexperienced navigators and 'show them the ropes.' In the years of peace that followed, he spent many years giving devoted service to the Air Training Corps 'showing the ropes' to the next generation.

CHAPTER FIFTEEN

Late Arrivals Club
Dennis Bebbington

Just after 2300 hours on the night of 7 September, 1942, Sergeant Carter and his second pilot, Segeant Dennis Bebbington, settled their Wellington 1c, T for Tommy of 70 Squadron, on to an easterly heading as they ran up to Tobruk with bomb doors open at 12,000 feet. Just short of the target, the aircraft was hit repeatedly by heavy ack-ack. So began an epic survival story which would highlight the determination, initiative and, above all, the courage of the quiet, self-effacing farmer's son from the tiny village of Wrentall situated deep in the Shropshire countryside.

As war approached Dennis Bebbington and his friend Tony Morris had joined the local Shropshire Yeomanry and as Hitler marched into Poland they were called up. Some eighteen months later, and with no sign of action, Bebbington volunteered for aircrew duties and was selected for pilot training. On 24 January, 1942, he was presented with his wings having successfully completed his flying training at 12 Service Flying Training School. He promptly rushed backed to Shropshire to marry his childhood sweetheart in the tiny Methodist Chapel where they had played the organ and sung in the choir. A

Dennis Bebbington's medals are Military Medal, 1939-45 Star, Africa Star with North Africa 1942-43 Clasp, Defence Medal, War medal.

Dennis Bebbington having just received his pilot's wings. (D B Bebbington)

Dennis Bebbington (front row, second from right) during recruit training. (D B Bebbington)

few days later he reported to **21 Operational Training** Unit at Moreton-in-Marsh to start a conversion **course on the Wellington.**

By mid-July he had completed **his course and** was heading for the Middle East where he joined 70 Squadron, **one of the** longest established and most experienced of the desert bomber **squadrons of 205 Group.** The Squadron was based at Abu Sueir, having conducted a **rapid retreat** from Benghazi ahead of the German breakthrough in the Libyan Desert. With a shortage of crews on the Squadron, Bebbington was soon in action flying as second pilot on a raid to Calato Lindos. This first operational sortie left him in no doubt that his training days among the peaceful Cotswold villages was a distant memory. Returning from the target, the navigator lost his way and, with the petrol tanks empty, the pilot had to make an emergency landing on the beach after a nine-hour flight. The Squadron Record Book aptly described the sortie as 'not altogether a successful operation'.

Dennis Bebbington's first full month in the Middle East, August 1942, was to prove one of the most significant months in the Desert war. Rommel's Panzer Army reached the Egyptian border and Montgomery arrived to assume command of the Eighth Army. The British retreat stopped at El Alamein and the Army dug in, having been told by its new Commander that there was to be no further withdrawal. Rommel's supply lines were stretched, yet he continued to mass his forces for one final thrust into Egypt and on to the Suez Canal. This exposed his rear positions and the Wellingtons of 205 Group turned their attention to his motor transport (MT) parks, forward landing grounds and supply dumps.

During a ten-day period in August Dennis Bebbington flew seven sorties against these ground targets in the battle area. Most were supported by flare-dropping Albacores of 826 Fleet Air Arm Squadron which carried out sterling work and attracted the greatest admiration from their Air Force colleagues. As Rommel prepared to launch his major attack on 30 August against the Alam el Halfa Ridge his positions were pounded once again by the Wellingtons with 'excellent support from the Albacores'. Bebbington and his crew, flying Wellington AD 641, carried 250 lb bombs and canisters of the 40 lb anti-personnel bombs to drop among the concentrations of enemy MT.

Attacks with the Albacores in support continued over the next four nights; those on 2 September proved decisive and were assessed as the most successful of all the battle-area night attacks. The Squadron despatched eleven aircraft, with Bebbington flying as second pilot in Wellington BB 477, and all crews returned to report many fires started. In all, twenty-four fires were claimed by the Squadron. The Squadron Record Book commented on the excellent co-operation given by the Albacores 'who did a great job of illuminating'. The next day Rommel's advance was halted and this marked the end of his efforts to reach the Suez Canal. Rommel was later to state: 'The continuous and very heavy attacks of the Royal Air Force . . . absolutely pinned my troops to the ground and made impossible any safe deployment or any advance according to schedule.' This intensive period of operations resulted in the loss of four Wellingtons of 70 Squadron.

With the enemy offensive halted, the Wellingtons resumed their attacks

A Wellington Ic of 70 Squadron in the Western Desert 1941. (Andy Thomas)

against the installations and shipping in Tobruk harbour. Acting as second pilot to his regular captain, Sergeant R Carter, Bebbington took off in Wellington Z 8976 for a night bombing attack against Tobruk. Three hours later the aircraft was crippled by anti-aircraft fire and the crew jettisoned the bombs over the target as both engines cut out. The starboard engine picked up and the aircraft was turned on to a south-easterly heading. Despite all available loose equipment and guns being jettisioned, the aircraft lost height rapidly. An SOS was transmitted and the two pilots prepared to make a forced landing which was skilfully achieved with the aid of the landing light and resulting in no injuries to the crew. Prior to landing, tracer had been seen a few miles to the north so it was decided not to risk attention by burning the aircraft and heavy axes were used to destroy all the aircraft systems and instruments.

The crew gathered up the emergency rations, compass, Very pistols, first-aid kit and local maps. All available water bottles were filled and, in accordance with their desert survival training, the crew drank the remainder as they prepared to trek off into the desert. With the likelihood of enemy nearby, they set off into the night walking for five hours before they came to some scrub and decided to stop for the day. They used this first day to rest and Pilot Officer B. E. Johnston, the Canadian wireless operator and only officer in the crew, took charge and together they devised a survival plan which included a strict 'water policy'.

The first six days were spent getting to the old Libya/Egypt frontier wire at Bir Sheferzen. En route they met small groups of Arabs and were able to replenish their water bottles and obtain some food. By the twelfth day they were south of Sidi Barrani, but the rough terrain had damaged the rear gunner's feet which had become badly infected and he was in considerable pain and having difficulty walking. The party headed north to intercept the main road in case the gunner, Flight Sergeant G. Croisiau, a Belgian who had posed as a French Canadian in order to join the RAF, could not continue.

The party arrived at a well and Johnston moved forward to a ridge where he spent the day observing traffic on the nearby road. He noticed two lorries parked well away from the remainder of a convoy. With Croisiau injured and in no state to complete the long march to the Allied lines, and with food getting low, the crew decided to wait for nightfall and then ambush the two lorries. While the navigator and front gunner remained at the well with the kit, the other four crew members crept forward to the lorries, which were parked fifty yards apart.

The group approached the first lorry with Croisiau in the lead; he had served with the guerrillas during the Spanish Civil War. With Johnston, he moved to the front of the lorry while Bebbington and Carter went to the rear. Johnston hit the driver over the head with the butt of his revolver, but he recovered quickly and was able to wrestle the revolver from him. In the meantime the two pilots had discovered a number of Italian troops asleep in the back of the truck and a gunfight started. This alerted the occupants of the second truck who rushed over firing into the dark and probably hitting Croisiau who was not seen again.

It was clear that, against such odds, the truck could not be captured so Johnston ordered a withdrawal, firing as he and Carter rushed back to the well. They rejoined the two crew left on guard and the four headed into the desert. In the confusion Bebbington had got into the driving seat of the truck, but he was soon surrounded by Italians. Fortunately, he had lost his hat in the skirmish and he was not identified and was later able to mingle with the soldiers searching for his comrades. As soon as possible he slipped away from the Italians and returned to the well where he drank as much water as he could, filled his bottle and headed south into the desert. Twenty-four hours later he

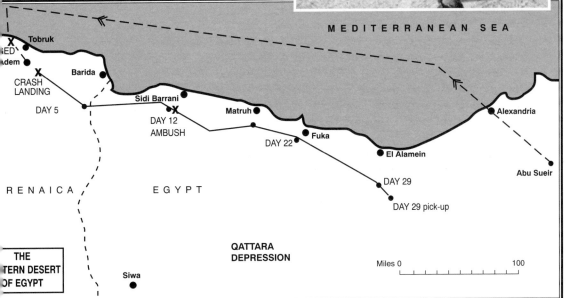

The crew relaxing at Seagull Camp, Alexandria on the day after their return. Bebbington is on the left with Pilot Officer B Johnston in the centre and Ivor Davies on the right. (Mrs P M Bridgewood)

Map showing the route followed by the Bebbington crew.

MEDITERRANEAN SEA

Tobruk
ED
dem
Barida
CRASH LANDING
DAY 5
Sidi Barrani
DAY 12 AMBUSH
Matruh
Fuka
DAY 22
El Alamein
Alexandria
Abu Sueir
DAY 29
DAY 29 pick-up

RENAICA
EGYPT

QATTARA DEPRESSION

THE
TERN DESERT
OF EGYPT

Siwa

Miles 0   100

met up with the four remaining members of his crew.

Over the next few days they met a number of friendly Arabs who gave them food and water and warned them of the proximity of the enemy. One Arab guided them through a difficult area and suggested they continue their travels at night. By the twenty-second day they were south of the Fuka Landing Grounds where they observed much searchlight and ack-ack activity. They decided to head south-east to keep well away from the coastal area which was dominated by the main positions of Rommel's Army. On the twenty-sixth day they were close to the salt marshes of the Qattara Depression when torrential rain allowed them to replenish their water bottles. A friendly Arab led them to Lake Magre where they rested overnight under a palm tree.

About half an hour after dawn on the twenty-ninth day two jeeps of an advanced patrol of a South African Armoured Car Unit were seen and soon the crew were being greeted by a South African Major who drove them to his advanced HQ. Within a short time they were back in friendly territory and were taken via the Unit's Rear Headquarters to Seagull Camp in Alexandria thirty days after they had taken off to bomb Tobruk.

With courage and determination, and by following implicitly the advice given during their training which emphasised the need to create a plan, stick together and ration food and water, this gallant Wellington crew had beaten the desert and crossed 350 miles of enemy territory. As the official report stated, 'It is never too late to come back.' This is perhaps a more appropriate accolade than the 70 Squadron Intelligence Officer's one-line comment in the Squadron Diary, 'After being missing for a month, Sergeant Carter's crew turned up at base having walked back.' The crew were made worthy members of the 'Late Arrivals Club', an unofficial and elite club for all those in the Desert Air Force who had returned from behind enemy lines.

A few weeks later the Squadron learnt that Flight Sergeant Croisiau was wounded but safe in a German prisoner of war camp. There was further delight when it was announced that Pilot Officer Johnston had been awarded a Distinguished Flying Cross and Dennis Bebbington and the observer, Sergeant Ivor Davies, had each been awarded the Military Medal. Their detailed joint recommendation concluded: '*Pilot Officer Johnston acted as leader throughout, being excellently supported by Sergeants Bebbington and Davies. This officer and the airmen displayed resolute courage and fortitude throughout the hazardous period.*'

The original submission had recommended Johnston for the award of the Military Cross and the two NCOs for a Military Medal. Just prior to his epic evasion Johnston had been considered for the Distinguished Flying Cross. The two citations were combined and so he was denied a specific award for his gallantry and superb leadership behind enemy territory. Many would agree that he should have received both. Changes were also made with regard to the awards for Bebbington and Davies. The War Office downgraded the awards to a Mention in Despatches but the Secretary of State for Air expressed his wish that they should be awarded the Military Medal as recommended by the Commander in Chief Middle East. After reviewing a more detailed report, the Military Secretary agreed that their 'exemplary conduct' justified the higher award and the recommendation was submitted to His Majesty The King for his approval, which was given, and the awards of the Military Medal were announced in January, 1943.

After six weeks' rest and leave Dennis Bebbington returned to operations just as the Eighth Army launched its great attack at El Alamein. As the battle raged, the Wellingtons of 70 Squadron flew at intensive rates attacking Rommel's guns, armour, advanced landing grounds and supply routes. As the Eighth Army surged forward the Wellington squadrons moved to airfields and landing grounds in the desert arriving at El Daba in mid-November and El Adem by the end of the month. On 25 November, Dennis Bebbington flew on operations for the first time as a captain with his own crew. By a strange coincidence, he took off from the airfield at El Adem just ten miles from where he had crashed landed a few weeks earlier. Flying Z 8765 he attacked the Germans' Advanced Landing Ground at Marble Arch.

During December there was some relief from the routine of bombing the retreating Axis armies when the Wellingtons attacked the German airfields in Crete. Dennis Bebbington and his crew bombed Tymbaki and then Heraklion before returning to hound the German concentrations as they continued their headlong retreat towards Tunisia. To keep within range, the Squadron was constantly on the move, arriving at Benina early in the New Year before continuing westwards to Magrun and then on to Gardabia. By February the Squadron was within range of Sicily and Bebbington and his crew attacked the port facilities at Palermo on three occasions in February. On the 20th they took charge of their own Wellington Mk III (DF 698) and flew it for the first time on a bombing raid against shipping in the Sicilian port.

By the middle of March, Rommel was preparing his defences along the Mareth Line in a final attempt to hold back the Eighth Army. Five Wellington squadrons were ordered to attack enemy concentrations and armour in the Mareth – Gabes area on 21 March. Bebbington and his fellow pilots claimed several good hits, but reported on the intensity of the flak, a number of aircraft being holed.

The following night similar raids were ordered and Dennis Bebbington settled into the cockpit of his Q for Queenie (DF 698) on what was to be the first of a double sortie. It was his twenty-ninth and penultimate sortie. He was no doubt anticipating the end of his tour and the opportunity to celebrate his commission which had been announced that morning. Acting as his second pilot was the new Flight Commander, Squadron Leader J A Tinne, who was flying the traditional introductory first sortie as a second pilot before taking his own crew on operations. The aircraft took off just after 2100 hours. Nothing further was heard. After six months, with no news of any member of the crew, Dennis Bebbington and his crew were officially posted as killed in action. They have no known grave and are commemorated on Column 269 of the Alamein Memorial in Egypt.

THE INSTALLATION OF THE ELECTRICITY FOR THIS CHURCH HAS BEEN GIVEN BY M^R & M^{RS} WILLIAM BEBBINGTON IN LOVING MEMORY OF THEIR SON PILOT OFFICER DENNIS BEBBINGTON, M.M. OF THE 70TH SQUADRON RAF. MIDDLE EAST, PRESUMED KILLED IN TUNISIA ON THE NIGHT 22ND 23RD MARCH 1943, BEING ONE TIME SCHOLAR TEACHER & ORGANIST OF THIS SUNDAY SCHOO

The memorial in the Methodist Chapel at Pulverbat Shropshire. (Author)

The people of the close-knit community round the Shropshire village of Pulverbatch still talk of, and remember, the kind, quiet but determined farmer's son who played the organ every Sunday in his local church. There is a small row of six council houses named in his memory and his framed picture still rests on the sideboard in the house of his old school friend fifty-seven years after they set off together to 'do their bit.' Some bit.

The memorial in Pulverbatch Church, Shropshire. (Author)

THIS TABLET COMMEMORATES THE INSTALLATION OF ELECTRIC LIGHTING IN THIS CHURCH BY THE PARISHIONERS, AS A MEMORIAL TO THE MEN OF THIS PARISH WHO MADE THE SUPREME SACRIFICE IN THE WORLD WAR 1939 – 1945.

SERGEANT E. G. BAILEY, K. S. L. I.
F/O D. BEBBINGTON, M. M., R. A. F.
DRIVER W. R. DOOGAN, R. C. S.
CAPTAIN J. HOLCROFT, R. T. C.
MAJOR J. Y. WEAVER, R. I. R.

GREATER LOVE HATH NO MAN THAN THIS, THAT A MAN LAY DOWN HIS LIFE FOR HIS FRIENDS.

CHAPTER SIXTEEN

Biscay Fighter Pilot – Jimmy Duncan

The four Beaufighter VI fighters of 248 Squadron closed in on the two-man dinghy and set up an orbit while they waited for the rescue sea-plane to arrive on the scene. With protection of the dinghy established, three of the twin-engined fighters departed the scene to leave Sergeant James Duncan to maintain the vigil. Ninety minutes later, the Beaufighter had reached its limit of endurance when Duncan and his navigator saw three Spitfires approaching and assumed that they were the relief. To their great surprise and discomfort, they looked in astonishment as the Spitfires turned towards them and opened fire. The Beaufighter escaped with minor damage and Duncan was able to fly back to the airfield at Takali in Malta. So ended James Duncan's third operational sortie since joining the Squadron a few weeks earlier.

At the outbreak of the war the lanky twenty-year-old Glaswegian, known as 'Jimmy', was keen to join up. He enlisted into the Army and served for eighteen months as a physical training instructor in the 9th Battalion Manchester Regiment. In March, 1941, Lance Corporal Duncan volunteered for aircrew

Jimmy Duncan's medals, Distinguished Flying Medal, 1939-45 Star, Atlantic Star with France & Germany Clasp, Africa Star, Defence Medal, War Medal.

Jimmy Duncan just after he transferred to the Fleet Air Arm in 1945. He does not yet have the ribbons on his uniform for the Defence and War Medals. (Author's collection)

training as a pilot with the Royal Air Force. After completing his initial training, he sailed for Canada to begin pilot training, first at Moose Jaw and then on to Medicine Hat where he gained his wings. Selected to fly twin-engined aircraft, he returned to the United Kingdom and completed the General Reconnaissance course at Squires Gate before converting to the Beaufighter at 2 (Coastal) Operational Training Unit (OTU) based at Catfoss in Yorkshire.

On 30 June,1942, Duncan travelled to Sumburgh to join 248 Squadron equipped with the Beaufighter VI. His stay in the Shetlands was short as the Squadron was earmarked to reinforce the RAF's depleted attack force in the Mediterranean.

By mid-1942, the island of Malta had suffered from an almost continuous assault from the Axis air forces. The immense fortitude and courage of the people of Malta had been recognised by the unique award of the George Cross to the island. By the end of July the situation had become desperate and there was an urgent need for supplies and a major effort was mounted to force a convoy through. Operation Pedestal was devised. This was to be the largest and most important convoy to be gathered for the resupply of the island and it required a considerable reinforcement of the air forces in Malta. 248 Squadron was earmarked for this operation and deployed south to Portreath to make preparations to move on to Malta.

Early in the morning of 2 August, the newly promoted Flight Sergeant Duncan climbed into his Beaufighter 'D' (EL 264) to prepare to take off for Gibraltar. The first formation of four aircraft were led by the Commanding Officer, Wing Commander J. Pike DSO, DFC, and they arrived at the crowded airstrip five hours later. The following day they took off for the airfield at Takali on Malta. Over the next few days the remainder of the Squadron arrived.

The Pedestal convoy included thirteen fast freighters, the oil tanker *Ohio* and a very powerful escort which included no less than four aircraft carriers, two battleships, seven cruisers and twenty-six destroyers. This mighty convoy sailed into the Mediterranean on the night of 10/11 August. Inevitably, over the next five days the convoy was constantly under severe attack and its passage to Malta is one of the epics of maritime history. The air battles in support of the convoy were just as intense.

As the convoy came in range of the Malta-based aircraft, the Beaufighters prepared to escort a Beaufort strike against units of the Italian Navy which posed a threat to the convoy. During the afternoon of 12 August the four remaining aircraft were made ready for an attack against the airstrip on the island of Pantellairia. This was Duncan's first operational sortie and he flew as the observer in Sergeant Sebring's aircraft. The formation leader ditched just after take-off and a Frenchman, Lieutenant Wiel, assumed the lead. The three Beaufighters arrived over the airfield just before dark and strafed a number of

Jimmy Duncan flew Beaufighter sorties from Malta. (Author's collection)

Italian S.79 bombers on the ground, destroying one and damaging others, in addition to setting a fuel store on fire.

At first light the following morning the Beaufighters set up patrols over the depleted convoy. The first pair were engaged by Me109s and one of the 248 Squadron crews was forced to bale out. Jimmy Duncan took off at 7.30 am with four other aircraft to continue the patrolling in support of the convoy. Inevitably, more Me 109s appeared and there were a number of running battles but the Beaufighters escaped and Duncan returned safely after a four-hour sortie. In the meantime the Malta Air Headquarters had set up a search for the missing airmen.

The search continued into the following day when aircraft spotted two men in a dinghy and hopes were raised for the safety of the 248 Squadron crew. The Squadron launched four Beaufighters to provide escort for a rescue aircraft with Duncan flying aircraft 'J'. They located the dinghy and circled low as the two survivors waved. With the position fixed, three of the Beaufighters left Duncan to continue the patrol. With his fuel running low, he was expecting a relief when the three Spitfires arrived and immediately opened fire, damaging the Beaufighter as he made his escape. His radio calls were intercepted and another Beaufighter was sent to the scene.

The rescue still had a dramatic twist. The French pilot, Lieutenant Maurice, and his English navigator, Flight Sergeant C. C. Corder, arrived on the scene. As darkness started to fall they had almost given up hope of the rescue aircraft arriving when they spotted a Dornier Do24 flying-boat approaching. Thinking the enemy aircraft was about to rescue their colleagues, they escorted the flying-boat as it alighted and taxied up to the dinghy and picked up the survivors. The Dornier then took off and turned for Sicily. It later transpired that the survivors were the crew of an Italian Ju 87 who had mis-identified the Beaufighter for a Junkers 88. The navigator of the lost 248 Squadron Beaufighter was eventually picked up by the Italians after spending three days in the sea, but no trace was found of his pilot.

This strange episode was Jimmy Duncan's last sortie during the brief Malta detachment. Seven days later the Squadron returned to the United Kingdom and moved to Talbenny to mount long-range fighter operations over the Western Approaches.

The Squadron soon settled in to its new Pembrokeshire airfield and operations began at the end of September. Duncan flew his first interceptor patrol on 30 September, flying Beaufighter 'D' (EL 264). Nine days later he took off in EL 304 as part of a three-aircraft formation led by Flying Officer Stringer. Halfway through their patrol the three aircraft spotted three Junkers 88s and closed in to attack. Hits were registered on one of the enemy aircraft and it fled into cloud. A second was attacked by all three aircraft and it burst into flames before it struck the water and sank. The three pilots were each credited with a 'shared destroyed'. It was the Squadron's first success since returning from Malta. The German aircraft was a Bordeaux-based Junkers 88C of *13/KG 40* flown by *Feldwebel* Wagner.

After a series of routine patrols flown throughtout October, the Squadron moved to Pembrey and continued to fly long-range patrols in the Western Approaches. Duncan was the first to see action after the move when he intercepted four Junkers 88s on 12 November. He closed and fired three bursts, but no hits were observed and there was no return fire. Ten days later he spotted another Ju 88 but was unable to engage.

During the latter part of 1942 German air activity in the Bay of Biscay had increased and the long-range Junkers 88 fighters were proving very troublesome to Coastal Command's aircraft hunting the increasing number of U-boats operating from the Biscay ports. The German fighters often operated in groups of four to eight, thus posing a formidable threat to the anti-submarine aircraft hunting alone. Allied bombers attacking naval targets and port facilities in

Western France were also troubled by the enemy fighter force based in the area. To counter these attacks and provide support at longer range, the Beaufighters of 248 Squadron moved to Predannack in Cornwall during January 1943. The redeployment soon paid dividends.

On 29 January, 248 Squadron met with success when four aircraft intercepted two Junkers 88s over the Bay of Biscay. The formation split into two pairs and attacked an aircraft each; within minutes both enemy aircraft had been shot down. The following day it was the turn of Duncan and his navigator, Flight Sergeant T. R. Weaver, to see more action. The weather was poor when three Beaufighters took off for a line patrol. During the patrol four Junkers 88s were encountered and the three fighters closed in to engage them. Duncan, who was leading, attacked one of the enemy aircraft and, after a long burst of cannon, the Junkers dived into the sea. As he pulled away Duncan saw another aircraft chasing a second which was on fire. Suddenly the chasing aircraft exploded and both aircraft dived into the sea. At this point, Duncan observed an enemy aircraft turning in for an attack and he began to climb just as the Ju88 opened fire. No damage was sustained and, after entering cloud, the enemy aircraft was not see again so Duncan returned to base. The other two Beaufighters failed to return and their crews were posted as missing.

Post-war analysis of this sortie shows that the enemy aircraft were four Junkers 88C night fighters of *14/KG 40* operating from Bordeaux airfield. Two of the aircraft, flown by *Hauptmann* Reicke and *Oberfeldwebe*l Hueur, failed to return. One of the surviving Junkers crews reported that a Beaufighter had collided with *Hauptmann* Reicke's aircraft and both were lost. This incident was probably that observed by Duncan. In the confusion of a hectic fight involving seven aircraft, a collision may have appeared as an explosion of two aircraft flying close astern. The other surviving Junkers pilot, *Unteroffizier* Hencke, claimed that he had jointly shot down one of the Beaufighters with Hueur. This seems unlikely since the first episode in the engagement was Duncan leading the other two Beaufighters into the attack in which he shot down one of the Junkers. If Reicke was involved in the 'collision', then the first aircraft to be lost must have been that of Hueur.

The next major action involving the Squadron occurred on 9 February, when Jimmy Duncan took off as part of a foursome led by the Flight Commander, Squadron Leader D Cartridge DFC. En route to the patrol area he suffered a complete electrical failure and was forced to return to Predannack. The other three aircraft pressed on into the Bay of Biscay and soon engaged four Ju88s. A fierce fight developed at sea level with the enemy aircraft forming a defensive circle before individual combats broke out. After two enemy aircraft had been shot down, another set up a head-on attack against the third Beaufighter. They opened fire on each other and the port engine of the Junkers fell away. The aircraft was seen to glide to the sea where it settled for three or four minutes before sinking. The heavy armament and superior tactics of the Royal Air Force pilots had resulted in three Ju88s being claimed as shot down. The Beaufighter pilot involved in the head-on attack was from Texas and flying on his first operational sortie. His combat report sums up his experience: 'I was a-commin', he was a-commin' – he was a-shootin', I was a-shootin' – and he got it!'

For the next three months, Jimmy Duncan flew regular patrols and escorts, often in excess of five hours, but he was not to see action again until mid-May. On 16 May, he took off on a cloudless morning for a routine line patrol looking for more Ju88s. There had been considerable U-boat activity during May and a number of attacks had been delivered against them by patrolling aircraft with two sightings earlier in the day. At 0930 Duncan was 120 miles south-west of Brest when he saw a U-boat on the surface and he immediately turned to attack. The submarine started a dive as Duncan raked the conning tower with a long burst of cannon fire. It continued its dive and nothing more was seen.

Duncan had attacked *U 591* a Type VIIC (*Kapitänleutnant* Hans-Jurgen Zetzsche). The U-boat's war diary briefly mentioned the attack 'by a small landplane', but indicated that no damage had been sustained. The submarine had sailed only four days earlier but was returning to St Nazaire under the command of the Executive Officer (*Leutnant zur See* Joachim Sauerbier) as the Commanding Officer and an Able Seaman had been wounded by gunfire in an attack the previous day by a Whitley from 10 OTU. A new captain (*Oberleutnant zur See* Reimar Ziesmer) was appointed and the submarine sailed again during June for a patrol in the South Atlantic where it was sunk on 30 July off Recife by a US Navy Ventura. Zetzsche survived the war.

Jimmy Duncan was a pilot instructor on Beaufighters at 79 OTU based in Cyprus. (Author's collection)

Duncan and his long-standing navigator, the newly commissioned Pilot Officer T. R. Weaver, flew four more patrols before completing their tour on 248 Squadron. After completing forty-eight operational sorties they were posted during June as instructors to 9 (Coastal) OTU, stationed at Crosby-on-Eden near Carlisle. Two months later Duncan was commissioned and, on 10 September, it was announced that he had been awarded the Distinguished Flying Medal. The citation recorded his participation in numerous air combats over the Bay of Biscay when he had displayed: *'great determination and a high devotion to duty'*. Reference was made to his attack on the *U-boat* and the citation concluded *'He has proved himself to be a keen and gallant operational pilot and has set a magnificent example as such to all ranks'*.

After a short period at Crosby Duncan transferred to 2 (Coastal) OTU at Catfoss in Yorkshire where he remained for six months. Another tour as a flying instructor followed when he was posted to the newly-formed 79 OTU established for general reconnaissance and strike training at Nicosia, Cyprus where he remained for most of 1944.

At the end of the war in Europe he transferred to the Fleet Air Arm at the request of the Royal Navy. He was commisioned as a Sub-Lieutenant in the Royal Navy Volunteer Reserve and attended a flying instructors, course at the Central Flying School graduating with a 'B' Category instructor rating. With almost four years of continuous service flying twin-engined strike aircraft, he was a natural choice to join 762 Squadron based at Ford. This squadron had been established as a heavy-twin conversion unit to train crews for service on the Sea Mosquito. The unit was equipped with Oxfords, Beaufort T II and Mosquito T 3 aircraft. After two years of instructing, he joined the Fleet Air Arm's Service Trials Unit, 703 Squadron, based at Lee-on-Solent, having recently been promoted to Lieutenant.

Jimmy Duncan spent four years on the RN's Service Trials Unit, the latter two years back at Ford (HMS *Peregrine*) testing and evaluating new weapons and equipments. On 24 January, 1952, he was flying an Attacker jet fighter (WA 509) when the engine failed as he approached the runway for a simulated deck landing. Too low to eject, he crash landed in a field short of the airfield sustaining serious injuries to his back. Fortunately, he made a full recovery. Five months later he completed his service and was transferred to the Emergency List.

Despite leaving the Royal Navy active list, Jimmy Duncan continued flying naval aircraft. He was employed by Airwork Ltd who provided numerous support flying activities for the Royal Navy, operating ex-naval aircraft relegated from the front-line squadrons. Initially Duncan flew Mosquitos and Meteors as a flying instructor operating from St Davids airfield in Pembrokeshire. In November, 1955, he joined the Fleet Requirements Unit (FRU) at Hurn flying the Attacker and Sea Fury. The main roles of the Unit were target towing with Rushden targets, radar direction exercises for the Fleet and ship's gun alignment sorties.

On 11 July, 1958, Duncan took off from Hurn Airport in Sea Fury VW 583. En route to the east coast, the aircraft had a complete engine failure and he made a perfect emergency landing at Biggin Hill. '*For his presence of mind and skill in executing an exemplary forced landing*', he was commended by the Flag Officer Air (Home), Vice Admiral Sir Walter Couchman.

Jimmy Duncan continued to fly with the FRU until he retired in November, 1972, by which time he had added the Seahawk, Hunter and Scimitar to the list of aircraft he had flown. Throughout his thirty years of flying, he had been almost exclusively involved in the coastal and maritime roles, an arena in which he clearly excelled. It was, therefore, no surprise to his friends that he should choose to retire by the sea.

A Sea Fury FB 11 - VR 936 - of the Fleet Requirements Unit at Hurn. Duncan force landed a similar aircraft at Biggin Hill after an engine failure. (T Stone)

CHAPTER SEVENTEEN

Burma Star – Gerry Osborne

At 1535 hours on 14 April, 1941, Sergeant Gerry Osborne released the brakes of his Blenheim IV (V 6029) and accelerated down the runway at Watton before climbing on an easterly heading. He joined up in formation with seven other Blenheims of 21 Squadron and set out at low level for the Dutch coast to attack a shipping convoy off Ijmuiden. Two hours later his was one of six Blenheims to return having survived the intense flak from the convoy's defending escorts and the lethal fire of the marauding Luftwaffe Me 109 fighters. It was his first operational sortie. Four years to the day he flew his one hundred and forty-eighth and final operational flight of the war when he landed his Spitfire VIII on the airstrip at Kwetnge south of Mandalay. With total air superiority over the skies of Burma, the routine fighter patrol had been uneventful. The two operations were very different, but, in the intervening years Gerry Osborne had rarely been away from the thick of the fighting.

Wyndham McKay Osborne, known throughout his Royal Air Force career

Gerry Osborne's medals are Distinguished Flying Medal, 1939-45 Star, Aircrew Europe Star, Africa Star, Burma Star, War Medal.

Blenheim IVs of 21 Squadron in April 1941. (Andy Thomas)

as Gerry, joined the RAF on his nineteenth birthday in June, 1939, to train as a pilot. He was awarded his wings and promoted to Sergeant on 19 November, 1940, and proceeded to Bicester to carry out his conversion course on the Blenheim with 13 Operational Training Unit. On 5 April, 1941, he joined 21 Squadron at Watton.

The Squadron operated the Blenheim IV as part of 2 Group which, at the time, had just been given orders to concentrate on anti-shipping attacks to halt the movement of all coastal shipping operating between the Brest peninsula and North Germany. Much of the shipping was transporting the iron-ore mined in Sweden and others were carrying the bulk of supplies from Hamburg to the occupying forces in Holland. Both of these supply routes were crucially important to the Germans; hence, the convoys were heavily defended by accompanying flak-ships, fighters were on call at nearby coastal airfields, and losses among the low-flying Blenheims were higher than in almost any other role during the war. Gerry Osborne's baptism to operational flying could hardly have been more daunting when he took off on his first war sortie on 14 April. The loss of two crews from the formation of eight aircraft merely reinforced the dangers.

Four days after his first sortie, he was part of an eight-aircraft formation tasked to attack a convoy off Heligoland. The Flight Commander, Squadron Leader 'Attie' Atkinson, was very uneasy about the tactics employed by the Blenheims, which involved flying line-abreast to attack the ships on the beam. He believed that the murderous flak from the escorts was able to be concentrated on such an attack and he decided to approach the targets at very low-level and to attack from astern where only an element of the anti-aircraft fire could be brought to bear. The ploy took the ships' gun crews by surprise and a successful attack was delivered against two merchant ships of 5,000 tons, which were claimed as sunk, but the price was again high as two crews were engaged by the flak ships and failed to return. Gerry Osborne's next attack was in very different circumstances.

A few days after the attack off Heligoland it was decided to send a small detachment of Blenheims to Malta to reinforce the limited attack force operating against the Italian convoys sailing to North Africa. Six crews of 21 Squadron were selected, including Osborne, and they set off from Watton on 26 April for Portreath and then on to Gibraltar under the leadership of Atkinson. With just one night's rest after the eight-hour flight from England, they took off on the equally long and dangerous leg across the Mediterranean for Luqa airfield on Malta.

After three days of acclimatisation, the Blenheims were ready to mount their first anti-shipping attacks. Marylands of 69 Squadron flew reconnaissance patrols to seek out shipping targets and radio back details for the bomber crews. On 1 May, the Squadron began operations and mounted two attacks against separate convoys; Osborne and his crew took part in both. The first proved uneventful, but during the afternoon Atkinson led an attack near the Kerkenah Islands against a convoy sailing from Palermo to Tripoli. The first echelon attacked a 3,000 ton merchant vessel and Osborne released his bombs from low level against an escorting destroyer scoring three hits despite facing intense anti-aircraft fire. The destroyer stopped and initial reports suggested that it had been sunk, but post-war analysis indicates that it was able to limp into harbour.

The following day Osborne gained further success when four aircraft attacked a convoy 140 miles south-west of Malta. Hits were obtained against another destroyer and Osborne's bombs struck a 1,200 ton merchant vessel and both ships were left enveloped in smoke. On 7 May, eight small merchant ships were sighted near the island of Pantellaria by the Marylands of 69 Squadrons and Osborne took off as part of a formation of five Blenheims escorted by three Beaufighters of 252 Squadron. The convoy was intercepted and Osborne attacked a 1,500 ton ship while other pilots aimed their bombs at a 3,000 ton vessel and a smaller ship. Hits were scored and two ships were left listing badly.

In a few days the Blenheims of 21 Squadron had achieved considerable success and it was decided to maintain regular six-week detachments, on a rotational basis, by the 2 Group Blenheim squadrons. Gerry Osborne and his colleagues returned to Watton in mid-May and, within a few days, it was announced that two of the pilots had been recommended for immediate awards. Pilot Officer D. F. Dennis was awarded a Distinguished Flying Cross, finishing the war with a Distinguished Service Order and a Bar to his DFC. The other immediate award went to Gerry Osborne who received the Distinguished Flying Medal, the recommendation stating: '*Whilst on overseas duties engaged on the interception of enemy convoys moving between Sicily and the North African coast, this NCO showed great skill and daring attacking both merchant ships and accompanying naval ships.... On each occasion, and in particular when attacking the destroyer in the face of intense flak, this NCO showed great*

181

determination and it is most strongly recommended that he should receive an imme-diate award.'

After returning to Watton, Gerry Osborne flew two more North Sea anti-shipping sweeps before he was posted with his crew to the Middle East to join 45 Squadron. Ferrying a Blenheim to reinforce the depleted Squadron, they arrived at Aqir near Haifa in Palestine on 7 July. Within three days Osborne was in action against the Vichy French, a day which the Squadron historian has described as 'one of the blackest days of the entire war for the Squadron'.

Twelve aircraft were tasked to bomb the ammunition dumps at Hamama. Osborne was at the controls of V 5926 and he successfully bombed the target from 4,000 feet. Repeated hits were seen together with a number of major secondary explosions. As the Blenheims turned away from the target they were attacked by six Vichy Dewoitine D 520 fighters which pressed home their attacks from below and three Blenheims were shot down in the first engagement. A number of the remaining bombers were damaged, including Osborne's aircraft before Tomahawks of 3 (RAAF) Squadron engaged the fighters, shooting down five of them. Approaching Aqir, Osborne was unable to lower his damaged undercarriage and he made a successful belly-landing sustaining slight injuries which kept him off flying for a few weeks.

Gerry Osborne's short but varied career soon included another variation when he took off from Habbaniya in Iraq on 26 August to bomb the Paytak Pass in Western Iran. For some time there had been concern about the attitude of Iran and three Blenheim squadrons, including 45 Squadron, had deployed to Iraq in early August. The bombing attack by the Blenheim force on the 26th had caused the Iranians to withdraw and the Gurkhas took the Pass without opposition. A few days later Osborne was part of a force of eleven 45 Squadron Blenheims that dropped leaflets ahead of the advancing Gurkhas; two days later, the Iranians capitulated. Before leaving Iraq, the three Blenheim squadrons provided a convincing demonstration of power by staging a mass flypast over the major Iraqi cities. This was Osborne's last flight before the Squadron moved to the Western Desert on 26 September to participate in Operation Crusader.

Osborne flew his first operational sortie in the North African theatre on

A Blenheim IV of 45 Squadron over North Africa 1941. (Andy Thomas)

Gerry Osborne left, wearing his DFM ribbon, and his 45 Squadron navigator Sergeant Robert Turton RNZAF. (via Jeff Jefford)

15 October when he took off from Fuka to bomb dispersed aircraft on the airfield at Gambut. Over the next six weeks he flew a further six sorties before the launching of Operation Crusader, the majority against stores areas and concentrations of motor transports. On the night of 30 October, flare-dropping Albacores of the Fleet Air Arm illuminated the stores area at Gazala and the Blenheims dropped their four 250 lb GP bombs from 3,000 feet. On 1 December, Osborne flew his last sortie in North Africa when he bombed parked vehicles at Sidi Rezegh. Shortly afterwards he received a posting to Kenya, where he was to become an instructor on 70 Operational Training Unit at Nakuru.

At the time of his posting from 45 Squadron. Osborne had flown just twenty operational sorties but he was one of the most experienced Blenheim pilots on the Squadron. Remarkably, he had operated in four different theatres of war, he had faced some of the most intense light flak, from ships and ground forces, he had been engaged by fighters of the *Luftwaffe* and the Vichy French, survived a crash landing and was the holder of an immediate DFM. Experience was gained quickly by twenty-year-olds in 1941.

Osborne never arrived in Kenya. Following the Japanese attack on Pearl Harbor, a number of Middle East Blenheim squadrons were earmarked for deployment to the Far East, including 45 Squadron. Osborne and his crew were recalled from leave in Egypt and rejoined the Squadron at Helwan in early January 1942.

In groups of five, the Blenheims of 45 Squadron took off on 9 February for Burma. A number of the aircraft became unserviceable during the transit but Osborne was one of the few to arrive at Mingaladon, a few miles north of Rangoon. Almost immediately the depleted Squadron detachment moved north to join small elements of other Blenheim squadrons at Zayatkwin, but the rapid Japanese advance forced a withdrawal to Magwe on 21 February. During the next few weeks 45 Squadron was heavily engaged in attempts to halt the Japanese advance and numerous moves had to be made to other

Blenheims bomb Japanese transports in Central Burma, 1942. (MOD)

airfields. Records for the period are very sketchy and Osborne's precise activities are difficult to trace. He had developed a reputation as one of the most aggressive pilots on the Squadron and it is difficult to imagine that he was not in the thick of the action.

On 21 March, the Squadron flew its last significant attack against the enemy before withdrawing to Akyab. Two days later the Japanese launched an air attack which destroyed a number of Blenheims. Gerry Osborne took the controls of the one surviving Blenheim and flew out to Calcutta with three crews on board. Within a few days a small detachment of six crews was established at Lashio in Eastern Burma and Osborne flew to the airstrip on 4 April; his was the only serviceable aircraft!

The Squadron's detachment at Lashio, together with the Headquarters of BURWING, retreated north on 27 April to an airfield at Loiwing and Osborne, who had just flown in to Lashio, took off in the only surviving Blenheim for Loiwing, an airstrip some miles to the north. The following day, his aircraft was destroyed on the ground during a Japanese air raid. With no serviceable aircraft, the aircrew were ordered to return to Calcutta but there is no indication of how they were supposed to get there. On 6 May, the Squadron Record Book states that 'Flight Sergeant Osborne and his crew are somewhere in Burma'! It appears that they had remained at Loiwing in the hope that one of the remaining Blenheims could be made serviceable, but their hopes of escape were dashed when this last aircraft was sabotaged by Japanese guerrillas. The crew then joined a party of ground crew and made a difficult overland journey to

Bombing up Blenheims on an Indian airfield during the desperate attempts to stem the Japanese advance in early 1942. (MOD)

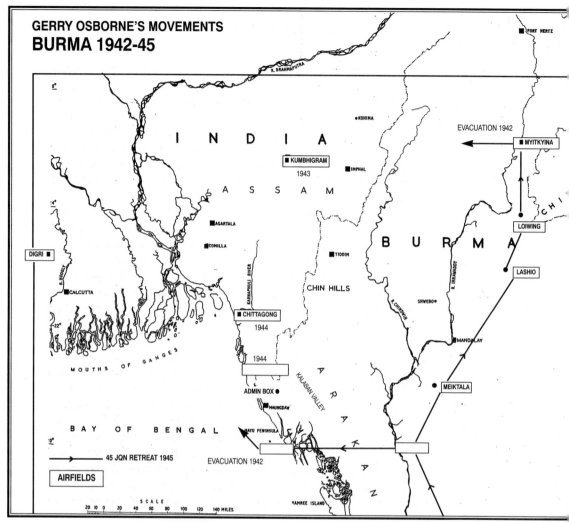

GERRY OSBORNE'S MOVEMENTS
BURMA 1942-45

Myitkyina in North-East Burma. On 9 May, they climbed aboard a 31 Squadron Dakota and returned to Calcutta on what proved to be the last flight out of Burma.

Gerry Osborne's adventures in escaping from Burma had occurred barely twelve months after his first operational sortie over the North Sea. In the meantime he had seen more varied action than many would see over much longer periods. However, in many respects his wartime flying career had hardly begun.

With the loss of all its Blenheims, 45 Squadron became non-effective and the majority of the personnel were detached for ground duties with units spread throughout India. Osborne's activities included an attachment to the Bengal Entertainment Services Association for 'script-writing and production purposes'. Unfortunately the records give no insight into the nature of these

186

duties but his reputation as something of an *enfant terrible* suggests that he might have been well qualified.

With the announcement that 45 Squadron was to be re-equipped with the American-manufactured Vultee Vengeance, all the Squadron aircrew were recalled at the beginning of November. The Vengeance carried a crew of two in tandem and was a large, single-engined aircraft designed as a dive-bomber and powered by a single 1,700hp Wright Double Cyclone engine. It was almost as heavy as a Blenheim and over 700 of these little-known bombers were delivered to the Royal Air Force.

Osborne rejoined 45 Squadron as a recently promoted Warrant Officer at Cholavaram near Madras in December and started converting to the Vengeance in January, 1943. The Squadron spent the next six months gaining experience on their new aircraft, participating in numerous exercises and developing tactics for the dive-bombing role. After six months of training the Squadron was ready for operations and, on 26 June, Gerry Osborne and his wireless operator/air gunner, Flight Sergeant A. R. Field, took off in Vengeance EZ 848 as part of an eight-aircraft detachment to Chittagong for operations in support of the 14th Army in the Arakan.

The day after their arrival the Squadron flew its first operation when six aircraft, led by Squadron Leader A Traill the Squadron Commander, took off to bomb Akyab town with an escort provided by Hurricanes of 261 Squadron. Osborne was flying EZ 848, loaded with two 500 lb GP bombs under the wings. Approaching the target from the sea, the formation climbed to 9,000 feet before rolling into an 80 degree dive, with the powerful airbrake extended to stabilise the speed at 300 mph, before releasing the bombs at 2,000 feet. The target was heavily damaged, with smoke visible several miles out to sea on the homeward flight. The Squadron's return to the front line had been marked by a very successful attack and was in stark contrast to the withdrawal almost twelve months earlier.

The eight Vengeance aircraft of 45 Squadron remained at Chittagong for three weeks, flying sixteen operational sorties. Gerry Osborne flew on ten of these dive-bombing attacks. The weather was a major consideration and the

A Vengeance II of 45 Squadron. The size of this dive-bomber is very apparent. (via Jeff Jefford)

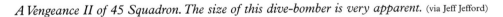

majority of sorties were planned to take off before 0700 hours in order to avoid the build-up of cloud in the monsoon weather. Sometimes the formation had to climb through solid cloud many thousands of feet thick before heading for the target area. On other occasions low cloud dictated that bombs had to be dropped from a shallow dive but results were good.

The sortie Osborne flew in EZ 848 on 30 June to bomb a concentration of buildings near Mychaung was typical of the operations mounted by the Squadron detachment. The eight aircraft formation, led by Squadron Leader Traill, took off at 0700 with seven Hurricanes of 67 Squadron as escort. Bad weather caused the outbound route to be changed and complete cloud cover over the target forced the formation to find a gap to the north of the target. The formation descended in two boxes of four to below cloud. A shallow dive-bombing attack from 3,000 feet was necessary because of the low cloud base with one box attacking one set of buildings and the second box attacking other buildings, each aircraft dropping two 500 lb GP bombs. One group of build-ings was seen to disintegrate and the others were damaged. The aircraft encountered small-arms fire which caused minor damage to two of them before climbing above cloud to return to base.

The detachment recovered to the Squadron's main base at Digri to the west of Calcutta on 14 July after a highly successful return to the front line. The Squadron had flown 102 sorties, often in very marginal weather conditions, and dropped 86,000 lbs of bombs. The Vengeance had established itself as a very accurate dive-bomber and a valuable addition to the offensive capability of the air forces in the Burma campaign.

Throughout the next two months 45 Squadron carried out a period of inten-sive training before the whole unit moved in early October to the newly constructed airstrip at Kumbhirgam in Assam for operations in support of the latest army probe in the Arakan. The Squadron's first sortie was flown on 16 October and Gerry Osborne took off in his faithful EZ 848. The formation of six aircraft attacked a Japanese Headquarters, diving from 13,000 feet before releasing their 500 lb bombs at 3,000 feet. The bombing was followed up by a machine-gun attack. Over the next two weeks Osborne flew five more sorties. Some involved Mohawks of 155 Squadron acting as pathfinders and marking enemy positions with 40 lb smoke bombs which the Vengeances dive-bombed from 10,000 feet.

By early November the build-up of Vengeance units was gathering pace and this included the re-equipping of two Indian Air Force squadrons. Both needed experienced reinforcements and a number of crews from the Royal Air Force squadrons were drafted, including Gerry Osborne and his air gunner, who joined 8 (Indian) Squadron in early November. After a period of intensive training, 8 Squadron moved to Double Moorings near Chittagong in readiness for operations in the Arakan in support of General Christison's XV Indian Corps.

The plan for the British offensive was to drive down the west coast towards Akyab with the 81 (West African) Division defending the Kaladan Valley on the eastern flank. Together with 82 Squadron, the Vengeances of 8 (Indian) Squadron were heavily engaged in providing close air support sorties against enemy strongpoints, supply dumps and headquarters positions. By the time of the offensive, Osborne was one of the most experienced pilots on the Squadron and he frequently led formations of twelve aircraft. On 16 January, 1944, he led an attack against enemy forces dug-in just a few hundred yards from the Indian army positions and marked by smoke bombs. He was the only non-commissioned pilot in the formation of twelve aircraft. Throughout the rest of January he flew almost daily on close support sorties as XV Corps advanced. The only diversion for him was a Spitfire-escorted attack by three aircraft to bomb the new Japanese airfield at Myohaung, scoring six hits on the runway. After completing the steep dive-bombing attack, Osborne, the other two Vengeances and their fighter escort strafed the aircraft parked in the dispersals.

The intensive flying rate continued throughout February when Osborne flew seventeen sorties, all in direct support of the ground forces whose distance from the enemy could often be measured in yards. The Squadron had moved south to an airfield in the Cox's Bazar area which reduced their reaction time to the urgent Army requests which were co-ordinated by an Air Support Cell; this cell was manned by a Wing Commander and co-located with the Corps Headquarters.

As the Japanese counter-attacked the sortie rate increased throughout March, with Osborne leading numerous attacks which were frequently escorted by a Flight of Hurricanes or Spitfires. Many sorties were flown in support of the West African Division that had been cut off in the Kaladan Valley. Each day twelve aircraft stood by from dawn to dusk waiting for tasking from the Army and two waves took off on most days. The activities of 19 March were typical, with the Squadron being informed at 1000 hours that special targets of the highest priority were to be attacked. An enemy gun position on a hill was holding up the advancing ground forces who were within 200 yards of the gun. Precision bombing was required to destroy this target and, led by the Squadron Commander, Squadron Leader N Prasad, twelve Vengeance IIAs took off and attacked the gun in a steep dive from 9,000 feet with a total of 6,000 lbs of GP bombs. Two direct hits were scored and all the bombs were within 30 yards. The photographic results showed one of the best groupings achieved by the Squadron against a pin-point target. One hour after Osborne and his colleagues landed, the Army signalled that the position had been taken. In the afternoon six aircraft took off to attack a gun that was shelling the vital airstrip in the

A Vengeance III takes off. Osborne flew his last few Vengeance sorties with 8 (Indian) Squadron in the Mark III. (Author's collection)

Kaladan Valley, the only source of re-supply for the beleaguered West Africans. Again, the gun was destroyed and a signal of congratulation arrived from the Army commander.

The month of April brought no respite for the dive-bombers and Osborne flew a further seventeen sorties. The advance by XV Corps along the coast had progressed well and the Japanese had transferred their main attack to the north at Kohima and Imphal. However, the troops in the Kaladan Valley were still cut off and relied entirely on air support. Enemy gun positions and dug-in troops were the main targets, often marked by smoke fired from mortars with aiming corrections being passed over the radio to the formation leader by a ground controller. On 26 April, Osborne led a twelve-aircraft attack against a school building being used as a Japanese Headquarters. The attack was a complete success. It was Osborne's fifty-third and final operational sortie with 8 (Indian) Squadron, to add to his sixteen Vengeance sorties with 45 Squadron.

There was little flying during the monsoon period and in June, 8 (Indian) Squadron was withdrawn for a rest and to re-equip with Spitfire XIIIs. During the period in the front line the Squadron had flown 1,470 sorties and dropped almost 1.5 million pounds of bombs; an incredible achievement for a single-engined bomber that carried just two bombs. The role and achievements of the Vengeance squadrons in the Far East are rarely mentioned but the Burma theatre proved to be the ideal environment for this outstanding but little-known aircraft. It had played a major role in the second Arakan campaign which General Slim described as 'the turning point for the Burma war'.

The Squadron moved to Quetta and in October started to exchange its Vengeance aircraft for Spitfire VIIIs. By mid-November it had been decided that 8 (Indian) Squadron would become an all-Indian manned unit and the British aircrew were posted out. After completing his conversion to the Spitfire, Osborne joined 155 Squadron and returned to the front-line when the Squadron moved to an airfield just north of Mandalay. By early January 1945, Slim's 14th Army had recaptured North Burma and was advancing on three fronts towards Rangoon. The role of the Spitfire squadrons was to maintain air superiority, thus allowing the bombers to support the ground forces unmolested. On 15 January, Osborne took off on his first Spitfire sortie to establish a standing patrol over Meiktila, seventy miles south of Mandalay.

By 1945 the Japanese air activity had almost ceased on the Burma front and the Spitfires encountered very little opposition. This created the opportunity for some sorties to be tasked in the ground support role. During a two week period in January Osborne flew fourteen patrols. The advance by 14th Army beyond Mandalay was rapid and 155 Squadron made regular moves to new and recaptured airfields in order to mount its standing patrols further south. February saw two moves and Osborne flew a further nineteen patrols and ground-strafing sorties. Although the threat from Japanese fighters had virtually disappeared, light anti-aircraft fire posed considerable problems for the ground attack sorties and a number of aircraft were lost.

Throughout March, Osborne continued to fly standing patrols, VIP escorts and bridgehead patrols over the advancing armies. He flew twenty-three sorties and, after a move to another captured airfield near Meiktila, he flew his final war sortie on 28 April; it was his fifty-fourth Spitfire patrol. Three months later he returned to England.

Gerry Osborne had arrived in Burma in early 1942, shortly after the Japanese invasion, and had begun flying operations immediately in his Blenheim in a valiant, but vain attempt, to stem the Japanese advance. Records are sparse, but he flew at least twenty sorties before his Squadron was wiped out. Throughout the rest of his stay in Burma, he flew a further 108 operational sorties in the

A long-winged Spitfire VIII DG-K of 155 Squadron on a Burmese airstrip in late 1944. (Norman Edwards)

A weary looking Gerry Osborne polishes the canopy of his Spitfire prior to a sortie. He flew 54 Spitfire patrols. (Author's collection)

Vengeance and Spitfire, often leading twelve-aircraft formations on precision close air support missions. Not only did he have to face an aggressive and ruthless enemy, but the violent weather and inhospitable terrain provided further formidable difficulties.

By any standards, Gerry Osborne's contribution to the air war in Burma was prodigious. It is open to speculation and conjecture, but, had he been serving in North West Europe, it is difficult to imagine that his efforts would not have been officially recognised with an award. Instead, like so many of his gallant comrades who served with the 'Forgotten Air Force', he had to be content with an un-named Burma Star. Because of his extended service overseas, he did not even qualify for the award of the Defence Medal. We have a strange way of recognising our heroes!

CHAPTER EIGHTEEN

Pathfinder Crew

The early months of 1943 heralded the opening of Bomber Command's 'Main Offensive' which unfolded around three major battles, the Battles of the Ruhr, Hamburg and Berlin. To many, this is the most famous period in the history of Bomber Command. The increased availability of the new four engined bomber force equipped with new bombing and navigation aids and led by the Pathfinder Force gave the Command a genuine strategic offensive capability. The entire operational career of Dennis Routen and his seven-man crew was condensed into this most significant, and perhaps most dangerous, period of the entire bomber offensive of the Second World War.

Coventry-born Dennis Routen had enlisted into the Royal Air Force Volunteer Reserve as a flight mechanic in June, 1940, but he was soon selected for pilot training which he carried out initially at the Flying Training School at Brize Norton, before proceeding to Bicester for twin-engined training. After

Medals awarded to four members of the Pathfinder Crew. Dennis Routen (pilot), Cyril Wolstenholme (navigator), Geoffrey Woodcock (rear gunner), James Kanelakos (mid-upper gunner). Distinguished Flying Medal, 1939-45 Star, Aircrew Europe Star, Defence Medal, War Medal.

The Crew from left to right; John Frewer (flight engineer), James Kanelakos (mid-upper gunner), Geoffrey Woodcock (rear gunner), Cyril Wolstenhome (navigatior), Dennis Routen (pilot). Leonard Noll (bomb aimer) is seated. Jack Simpson, the wireless operator, took the photograph. (James Kanelakos)

receiving his wings and promotion to Sergeant, he was posted to Chipping Warden to join 12 Operational Training Unit (OTU) for training for the heavy bomber force. He formed an immediate friendship with a tall, Cardiff-born navigator, Sergeant Cyril Wolstenholme, and they agreed to fly together. They were soon joined by two more Sergeants, Leonard Noll, a Canadian bomb aimer, and Jack Simpson, who had trained as a wireless operator/air gunner. Finally, they invited two Sergeant air gunners to join them, Canadian James Kanelakos and Englishman Geoffrey Woodcock, who had both recently completed their training at 7 Air Gunnery School, Stormy Down. These six young men formed a crew that flew together on every one of their operational sorties and they became very close friends. During their operational training

194

they soon developed a reputation as an above-average crew. Their subsequent operational record more than justified this initial assessment made during their training days on the Wellingtons of 12 OTU.

Posted to 1651 Heavy Conversion Unit at Waterbeach in November, they were joined by the seventh and final member of the crew, flight engineer Sergeant John Frewer. Once they had completed converting to the Stirling, they were posted to the recently re-formed 90 Squadron stationed at Ridgewell in Suffolk and part of 3 Group. Their arrival in February, 1943, coincided with a concentrated phase of attacks directed against the U-boat bases on the Biscay coast.

After a brief spell of training on the Squadron, twenty-two-year-old Dennis Routen and his colleagues flew their first operational sortie on the night of 13 February when they joined a large force of 466 bombers to attack the French port of Lorient. Flying Stirling I F for Freddie (BF 414), they arrived over the target at 10,000 feet at 2133 hours with a load of 1,000 lb HE bombs and incendiaries and made a timed run from the Ile de Groix. Sergeant Leonard Noll, the Canadian bomb-aimer, had a clear view of the docks and released the bombs onto the target, which was already well ablaze. On the following night their target was a cloud-obscured Cologne and the bombs were dropped on the Pathfinder's sky marking.

The last week of February brought a concentrated series of attacks and the crew took F for Freddie to Nuremberg on the 25th and to Cologne the following night. Two nights later the second of the U-boat ports on the Biscay coast, St Nazaire, was attacked by a large force of bombers. The Stirlings of 90 Squadron carried a large load of incendiaries and the raid caused widespread destruction.

On 1 March, Routen and his crew flew their fourth sortie in five nights; their first visit to the 'Big City'. They arrived over Berlin at 13,000 feet at 2213 hours to find no cloud and good visibility. The target was identified and had been well marked by red and green TIs (Target Indicators) and the 1,200 x 4 lb incendiaries were released on the aiming point. The crew were able to see the glow from the target eighty miles away on the return flight.

The giant Krupps factory complex was crucially important to the German war machine and it was one of the most frequently attacked locations during the Battle of the Ruhr. Not surprisingly, it was one of the most heavily defended targets that the bomber crews had to face. It was Essen that provided Routen and his friends with their next test when they visited the city on the night of 12 March. The weather was good, the green TIs were well placed and the incendiaries were dropped. On the run-up to the target F for Freddie was coned by searchlights, but Dennis Routen continued his run until the bombs had been released. On return, the aircraft was seen to have suffered flak damage to the tail, bomb doors and fuselage.

After a second successful sortie to Berlin, severe icing prevented the crew reaching the 'Big City' on 29 March. The Stirling's great weakness was its limited ceiling. On the outbound leg of the operation to Berlin the bomber became so badly iced-up in cloud that it could not climb above 16,000 feet. In an attempt to climb above the icing level, Routen gave the order to jettison part of the bomb load and the aircraft staggered to 18,000 but it was still unable to break clear of cloud. Despite skilful work balancing the fuel by John Frewer, the flight engineer, the petrol consumption had risen to such an extent that the Stirling was unable to reach Berlin and the crew had no option but to abandon the sortie and return to England . Such events were commonplace in the Stirling force and they highlight the range of difficulties that their crews had to face.

After returning from Duisburg on three engines after his aircraft had been hit by flak, Routen attacked Stuttgart on 14 April. On completion of the bombing run, he descended to 500 feet to return through the fighter belt. This method of return was approved on a moonlit night and, such was the spirit in this close-knit crew, that they took every opportunity to return at low level and continue their attacks against the enemy. Three trains were machine-gunned and the engine of one was seen to explode. Following a mining sortie to the Bay of Biscay on 17 April, Routen and his crew were selected for the Pathfinder Force and they left 90 Squadron to join 7 Squadron based at Oakington.

Training for the Pathfinder role occupied most of the next five weeks, although the crew flew sorties in the bombing role to Dortmund and Bochum, both towns suffering heavy damage. The Stirlings were equipped with the new navigation and bombing aid H2S. In the Pathfinder Force the navigation load was shared between the navigator and the bomb aimer with the latter spending most of the outbound leg working the H2S. Wolstenholme and Noll soon formed a very effective team. Much of this additional training was directed towards navigation exercises, culminating in high-level bombing runs using the H2S. The exercises also provided a good opportunity for fighter affiliation training which kept the two air gunners happy.

After an excellent attack against Dortmund on 23 May, the Pathfinders achieved one of their greatest successes on the night of 29 May. A force of 719 bombers took off to attack Wuppertal with the Routen crew flying a Stirling I (EF 363). The OBOE-equipped Mosquitoes of 109 Squadron hit the aiming point with their red TIs and the crews of the backers-up maintained very accurate marking, allowing the main force of bombers to deliver a devastating attack which was later described in the official reports as 'one of the most highly concentrated blitzes of the war'. After dropping the 500 lb bombs and the load of incendiaries, Wolstenholme gave his captain a heading to steer to clear the target and to start heading for home. Ten miles clear of the target Sergeant

Geoffrey Woodcock in the rear turret saw a Me 110 night fighter closing on the bomber from 500 yards and he ordered Routen to corkscrew port just as the enemy fighter opened fire. Sergeant James Kanelakos in the mid-upper turret also saw the fighter, and the two Stirling gunners opened fire as the fighter dived away. Shortly afterwards it re-attacked and closed from below on the starboard

Bombing up a Stirling of 7 Squadron. (MOD)

side. Again the gunners engaged and the enemy fighter broke off at 300 yards with its port engine on fire. The Me 110 was last seen in a vertical dive, but the intensity of the fires below prevented the gunners from seeing the final outcome. The enemy fighter could only be claimed as 'probably destroyed'.

Stirlings of 7 Squadron climb out over the Fens. (Author's collection)

There was a brief interlude in the Battle of the Ruhr on 19 June when 290 bombers made a daylight attack on the Schneider armaments factory at Le Creusot in Eastern France. This was the first sortie that the crew flew in the Pathfinder role when they dropped flares for the Main Force. They were the second crew over the target and they obtained a perfect aiming-point photograph. Flushed with their success, the crew returned at low level and continued with their successful train-busting role when they blew up a goods train near Orleans with machine-gun fire. On landing, they were congratulated by the Air Officer Commanding on obtaining an excellent aiming-point photograph and each member of the crew was given a copy.

Dennis Routen and his crew drop their flare directly over the Schneider armaments factory at Le Creusot on the daylight raid of 19 June, 1943. (James Kanelakos)

As a relatively inexperienced Pathfinder crew, the next few operations were flown as a 'backer-up', dropping their green TIs visually, together with their load of four 2,000 lb GP bombs. They observed that 'there were plenty of fighters' on sorties to Krefeld and Cologne. On the former the Squadron suffered very badly when four crews failed to return, including a veteran Flight Commander, Squadron Leader Hughes.

On 15 July, Flight Sergeant Dennis Routen was recommended for the Distinguished Flying Medal, the citation recognising his *'cool courage in pressing home his attacks in spite of fierce opposition having displayed a keen, aggressive spirit which has reflected in his crew.'* His Station Commander commented: *'This NCO's determination and offensive spirit is an inspiration to his crew and an outstandingly good example to other captains.'* There is no doubt that he led an outstanding crew who had developed a sense of teamwork and loyalty that was the trade mark of many bomber crews. Colleagues have gone further and commented that this crew stood out as one of the best.

During July, 7 Squadron started converting to the Lancaster III and Routen's crew carried out more advanced Pathfinder training, being awarded their Pathfinder badges on 25 July. As a result of this training and conversion to the Lancaster, they missed the initial raids of the Battle of Hamburg, one of the most destructive strategic bombing actions of the war. Outside the range of OBOE, the port was marked, using the H2S as the primary aid, but the most significant feature of this attack was the first use of the electronic counter-measure known as Window, a cloud of thin metal strips dropped ahead of the main bomber force to confuse the enemy ground and airborne radars. It was so effective that the staff of Bomber Command assessed that over 100 bombers were saved throughout the four attacks of the Battle.

Dennis Routen and his newly qualified Pathfinder colleagues flew on the fourth and final night of the Hamburg raids. Although 7 Squadron had virtually re-equipped with the Lancaster, there were still a small number of Stirlings on strength and the crew found themselves allocated Stirling (R 9829). They

A 7 Squadron Lancaster III stands on its dispersal at Oakington. (7 Squadron archives)

carried green TIs, flares and six 500 lb bombs. The attack went badly from the outset, with severe weather being encountered over the North Sea. The quiet, efficient wireless operator, Jack Simpson, sent a stream of weather reports and wind velocities back to Bomber Command Headquarters for the operations staff to assess together with other reports. Once the Force arrived over Germany they encountered very large thunderstorms and many of the bombers experienced serious difficulties due to icing and were forced to return. However, the Routen crew pressed on but found cloud up to 15,000 feet obscuring the target and they saw no evidence of any marking. In keeping with the superb reputation this crew were developing, Routen took the bomber down to a lower level as Wolstenholme guided the Stirling back towards the target for a second run, but this also proved abortive. The bomber descended further and another run was commenced, this time at 5,000 feet and Noll placed the markers three miles from the aiming point. Subsequent analysis of the photograph taken by the crew showed that they had been one of only two crews to be this close to the target.

Despite the persistence of Routen and his entire crew, this final raid on Hamburg had been a failure, due almost entirely to the appalling weather, and it had cost the lives of thirty bomber crews. However, the overall success was one of the most significant events in the strategic bombing campaign.

The Hamburg raid was the last Stirling sortie for the Routen crew, and their first Lancaster operation proved to be an uneventful raid on Nuremberg on 10 August in JA 706. For the next week Bomber Command turned its attention to North Italy with attacks against Turin and Milan. On 12 August, the crew operated in the 'backer-up' role over Turin and two nights later flew their first sortie as a 'blind marker' against Milan. Blind marking was always carried out on H2S and was a task given to the more experienced crews. On this raid only one bomber was lost but it was a grievous loss for 7 Squadron as it was Flight Lieutenant Matkin on his forty-fourth operation who failed to return. The following night the long haul to Milan was carried out again when the crew acted as one of the 'visual marker' crews. This type of marking was code-named 'Newhaven' and the Bomber Command Summary for the attack claimed this raid to be 'The best Newhaven so far.' A few days later, Routen was commissioned as a Pilot Officer.

Following the Italian interlude, the campaign known as the Battle of Berlin began. Berlin posed enormous difficulties to an attacking bomber force. It was very heavily defended by an extensive searchlight belt and by a multitude of anti-aircraft guns of many different calibres. Due to the city's geographical position, attacks involved deep penetration into Germany, with the bombers operating at maximum range which gave the planning staff limited flexibility in choosing diverse routeing. This made the rapidly expanding German night fighter force, the *Nachtjagd*, under the capable command of *General der Flieger*

Joseph Kammhuber, a fearsome threat, and the night fighters took a heavy toll of the British bombers.

The first raid in the initial phase of the Battle of Berlin took place on the night of 23 August when 727 aircraft were sent to the city; this was the biggest raid mounted on Berlin at the time. Routen and his crew took off in their Lancaster JA 849 at 2038 hours to join the stream heading for the Zuider Zee and then an almost direct route to Berlin which was marked by flare-dropping Mosquitos. They were part of the 'blind-marker' force and they dropped their green TIs and 4,000 lb HC bomb using H2S having identified the bombing offset at Lake Wolzig. They then turned north to return via Denmark. The *Nachtjagd* were out in force and the bombers suffered heavy casualties, with fifty-six aircraft lost, including Squadron Leader Lofthouse, the very experienced Flight Commander of 7 Squadron. Although extensive damage was caused, the bombs fell over a wide area and the raid was only partially successful. The official Pathfinder report summed up the raid as follows: 'A big proportion of the bombs dropped may be considered to have done useful damage, but the credit for that is due to the Germans for building so large a city.'

After a successful attack against Nuremberg on the 27th, Air Chief Marshal Sir Arthur Harris selected Berlin for another attack on 31 August. There was almost complete cloud cover over the target and a blind marking attack, which was known by the code name 'Paramatta', was delivered. Routen's crew were one of the first over the target dropping red TIs and their heavy bomb load, using the H2S radar to identify the aiming point. However, the marking was scattered and a significant 'creep back' by the Main Force developed and the raid was not considered successful; very little damage was caused to the city.

Three nights later Harris ordered another raid on Berlin, but he limited it to an all-Lancaster attack following the high casualties sustained by the Halifax and Stirling forces. The bombers were routed directly to the 'Big City' and, on arrival, cloud cover again dictated the need for a blind 'Paramatta' attack. Just before Leonard Noll released the red TIs and the 4,000 HC and 1,000 lb GP bombs from 15,000 feet, about forty searchlights 'coned' the Lancaster. As soon as the bombs had been released the Lancaster came under severe attack from heavy and light flak and Routen put the aircraft into a series of violent manoeuvres, finally pulling out of a dive at 2,000 feet. Almost immediately, Geoffrey Woodcock in the rear turret saw a Me 210 night fighter closing in and start firing at 300 yards. Routen turned the Lancaster hard to starboard and Kanelakos, in the mid-upper turret, opened fire simultaneously with Woodcock, and, after a four-second burst, the enemy fighter was hit. It passed astern and very shortly afterwards hit the ground in flames. As the crew broke clear of the Berlin defences Wolstenholme gave the pilot a heading to steer north

FROM:- No. 7 Squadron, P.F.F.

TO:- Headquarters, Path Finder Force.

DATE:- 5th September, 1943.

Ref:- 7S/2021/4/OPS.

AT 43/8863   79

Duplicate

Doble Rounds fired 400 (approx)

COMBAT REPORT.

Target Berlin

Captain:	P/O D.A.Routen
Navigator:	F/S C.H.Wolstenholme
W.Operator:	F/S J.J.Simpson
Engineer:	F/S J.Fraser
Bomb Aimer:	Sgt.L.C.Moll.
Mid-Upper Gunner:	F/S J.Kanelakos - Trained at 31.AGS.Canada, 7.AGS Stormydown, and 1483 Flight,Marham
Rear Gunner:	F/S G.Woodcock - Trained at 24 G.A.O.S.Rhodesia, 7 AGS Stormydown, and 12 OTU.

Lancaster J.A.   *ME. 210.*

BC/3

Reference Form Y, No.376. On the night of the 3rd/4th September 1943., Lancaster A/C J.A. 849 F/7 over target, heading due north, height 3,500, Rear Gunner saw an ME.210 approach from starboard beam, and below, e/a/c showed no lights.

ME.210 attacked opening fire at 300 yards, Lancaster F/7 turned hard to starboard, both Mid-Upper and Rear Gunner fired, about four second bursts at 200 yards range, and e/a was hit; e/a then passed astern of Lancaster F/7 and was seen to hit the ground in flames.

Previous to the attack Lancaster F/7 had been coned by approximately 40 searchlights when at 15,000 feet, and had been subjected to both heavy and light flak, Lancaster F/7 took violent combat manoevres, pulling out of the dive at 2,000 feet.

When ME.210 attacked Lancaster F/7 was held by only two searchlights, one on each side, which went out immediately the e/a opened fire.

ME210 claimed as definitely destroyed. Neither Booser nor Monica were fitted.

...................P/O
Captain's signature.

for Wing Commander, Commanding. S/L
No. 7 Squadron.   P.F.F.

The combat report submitted by Denis Routen after his two gunners shot down a Me 210 over Berlin on the night of 3/4 September, 1941.

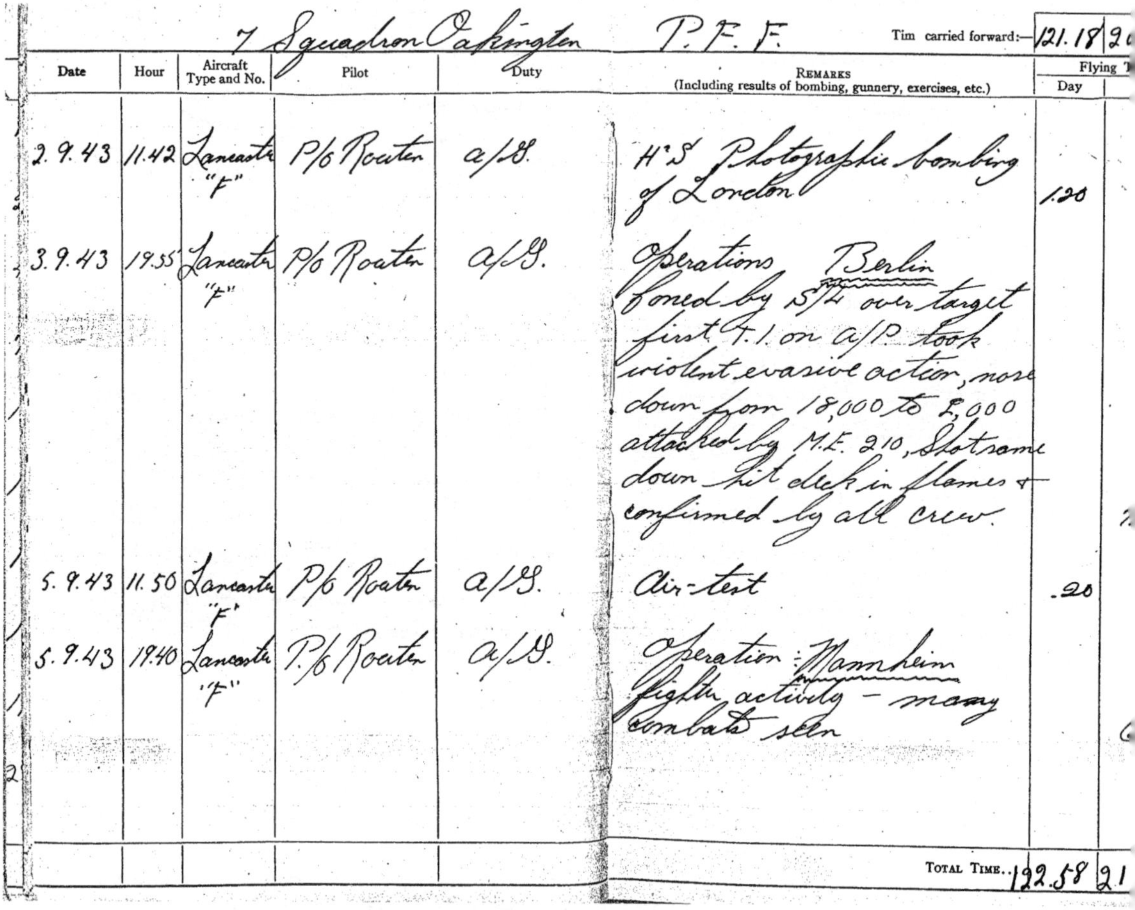

Date	Hour	Aircraft Type and No.	Pilot	Duty	REMARKS (Including results of bombing, gunnery, exercises, etc.)	Flying Day
2.9.43	11.42	Lancaster "F"	P/O Routen	a/c	H²S Photographic bombing of London	1.20
3.9.43	19.55	Lancaster "F"	P/O Routen	a/c	Operations Berlin. Bombed by S/L over target first. T.I. on a/P. took violent evasive action, nose down from 18,000 to 8,000 attacked by M.E. 210, Shot same down hit clerk in flames + confirmed by all crew.	
5.9.43	11.50	Lancaster "F"	P/O Routen	a/c	Air-test	.20
5.9.43	19.40	Lancaster "F"	P/O Routen	a/c	Operation: Mannheim fighter activity – many combats seen	

Time carried forward: 121.18

TOTAL TIME.. 122.58

An extract from James Kanelakos' log book showing the sortie over Berlin on 3/4 September, 1943, when he and the rear gunner shot down a Me 210 night fighter.

and the Lancaster left Germany south of Sweden and finally headed home from the northern tip of Denmark. At this late stage of the flight the wireless operator, Jack Simpson, was kept busy obtaining bearings and airfield weather reports for landing and John Frewer was carefully balancing the fuel tanks to ensure that every drop of fuel was available for the long haul back home. After an eight-hour flight, Routen eased Lancaster JA 849 on to Oakington's main runway after another eventful sortie in which every member of the crew had played a crucial role.

That morning the crew celebrated their safe return and the gunner's second success against German night fighters. They had cause for further celebration

James Kanelakos and the armourers pose by the rear turret of a Lancaster at Oakington, August 1943. (James Kanelakos)

when they were informed that their excellent navigator, Cyril Wolstenholme, had received his commission.

The Commander-in-Chief recognised that the initial three raids against Berlin had not been entirely successful and he decided to leave the city alone for a few weeks while waiting for the more accurate navigation and bombing aids that were shortly due to become available. Two nights later Mannheim was attacked and the weather conditions dictated that the Pathfinders employ a 'Newhaven' attack. Routen's crew were tasked as 'blind markers'; their red TIs were dropped accurately and they could see that a good concentration of markers had been achieved by the Pathfinders. At their subsequent de-briefing they commented that it 'looked like best blind marking yet seen'. Their enthusiastic report was confirmed in the official Pathfinder Narrative of Operations No 85 which said, 'This was undoubtedly one of the best Y (H2S) attacks the Pathfinders have ever achieved.'

With thirty-five operations completed, the Routen crew took some well-earned leave but not before the announcement that their navigator had been awarded the Distinguished Flying Medal. The recommendation for Cyril Wolstenholme's award covered the period before he was commissioned and it commented on '*his fine accuracy maintained throughout the flights allowing him to direct his captain with such precision that very successful bombing runs resulted. The courageous execution of the NCO's work has in large measure contributed to the success of his crew.*'

After three weeks' leave Routen and his friends prepared for their thirty-sixth operational sortie; all flown together as a crew. The target on the night of 27 September was Hanover and they took off in their usual Lancaster (JA 849) at 1939 hours. Nothing was heard from them after take-off. The 7 Squadron Record Book recorded: 'Pilot Officer Routen and his crew were missing from this raid, one of the Squadron's most experienced crews, a great loss.'

A few days later the Squadron learned from the International Red Cross that there was one survivor. The Canadian mid-upper gunner James Kanelakos had literally been blasted out of his turret, sustaining serious injuries on landing. It transpired that the Lancaster was at the head of the Pathfinder attack approaching the target when it was attacked by a German night fighter. Neither gunner saw the fighter approach and the bomber was almost certainly a victim of a classic *Schräge Musik* attack where the fighter approached directly below the bomber before engaging the bomber with its upward-firing cannons.

The Lancaster came down near the town of Quakenbruck. Sadly, six of this close-knit crew lost their lives and they are buried together in Rheinberg. It was too late for the rear gunner, Geoffrey Woodcock, to know that he had been awarded the Distinguished Flying Medal. James Kanelakos spent many months in a German hospital but eventually made a good recovery and he was re-patriated at the end of the war to learn that he was the fourth member of this gallant crew to be awarded the DFM. His citation recorded '*his great keenness, devotion to duty and fine fighting spirit as an air gunner*'.

Dennis Routen was an inspiring and brave captain, but he had the good fortune to have a crew which shared these qualities in equal measure. They were a devoted team working entirely for each other. James Kanelakos continues to mourn their loss. He described his friends as 'not just a crew; we were more like brothers.' They were typical of very many of the crews who went out time after time to face one of the most efficient and deadly anti-aircraft defence systems ever devised. Sadly, their fate was shared by many gallant young men of Bomber Command who 'failed to return.'

CHAPTER NINETEEN

Fighter Reconnaissance Pilot
Peter Perry

On the morning of 12 May, 1944, the German artillery and self-propelled guns in the Atina valley north of Monte Cassino were reluctant to open fire. The Allies had complete air superiority and the Spitfire Vs of 208 Squadron were able to maintain continuous patrols over the area seeking out any enemy gun activity and passing details of its precise location to the waiting Kittyhawk and Mustang fighter bombers and to the Allied artillery. Leading the early morning patrol was 208's Flight Commander, Peter Perry, who had been with the Squadron for almost two years during which time he had more than lived up to the Squadron's appropriate motto 'Vigilant'.

Pete Perry was born in Wallasey and, at the outbreak of the war, he was halfway through his veterinary studies at Liverpool University when he was called up. Having served in the Officer Training Corps, he was immediately sent to 165 Officer Cadet Training Unit where he completed his officer training before

Peter Perry's medals are Distinguished Flying Cross, 1939-45 Star, Africa Star with North Africa 1942-43 clasp, Italy Star, Defence Medal, War Medal with Mention in Despatch.

Pete Perry in the cockpit of his Hurricane. (P Perry)

being posted to the King's (Liverpool) Regiment in January, 1940. After ten months with little sign of any action, he and a number of colleagues volunteered to join the King's African Rifles and set sail for Kenya. His arrival in Nairobi in October, 1940, coincided with the end of fighting in Abyssinia; his quest for action was again frustrated.

During the next six months he lived a very peaceful life in the tranquillity of Kenya but the war had been in progress for eighteen months and he saw little prospect of any action unless he took some drastic steps. He volunteered for aircrew duties in the Royal Air Force but his Commanding Officer refused to release him; so he resigned his commission as a Lieutenant and, the following day, joined the RAF as an Aircraftman 2. For the next month he manned the fire engine at Nairobi's Eastleigh airfield before setting off with a number of other aircrew recruits on a three-week drive by truck to join the Initial Training Wing at Bulawayo. On 24 August, he finally started pilot training at 25 Elementary Flying School at Belvedere, near Salisbury.

The Flying School at Belvedere had been created as part of the remarkable Commonwealth Air Training Plan which had been introduced a few months earlier. With the constant air attacks by the *Luftwaffe,* the skies over the British Isles were no place for initial aircrew training and the Commonwealth plan was devised. It proved to be one of the great organisational feats of the war. The perfect weather in Rhodesia allowed for rapid progress and Pete Perry went solo in Tiger Moth T 8025 three weeks after his first flight. With fifty-five hours in his log book, he moved to 20 Service Flying Training School at Cranbourne to start training on the Harvard. On 2 December, he was awarded his wings and he completed his advanced training two months later when he was commissioned as a Pilot Officer.

The majority of pilots trained in Rhodesia were posted to the Middle East. With his Army background, Pete Perry was selected for training as an Army Co-operation pilot and was posted in May 1941 to 74 Operational Training Unit at Aqir in Palestine. The flying training syllabus on Harvards and Hurricane Is concentrated on low flying and all aspects of tactical, photographic and artillery reconnaissance. Evasion tactics and air-to-ground firing also formed an important part of the training of an 'Army Co-op' pilot. After sixty hours' flying, Pete Perry was assessed as above average in this specialist role and was posted to 208 Squadron which was equipped with the Hurricane II.

208 Squadron had started life as Naval 8 Squadron, fighting with great distinction on the Western Front during the First World War. In 1920 the Squadron started its long association with the Middle East when it re-formed in Egypt and it served continuously in the area until the outbreak of war. When the Italians declared war in June, 1940, the Squadron was immediately in action with its Lysander aircraft and was involved in some of the bitterest fighting before joining the ill-fated expedition to Greece where it fought with great gallantry before being virtually wiped out.

Pete Perry joined 'A' Flight of 208 Squadron on 7 July, 1942, at Heliopolis just as it completed its redeployment from the advanced desert landing grounds. The Squadron had been very heavily engaged during the retreat to the El Alamein defensive position and it had suffered heavy casualties from the intense, light flak and the marauding Me 109s. After a brief area familiarisation flight, Perry flew his first operational sortie in Hurricane BG 567 on the day after his arrival, acting as a 'weaver' to Flying Officer J. Moss DFC who was conducting a tactical reconnaissance sortie in the El Alamein area.

The Army Co-op role was particularly dangerous and the Hurricanes flew in pairs. Teamwork and disciplined flying were crucial if the vulnerable aircraft were to survive and return with their vital information. The pilot carrying out the reconnaissance spent the majority of his time seeking out enemy positions and noting the precise locations while balancing a map on his knee. He had no time to scan the skies for enemy fighters and he relied entirely on his number two, the weaver, whose sole job was to protect his leader and warn of any attacks by enemy fighters. By definition, the Squadron flew in direct support of the Army and it was crucial to establish a very close relationship between the ground units and their Desert Air Force colleagues who were their 'eyes in the sky.' To establish this close co-operation three Army Liaison Officers (ALOs) were assigned to the Squadron and 208 was particularly fortunate in being served by some outstanding Army officers throughout the war.

By July, 1942, the ground battle had stabilised with the Allied troops entrenched on the El Alamein line and the German Commander, General Rommel, probing with numerous minor attacks designed to give the Allies no time to recover from their recent reverses. Pete Perry and his fellow pilots on 208 Squadron were kept very busy flying tactical and photographic reconnaissance sorties over the El Alamein region. To give the Hurricanes maximum time in the operational area, the Squadron moved forward to Landing Ground (L G) 100 at Wadi Natrum and to L G 39 at Burgh el Arab, both situated closer to the forward Army positions.

Early August saw Perry co-ordinating the artillery fire of 64 Medium Regiment, Royal Artillery against enemy gun positions on the El Alamein line, and on two successive sorties flying his Hurricane Z 2416, he had two full squadrons of Hurricane fighters acting as escort. With the German Command recognising the importance of the Squadron's reconnaissance sorties, such a heavy fighter escort became an essential requirement throughout the next two months. However, despite the presence of such a strong force of fighters, 208 Squadron lost three pilots during July and seven failed to return in August. By the end of August Pete Perry had completed twenty hazardous operational sorties.

The situation on the ground remained static during most of September, but this in no way reduced the requirement for reconnaissance. Although pilots often returned with little activity to report, such 'negative' information was valuable to the Army planning staffs. The daily routine for 208 Squadron was to generate two dawn sorties looking for enemy movements and changes in dispositions and, during the afternoon, fighter-escorted tactical or photographic reconnaissance sorties covering the whole front. As one of the more experienced pilots, Perry was frequently tasked with these important flights. With his weaver, he would fly to the advanced landing ground occupied by the fighter escort squadrons and attend a joint briefing before the whole formation of up to twenty-four aircraft took off in mid-afternoon for the battle area. On 14 September, no less than three fighter squadrons of 244 Wing escorted him as he sought out enemy tanks and motor transport. He returned to report 'considerable movement' in the Rahman area but the fortifications in El Qattara were non-existent; the latter was an important piece of 'negative information' which confirmed other information gathered by Army intelligence.

The Squadron again suffered badly during September with the loss of five pilots, including the Squadron Commander, Wing Commander J. K. Rogers, who was killed in action. During the month Lieutenant General Brian Horrocks, the dynamic Commander of XIII Corps, visited the Squadron and briefed the pilots on the ground situation and future plans. The unique relationship that existed between the Eighth Army and the Desert Air Force extended down to unit level and it contributed greatly to the ultimate success in North Africa.

As General Montgomery prepared for the forthcoming battle at El Alamein the requirement for reconnaissance became crucial. Perry was flying operations almost daily. With 80 and 1 (SAAF) Squadrons as escort, he carried out a tactical recce south of Qattara on 15 October, followed two days later by a photographic reconnaissance, with vertically mounted cameras, of the German positions. On the 19th the RAF opened their air offensive prior to the main ground attack and Perry carried out a tactical recce. Twenty Me 109s jumped the fighter escort and Perry had to take immediate cover and break off his sortie but not before he had observed over 500 enemy motor transports.

During the afternoon of 23 October, General Horrocks again visited the Squadron and briefed the pilots on the opening of the Battle of El Alamein which was planned to start later that day. He emphasised the type of information required from the afternoon reconnaissance sortie, which was again to be flown by Pete Perry. With two squadrons of Spitfires from 243 Wing as escort, he took off in BG 815 to reconnoitre the northern sector where the main battle was to be launched. He reported 800 stationary and dispersed transports near the coast road and a further 500 on the southern road, but, more important for the Army commanders, there was no evidence of movement or preparation for a battle. Later that night, the 900 guns of the Eighth Army opened their barrage on the enemy positions and the battle, which ultimately proved to be the turning point of the Desert War, had begun.

At first light the following morning Perry took off to reconnoitre the same area to report any changes to the German dispositions; he was the first pilot to fly over the battle area. He reported that tanks on transporters were moving east and there was heavy artillery activity. Over the next forty-eight hours there was a constant requirement for reconnaissance and the pilots of 208 Squadron, operating from the rudimentary advanced landing grounds, flew at maximum effort. On the 28th the Squadron located over 200 tanks and 2,000 transports massing for a counter-attack in the north. During the afternoon, with 80 Squadron providing the escort, Perry conducted an artillery shoot. At the successful conclusion of the shoot, he descended to low-level and machine-gunnd forty transports in a wadi, reporting that all the rounds impacted in the target area.

The Eighth Army broke through the enemy lines on the early morning of 2 November and the call for reconnaissance increased to such a degree that sorties had to be flown without a weaver. Pete Perry took off to report on the northern sector and found 800 motor transports with 'much milling in area'. He had just identified a further 400 vehicles dug-in when he was bounced by

208 Squadron pose in front of their Hurricane IIs in Iraq, February 1943. (Author's collection)

three Me 109s and he took cover in some cloud before returning to land. Later in the day the Squadron lost a pilot, and Captain J. Becourt-Foch, a relative of the French Marshal Foch, was severely wounded when his aircraft was hit by flak.

Dispensing with the weavers had proved costly. Two days later the Squadron was withdrawn from the front line for a rest period, having given outstanding support to the Army. The Corps Commander, who had taken such a close personal interest in the Squadron's activities, signalled a message of congratulation and thanks for 'the excellent tactical reconnaissance reports'. As always, throughout this hectic and dangerous period, the 208 Squadron pilots had been admirably supported by their loyal ground crew, who had to work in primitive conditions keeping the old Hurricanes and their delicate cameras serviceable. Pete Perry had completed forty-three hazardous operations during the period and he was due for a rest from operations. However, with the Squadron being taken out of the front-line, he avoided a posting as an instructor to one of the Operational Training Units and he remained with 208 Squadron for his 'rest.'

In early January, 1943, a move was made to Aqsu, near Kirkuk in Iraq for winter training with 21 Corps. Perry's 'A' Flight was detached to Landing Ground K 1 near Baghdad and carried out numerous exercises with the 5th

Indian Division. To celebrate the Silver Jubilee of the formation of the Royal Air Force on 1 April, eight Hurricanes of 'A' Flight conducted a formation flypast and 'shoot up' over Baghdad. The Flight received a 'strawberry' from the Group Captain who commented, ' I was pleased and relieved to see that Pilot Officer Prune was not present'; an oblique reference to the inept activities of the RAF's cartoon character. The *Iraq Times* was rather more complimentary and reported, 'It seemed as though the RAF transferred Hendon air display to Baghdad in honour of the RAF anniversary.' Forty-eight years later 208 Squadron carried out a very different 'air display' over Baghdad when it destroyed numerous key targets during the Gulf War. There is no record of how the *Iraq Times* reported the later Squadron 'display'!

During April it was announced that Army Co-operation Squadrons were to be re-designated 'Fighter Reconnaissance' Squadrons. During the summer 208 moved to Rayak in Syria and Pete Perry was promoted to Acting Flight Lieutenant to take command of 'A' Flight. Intensive training was carried out throughout the summer, but the Hurricanes began to show their age; Perry having to make two forced landings after engine failures. During this time he

Hurricane IIs of 208 Squadron formate over Syria, September 1943. Pete Perry is flying HK 822. (Author's collection)

lost his good friend Flying Officer J. D. Wilson, who was killed when his engine failed over the mountains. The two friends had joined the King's African Rifles at the same time two years earlier and had remained together since then.

The Squadron started to re-equip with Spitfire Vs later in the year and the Squadron Record Book noted that 'the pilots have taken on a new lease of life'. Pete Perry flew his last Hurricane sortie in December before converting to the Spitfire V at Muqeibila in Palestine. On 31 December, it was announced that he had been awarded a 'Mention in Despatches' for his valuable work during the North African campaign.

With sixteen Spitfires on strength, the Squadron began a comprehensive work-up in January for a return to operations, and, in preparation, it participated in a major exercise in the Suez area. The Army was so impressed by the accuracy of the pinpointing of targets that it suspected the Squadron of 'fixing'

Pete Perry with his groundcrew in Italy 1944. (P Perry)

the sorties beforehand. The exercise afforded the Squadron pilots an excellent opportunity to assess the Spitfire. They all agreed that the aircraft was a great improvement over the Hurricane, particularly in the photographic reconnaissance role. Early in March the Squadron was ordered to prepare to move to Italy.

Since October, 1943, the Allied armies had made significant progress in advancing through Southern Italy and by March, 1944, they had secured the beachhead at Anzio and were preparing a further assault on Monte Cassino as they pressed towards Rome. The demands on the only Tactical Reconnaissance Wing had reached the point where it was essential for reinforcements to be provided and on 17 March, 208 Squadron flew in to the recently constructed 1,200 yard airstrip situated almost on the beach at Trigno on the Adriatic. Perry was a day late in arriving from Egypt having to divert to Malta when the engine of his Spitfire misbehaved.

Commanded by the South African Lieutenant Colonel Johnny Blaauw, 208 Squadron flew its first operational sorties under the control of 285 Wing twenty-four hours after arriving in Italy. Some of the Spitfire Vs had been replaced with Spitfire IXs and the Squadron flew with the mixed fleet for some months. Pete Perry flew his first sweep over the battle area on 20 March, followed by a number of weaver sorties in support of 40 (SAAF) Squadron, who had been with 285 Wing for many months, gaining considerable experience in the area.

On 27 March, Perry was flying a Spitfire V, modified to carry vertical and oblique cameras, on a reconnaissance sortie in the Chieti area north of the German Gustav Line where the Germans had massed a large array of artillery. He had just started his first photographic run when his aircraft was hit by an 88 mm shell which severely damaged the tailplane, fin and rear fuselage. Nevertheless, he continued to take photographs, despite the heavy anti-aircraft fire, until the task was complete and he returned to the airfield with his vital information. The reconnaissance pilot's task was incomplete unless he returned with his photographs and visual report.

In the build-up to the Spring offensive the Spitfires of 208 were kept very busy monitoring the German lines of communications, observing enemy movements and finding targets for the fighter-bombers. There were few *Luftwaffe* fighters in the skies over Italy by this time, but the anti-aircraft defences were formidable. On 2 April, the Squadron lost its second-in-command, Flight Lieutenant A.V. Maslen DFC, who was flying his 100th operational sortie. Two more pilots were lost later in the month.

Towards the end of April, artillery reconnaissance became a major activity for the Squadron and Perry found himself controlling a number of shoots in the Miglianico area. With his weaver above, he would fly at 5,000 feet seeking out enemy artillery before calling up the Divisional artillery and reporting that

During the advance north through Italy, the Squadron personnel were able to inspect the destroyed and abandoned German artillery. (Ken Pugh)

a particular area was active. He would then correct the fall of shot until the enemy guns had been silenced. On 21 April, he registered three gun positions as targets and, two days later, he registered a further two. At the end of April the Squadron started a series of moves which would see it occupy a succession of eight airstrips over the next three months.

The ubiquitous 88 mm gun of the German Army was a great threat to both ground troops and aircraft, and a battery near Francovilla just to the north of the Gustav Line was proving particularly troublesome; Pete Perry was tasked to fly a low-level oblique photographic sortie so that its location could be fixed precisely. He and his weaver encountered severe anti-aircraft fire, but he completed his sortie successfully and returned with photographs which allowed the gun position to be pin-pointed for a follow-up attack by the fighter bombers.

During the afternoon of 11 May, the pilots were briefed by the Squadron's

Army Liaison Officer, Major Tipper, on the offensive which would herald the opening attack in the drive to reach Rome. At a mass briefing he outlined the Squadron's role in the forthcoming attack which started a few hours later with a major offensive against the Gustav Line. For the next eight days, 208 maintained continual artillery reconnaissance patrols over the Atina valley as the gallant Poles and Gurkhas made yet another assault on Monte Cassino.

Ground equipment was in short supply during the rapid advance north. Willing hands lift a clipped-wing Spitfire LF IX for a wheel change on the temporary hardstanding. (Ken Pugh)

Spitfire LF IX - PV 117 - of 208 Squadron sets off on a reconnaissance. (via Peter Green)

Perry flew eleven artillery patrols during this period, calling down Allied fire as soon as any enemy gun opened fire. Finally Cassino was taken and the Germans began a large-scale withdrawal.

The Squadron now reverted to tactical reconnaissance sorties along the major withdrawal routes, finding targets for the fighter-bombers which formed a 'cab-rank' waiting to be called in to attack. Over the next few weeks the Squadron was constantly on the move in order to keep up with the rapidly advancing armies and the ever-cheerful ground crew became expert at rapid moves. They also gained a great deal of experience changing aircraft wheels after the many tyre bursts caused by the very rough surfaces of the temporary airstrips. However, this constant progress was a great boost for morale as the ground crew could see the results of the many air attacks which had preceded the offensive. By the end of June, the Squadron was at Osa, just eight miles outside Rome.

The rapid advance of the ground forces created a huge demand for reconnaissance sorties and all the pilots flew at intensive rates. During a sixty-day period in May and June, Perry flew forty-nine operations. On 17 June, he flew his 100th operational sortie when he carried out a tactical recce in the Perugia area. Following the capture of Rome on 5 June, the Germans fell back on the next main defensive line known as the Gothic Line at the foot of the northern Apennines between Pisa in the west and Rimini in the east. Shortly afterwards, the Squadron started to receive Spitfire VIIIs and moved north to Castiglione which proved to be one of the most pleasant of all the Italian airfields.

Throughout July the demands for reconnaissance continued, with special emphasis on monitoring the German lines of communications and on artillery shoots. The latter were particularly difficult as the Germans had their artillery well dug-in and withheld fire whenever aircraft were in the vicinity. Perry flew thirteen more operations during July, including the first sorties north of Florence. On 14 July, he received a signal from the Air Officer Commanding the Desert Air Force congratulating him on the immediate award of the Distinguished Flying Cross. The recommendation cited the skill with which he continued his photographic sortie after being severely damaged by flak and concluded: '*This officer has already completed 109 operational sorties and has served continuously with 208 Squadron since July, 1942. He has at all times been a source of inspiration to his colleagues by his unfailing determination and courage. I cannot too strongly recommend this award.*' This was the first award to the Squadron during the Italian campaign.

As the Germans consolidated their positions behind the Gothic Line, the demands for aerial reconnaissance became even more pressing and the Officer Commanding the Wing had to reassess the dispositions of his scarce resources. He decided to move two squadrons to support the advance in the east but he opted to leave 208 in the centre to operate in support of 5th Army. Behind the Gothic Line there existed a limited number of main roads running north to the Po Valley and the Germans were dependent upon these roads for re-supply; 208 was required to maintain a constant watch in the area. This necessitated another redeployment for the Squadron and they moved further north to Magliano which was very close to the front line. One Squadron pilot commented that he didn't need to leave the airfield circuit to complete his reconnaissance!

Throughout August the Squadron mounted a maximum effort and during the first fifteen days of the month Perry flew no less than twenty-two sorties in support of 5th Army on the west coast of Italy. By this stage, tactical reconnaissance sorties were being flown to Pisa and Pistoia, and Perry flew the first sortie to this area. On 15 August, he flew Spitfire V EP 893 on a sortie to photograph the Prato to Florence road using a 12 inch oblique camera, obtaining 'excellent results'.

By the middle of August, Perry's long and distinguished career with 208 Squadron was coming to an end. On the morning of 22 August, he climbed into the familiar cockpit of his Spitfire IX (MK 229) for the last time. His final sortie was to fly as weaver to Flying Officer R Knowlton on a tactical reconnaissance to the Pisa area. After one-and-a-half hours, he landed and completed his 150th operational sortie in one of the most demanding and hazardous roles, having served continuously on 208 Squadron for over two years. A month later

Gun harmonisation for Spitfire IX - MJ 659 - North Italy. (Ken Pugh)

he boarded a Liberator at Naples and returned to England after an absence of almost four years.

After a period of leave Perry started a flying instructor course at Montrose, qualifying in January, 1945. For the remainder of the war he trained student pilots on the Harvard, before moving to the Royal Air Force College at Cranwell where he instructed cadets on the Tiger Moth and later the Harvard. His last flight in the Royal Air Force was on 15 December, 1945, in Harvard 2b FS 847 on a training sortie with Cadet Bower. A few weeks later he was demobbed.

Pete Perry returned to Liverpool University to complete his veterinary studies. Over the following years he built up one of the biggest veterinary practices in the West Country and finally retired in 1985.

CHAPTER TWENTY

Conspicuous Gallantry – Stuart Sloan

Stuart Sloan had always wanted to be a pilot but he had been selected for training as a bomb aimer. He was just twenty when he joined his first squadron and, within a few months, he had completed seven operations. On his eighth bombing sortie, he had an unexpected opportunity to display his ability as a pilot. Six years later the young bomb-aimer was a senior pilot flying with the King's Flight.

Lanark-born Stuart Sloan was just nineteen when he volunteered for aircrew duties in the Royal Air Force. After completing his initial training at Dyce near Aberdeen, he was selected for air observer and bomb-aimer training and sailed from Liverpool in the *Arundel Castle* for South Africa where he undertook his flying training. By the time Sloan arrived at 42 Air School in early 1942 the Commonwealth Air Training Plan was beginning to gather momentum with most aircrew being trained at the many flying training schools that had been

Stuart Sloan's medals are, Member of the Royal Victorian Order (Fifth Class), Distinguished Flying Cross, Conspicuous Gallantry Medal, 1939-45 Star, Aircrew Europe Star with France and Germany Clasp, Defence Medal, War Medal.

established in the Commonwealth countries. For the trainee aircrew this was an experience of a lifetime. Far away from the theatres of war, with mostly ideal weather conditions for flying, they were taught the basic skills of their flying trade before completing their training in the United Kingdom.

After six months in South Africa, Stuart Sloan was posted to Dumfries for further training; 10 Bombing and Gunnery School had moved there in mid-1940 and had been redesignated as 10 Air Observer School in September, 1941, and 10 (Observer) Advance Flying Unit shortly before Sloan arrived. Following completion of his course there, he began converting to Wellingtons at 11 Operational Training Unit based at Westcott near Oxford; it was here that he finally qualified as a bomb-aimer. Just before Christmas, 1942, he travelled to Burn in South Yorkshire to join the recently formed 431 (Iroquois) Squadron of the Royal Canadian Air Force which was equipped with the Wellington Mk X.

For three months the new Squadron conducted an intensive training programme in readiness for bombing operations over Germany. By the Spring of 1943 the main bomber offensive was gathering momentum. The Pathfinder Force had been established and new navigation and bombing aids were being introduced; the Commander-in-Chief of Bomber Command Air Chief Marshal Sir Arthur Harris, had just launched what he termed 'The Battle of the Ruhr'. The aircrews dubbed it 'Happy Valley'.

On 12 March, Sergeant Stuart Sloan was detailed to fly with his Squadron Commander, Wing Commander J. Coverdale, in Wellington 'A' (HE 182) for a raid on the Krupps factory at Essen. Twelve squadron aircraft lined up on the runway behind the Wing Commander who was the first to roll at 1915 hours. The bomber stream climbed on an easterly heading and set course for the Ruhr. From his position in the nose of the Wellington, Sloan picked up the green TIs in his bomb sight and gave corrections to his pilot before releasing the bombs from 17,500 feet. He saw large explosions in the target area and the fires were still visible 100 miles distant on the return flight. This was the second raid on Essen within a week and it was judged to have been very successful with the OBOE-equipped Mosquitoes marking very accurately.

Over the next few weeks Sloan flew six more sorties, including one mine-laying operation off St Nazaire and two bombing attacks against Duisburg. The attacks against Duisburg, the largest inland port in Germany, had been only partially successful and a third was ordered for 12 May. With the Wing Commander at the controls, 'J' (HE 183) took off at 2350 hours and Sloan moved forward to his position in the nose to prepare his bomb release equipment. In good weather they arrived over the target at 16,000 feet and encountered moderate flak as Sloan lined-up on the green TIs and released his bombs. During the run-up he had seen numerous large explosions and post-sortie reports confirmed that it had been a very successful attack, causing extensive damage.

Four nights after this raid, Bomber Command mounted one of the most famous and daring bombing attacks of the entire war – the attack against the Möhne and Eder Dams by 617 Squadron. For the rest of the bomber squadrons it was a night off.

The biggest raid of the Battle of the Ruhr so far was mounted on the night of 23 May when 826 bombers attacked Dortmund. Sloan and his usual crew were detailed to fly with a pilot who had recently arrived on the Squadron. The five-man crew were allocated Wellington 'D' (HE 198) and were one of the first to take off as they rolled down the runway at Burn at 2040 hours. The outbound flight was uneventful and Sloan released the bombs on to the green TIs from 17,000 feet.

As the pilot turned away from the target area the aircraft was 'coned' by a large concentration of searchlights. The pilot immediately put the Wellington into a steep dive, but was unable to recover. Sloan came to his assistance by putting his back against the instrument panel and pushing against the control column. This was effective, but the aircraft was still held by the searchlights and heavily engaged by intense flak. The pilot immediately put the aircraft into another steep dive just as the rear gunner reported that they had been hit and were on fire. The order to bale out was given and Sloan went forward to the nose to collect his parachute. In the meantime, the pilot opened the escape hatch and jumped. Sloan realised that other members of the crew were still aboard and, with the aircraft still diving, he decided to try and get the aircraft under control. After a great struggle, he was able to level out the Wellington. The navigator, Sergeant G. Parslow, came forward and found Sloan with his parachute on but having to sit sideways in the pilot's seat. He immediately came to his assistance and Sloan settled into the pilot's seat.

Having found that the aircraft was handling satisfactorily, Sloan immediately took command and decided to try and keep the aircraft flying although it was still held by searchlights and was being subjected to intense light *flak*. He confirmed that the navigator and the wireless operator were still on board the aircraft. The intercom emergency call light came on, but he could get no reply from the rear gunner and he assumed that he too had baled out. By some aggressive flying, the bomb-aimer was able to shake off the searchlights but this initial success was short-lived and the Wellington was picked up by more searchlights and again came under heavy fire. Once more, he was able to escape the beams. The crew estimated that they had been held by searchlights for over 45 minutes.

Once clear of the searchlight zone, Sloan concentrated on trying to get the aircraft home. With the loss of the escape hatch and the rear turret doors open, most of the navigation charts and radio logs had been lost and a gale was blowing through the aircraft. Sergeant Parslow and the wireless operator, Flying Officer J. Bailey, established some order under extreme difficulties and gave Sloan courses to steer. The aircraft was established at 9,000 feet over the enemy coast where the navigator obtained a visual fix and gave a heading for the nearest point on the coast of East Anglia.

Over the North Sea revolutions on the port engine started to rise. The wireless operator had previously reported a fault in the generator and Sloan decided to put the propeller in fixed pitch and to switch off all un-necessary electrical services. Over Orfordness Sloan turned towards base and headed for the Cottesmore beacon. Fixing the pitch of the propeller had not been entirely successful and Sloan had to progressively reduce the revs. Over Cottesmore he was having difficulty maintaining height and decided to land at the first airfield showing the Drem lighting system. He gave his two colleagues the option of parachuting to safety while he attempted to land but they both chose to stay and help. The first flarepath they saw was of a simpler type, but the aircraft was becoming difficult to control and he decided to land as soon as possible. He circled the airfield three times as Bailey fired Very signals. Once given a green, he lowered the undercarriage and started his approach. As he crossed the boundary fence, the engine failed but he made a good landing without further damage to the aircraft.

This very gallant crew, led by the young bomb-aimer Stuart Sloan, had landed at Cranwell. In addition to their gallantry, they had displayed an outstanding sense of crew co-operation and loyalty to each other. Remarkably, Sloan had no previous piloting experience but had always shown the greatest interest and often stood by his pilot in the cockpit and monitored his actions. He had also shown a keen interest in flying the Link trainer.

When the Cranwell Intelligence Officer telephoned Burn to report the safe arrival of Wellington 'D', but without a pilot, the Station Commander was incredulous and news rapidly spread of the epic flight. Within a few days, it was announced that Stuart Sloan had been awarded an immediate Conspicuous Gallantry Medal, the highest award for gallantry open to a non-commissioned man other than the Victoria Cross. The citation for his award concluded: '*Throughout the return journey Sergeant Sloan showed courage, resource and determination, in keeping with the highest traditions of the Royal Air Force. His fine example of leadership and devotion to duty has been an inspiration to the Squadron.*' In addition to his gallantry award, he was commissioned in the field. Finally, he was sent on a pilot's course!

His two gallant colleagues were also given immediate awards. Flying Officer Bailey was awarded the Distinguished Flying Cross and Sergeant Parslow received the Distinguished Flying Medal. Tragically, both were lost three weeks

Stuart Sloan is congratulated on the announcement of the award of the Conspicuous Gallantry Medal. Looking on are Flying Officer J Bailey who was awarded the DFC and Sergeant Parslow who received the DFM. (Author's collection)

later on a raid to Krefeld while flying with Wing Commander Coverdale.

Stuart Sloan had to wait until the end of the year before starting his pilot training at 28 Elementary Flying Training School in a Tiger Moth. Just before Christmas 1943, he reported to the RAF College Cranwell, the scene of his epic landing, and began his advanced training at the Service Flying Training School. He made steady progress and was awarded his wings on 27 June before proceeding to 19 OTU at Kinloss for bomber training on the Whitley. After converting to the four-engined Halifax with 1652 Heavy Conversion Unit at Marston Moor, Sloan was posted in the New Year of 1945 to Lissett to join 158 Squadron.

The 'Final Offensive' was under way when Sloan took off on his first operational sortie as a pilot on 28 January. His Halifax III 'Y' (MZ 813) was one of

Halifax III - NA 570 - starts the take-off run. (J Pelly-Fry)

twenty-two launched by the Squadron for an attack on Stuttgart which was bombed from 12,000 feet. With heavy cloud cover, the Pathfinders dropped sky-markers and Sloan's bomb-aimer released on the red-yellow markers. This last raid on the city of Stuttgart was considered a success despite a number of aircraft bombing one of the sophisticated fire decoy sights.

During the latter stages of the war, the bomber offensive was directed at oil targets and communications centres, and Sloan and his crew bombed Mainz and then the Nordstern synthetic-oil plant at Gelsenkirchen. The town of Goch, situated on the edge of the Reichswald Forest, was a fortified town and a key defensive position. The British XXX Corps planning staff had asked for the town to be destroyed prior to a major attack they intended to mount in the run-up to the crossing of the River Rhine. The town was bombed by a large force of 4 Group Halifaxes on 7 February. Before Sloan could bomb, the Master Bomber called off the attack when smoke from the accurate first wave obscured the target and he assessed that the town had been destroyed; only four of the twenty-five aircraft launched by 158 Squadron had dropped their bombs on the target before the raid was discontinued. A few days later Sloan attacked the oil refinery at Wanne-Eickel.

After a brief spell of leave, during which the Squadron participated in the attack on Dresden, Sloan returned to operations at the end of February when he attacked Mainz. Due to cloud cover, sky-marking was again employed in this last raid on the town. The campaign against the oil targets continued and the synthetic-oil plant at Kamen was bombed on 2 March. Sloan was flying his new aircraft 'U' (NR 170) on the 5th when he attacked the town of Chemnitz which was proving a major obstacle to the advancing Russian Army in the east. This proved to be a costly raid for Bomber Command. Two nights later, the target was again an oil refinery, this time at Hemmingstedt. Just after leaving the target, Sloan's Halifax was engaged by a Junkers 88 which his gunners managed to fight off. Over the next seven days, he bombed five major towns in the Ruhr area which had now become part of the front line. These towns had major rail centres and their destruction was part of the plan to destroy the remaining major communications systems which severely restricted the Germans' flexibility to move troops in the defence of their homeland. These targets, which had been crucial to the strategic plan had, in effect, become tactical targets.

Throughout February and March, 158 Squadron regularly provided more than twenty aircraft for each raid. The overall Bomber Command effort during this period was prodigious and more bombs were dropped during March, 1945, than in any other month of the war. While bomber losses still occurred, they had been reduced to a trickle compared to earlier years. When Sloan attacked Wuppertal on 13 March in daylight, there were no losses among the 354 heavy bombers. However, the anti-aircraft defences were still effective and Sloan's aircraft was hit by flak seven days later just after he had released his bombs on the railway yards at Recklinghausen. He landed safely.

A daylight attack on 24 March against Gladbeck was carried out in good weather and the crews had the unique experience of being able to map read their way to the target. The skies were virtually clear of enemy fighters and any that risked an attack were soon engaged by the escort fighters which now accompanied every bombing raid. Sloan bombed the Pathfinder's markers from 16,500 feet and the target was assessed as having been 'devastated'. On 4 April, 158 Squadron generated twenty-one aircraft for its final attack against an oil target. With excellent marking from the Pathfinder Force, the Rhenania oil plant at Harburg was destroyed. On this raid heavy flak was encountered, a testimony to the tenacity of the anti-aircraft units at this very late stage of the war when the whole German military machine was collapsing.

By the middle of April the strategic bomber offensive was over and targets were selected on the basis of their importance to the final land and maritime offensives. On 18 April, Sloan and his crew took a Halifax VI (NP 876) on the huge raid that devastated the German Naval Base on Heligoland. No less than 969 bombers reduced the island to a moonscape. Among the bombers were a number of Lancasters carrying the 22,000 lb Grand Slam bombs. There was just one more raid for the Halifax force of 4 Group and Sloan took his faithful Mk III Halifax 'U' (NR 170) on the daylight raid which attacked the major coastal guns on the island of Wangerooge which protected the approaches to the major German North Sea ports. At 1810 hours Flight Lieutenant Stuart Sloan eased his Halifax on to the runway at Lissett at the end of his twenty-first operation, taxied into his dispersal and shut-down the four Hercules engines. His war was over. This raid marked the end, too, for arguably the most famous aircraft that ever served in Bomber Command; 158 Squadron's LV 907 which carried the nose-art 'Friday the 13th'. Following its safe return from Wangerooge, the aircraft had one more symbolic bomb painted on its nose (bringing the total to 128) before being put on public display in Oxford Street. The original panel bearing that remarkable tally was eventually displayed at the Royal Air Force Museum, Hendon. The Yorkshire Air Museum's recently restored Halifax now bears the markings of that legendary bomber.

At the end of the war 4 Group was disbanded and 158 Squadron transferred to Transport Command but spent the first few weeks 'jettisoning bombs' in designated areas at sea. During June numerous low-level cross-country flights over Germany were flown which allowed aircrew to see the devastation caused by the bombing campaign. On many of these 'Cook's Tours' flights the hard-working ground crew were taken along as passengers. 158 Squadron moved to Stradishall in June where Sloan flew the Halifax VI and converted to the Stirling which the Squadron used for flying the long-range routes to the Mediterranean and Near East.

On 17 July, 1945, an entry in the *London Gazette* announced that Stuart Sloan had been awarded the Distinguished Flying Cross, the recommendation concluding: *'An officer of proven courage he has shown the greatest possible determination to press home the attack upon the enemy and he has faced the severest enemy defences with a coolness which has been a constant source of inspiration to the men of his crew. It is strongly recommended that this pilot's record of skill, courage and devotion to duty throughout an excellent tour be recognised by the award of the Distinguished Flying Cross.'*

During October, 158 Squadron was involved in Operation Sketch, the

A York C 1 - MW 290 - of 59 Squadron. Sloan became a training captain on the York.
(via Andy Thomas)

transfer of 10,000 Indian troops from Shallufa, on the Suez Canal, to India using converted ex-bomber Stirling Vs with each aircraft carrying twenty-four troops. At the end of the year 158 Squadron was disbanded and Sloan transferred to 51 Squadron which was being re-equipped at Waterbeach with the four-engined Avro York which it operated on routes to the Far East. After nine months he left for Canada where he completed an instrument rating examiners' course at Trenton, returning to 51 Squadron at Waterbeach in December 1946. He remained with the Squadron for another twelve months flying the long range-routes to the Far East

On 1 December, 59 Squadron re-formed at Abingdon with half the crews from 51 Squadron and Sloan was transferred to the new Squadron and appointed as one of the Flight Commanders. 59 Squadron was established at Abingdon as a long-range transport squadron with scheduled passenger and

Officers of the King's Flight stand by a Viking at Benson, May 1951, Stuart Sloan is standing directly beneath the propeller. (32 'Royal' Squadron archives)

Stuart Sloan (left) with his King's Flight crew, left to right Flt Lt F Gray (WOP), Flt Lt Ted Brewin (navigator), Flt Lt F Pennycott (flight engineer). Sgt D Griffiths (steward). Benson 1951. (Ted Brewin)

transport flights to Singapore, India and the Middle East. The Squadron also flew many 'specials' and Sloan took aircraft to Southern Rhodesia and the Gold Coast during the first months of 1948. In April he was awarded an 'A' Category (Exceptional) as a transport pilot.

Tension increased between the four Allied Powers in Berlin during May 1948 and the Russians imposed an overland blockade. The western powers decided to re-supply the city of Berlin by air and RAF Transport Command took a leading role. Operation Planefare began on 28 June and two days later sixteen crews from 59 Squadron deployed to RAF Wunstorf, near Hanover. Three air corridors from the Western zone of Germany ran to Berlin, terminating at Templehof in the American sector and RAF Gatow in the British sector. Within twenty-four hours of the order being given, the Dakotas and Yorks of the Royal Air Force began operations. On 1 July, Sloan was the captain of the first York aircraft to carry supplies into Berlin.

The Berlin Airlift proved to be another epic chapter in the history of the Royal Air Force but Sloan's involvement amounted to seven return sorties. In mid-July he was selected to join the King's Flight at Benson which was in the process of building up to five crews and five Viking aircraft in readiness for a Royal Tour of Australia. Unfortunately, a few months later the King became ill and the Royal Tour was cancelled. The Flight was reduced to two crews with Stuart

The Captain of the King's Flight, Air Commodore 'Mouse' Fielden escorts His Majesty King George VI and Princess Margaret from the Viking with Stuart Sloan and his crew in the background 21 May, 1951. This proved to be the last flight made by The King with the Flight.
(Ted Brewin)

Sloan remaining as one of the captains. His friend and navigator from 51 Squadron days, Ted Brewin, also remained and they were crewed together again. For the next three years they transported members of the Royal Family around Europe and the British Isles. Regular visits were made to Malta where Prince Philip was serving with the Royal Navy. In March, 1950, a long-range trip to Nairobi was undertaken with the Duke and Duchess of Gloucester who were attending civic celebrations.

The King was renowned for his deep interest and knowledge of medals and awards and also for his superb memory. At a Balmoral reception for his staff on 26 August, 1949, he noticed Sloan was wearing the ribbon of the Conspicuous Gallantry Medal, an extremely rare award. He engaged him in conversation and remarked that he did not recall presenting the medal to him. Sloan replied that he had still not received the medal and the conversation passed to other matters. Within a few weeks the King had arranged to present the gallantry medal to Sloan.

In August, 1951, Stuart Sloan's tour with the King's Flight came to an end and he decided to retire after ten years of service in the Royal Air Force. During this relatively short time, he had distinguished himself with his conspicuous gallantry as a bomber pilot, participation on the Berlin Air Lift and finally as a captain in the King's Flight. Just after retiring, he received his final award when it was announced that he had been made a Member of the Royal Victorian Order (Fifth Class).

Sloan joined Vickers-Armstrong as a test pilot where he joined his King's Flight colleagues Jock Bryce and Brian Trubshaw. He became a production test pilot flying Valettas and then the Viscount. After a few years he returned to his native Edinburgh to run the family motor dealership and immediately took up a commission in the Royal Air Force Volunteer Reserve (Training), giving many years service to the Air Training Corps. He commanded the Edinburgh Wing and retired with the rank of Wing Commander in 1975.

CHAPTER TWENTY ONE

Coastal Strike Pilot – Peter Branton

Just before mid-day on 28 November, 1940, Peter Branton settled himself in to Beaufort L 4502 prior to taking off from Wick on his first operational sortie. Acting as co-pilot to Pilot Officer Harvey, he was heading for the Norwegian coast to carry out an anti-shipping patrol off Utsire. Landing three hours later, the post-mission debrief report was a terse 'No shipping seen, returned to base'. Three more 'offensive recces' to the Norwegian Coast were to be flown as second pilot to Harvey with similar results. A combination of poor weather, poor navigational aids and limited intelligence was a feature of these early sorties by Coastal Command's two strike squadrons. Four years later Peter Branton was taking part in large, complex, co-ordinated strikes involving up to one hundred aircraft as the Coastal Strike Wings wreaked havoc with enemy shipping off the same Norwegian coasts and the waters around the Dutch Islands. Engaged on flying duties throughout the war, he was to play numerous roles

Peter Branton's medals, Distinguished Flying Cross, 1939-45 Star, Altlantic Star with France and Germany Clasp, Defence Medal, War Medal, Air Efficiency Award.

Peter Branton, second from the right in the back row with his crew below him, at No 1 (C) OTU at Silloth in 1940. (Ron Chadwick)

as Coastal's strike squadrons developed from a Cinderella force into one capable of wielding awesome power.

Having enlisted in the Royal Air Force Volunteer Reserve in March 1939, Peter Branton, a tall, fair-haired Yorkshireman from Hull, had to wait six months before he was called up to train as a pilot. The two-month course at No 1 Initial Training Wing at Cambridge was followed by pilot training at 12

Elementary Flying Training School and 15 Service Flying Training School, where he was awarded his wings on 20 June, 1940. He celebrated his twenty-first birthday by arriving at Thorney Island to join a detachment of 42 Squadron, having just completed his Beaufort conversion course at No 1 (Coastal) Operational Training Unit (OTU) at Silloth. He was ready to start his operational career as a strike pilot with one of only two Coastal Command Torpedo Bomber squadrons in the Royal Air Force's order of battle at the start of the Second World War.

Peter Branton came face to face with the enemy on his third sortie as a newly qualified captain. After two sorties escorting coastal convoys, he took off from Leuchars for a shipping strike off the Norwegian coast. Approaching a group of six fishing vessels showing mast lights, his gunner reported a shadowing enemy aircraft above and behind. Within a minute an Me 110, with an Me 109 in company, attacked from the starboard quarter. The bombs were jettisioned and violent evasive action taken. Assisted by the wireless operator who was manning the side guns, Sergeant John, the gunner in the dorsal turret, was able to drive the two fighters off and Beaufort NE 217 was brought home safely.

During May, 42 Squadron found itself on alert for strikes against the heavy

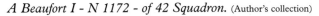

A Beaufort I - N 1172 - of 42 Squadron. (Author's collection)

cruiser *Prinz Eugen* and the pocket battleship *Lutzow* which had escaped to Norwegian waters. After one or two false alarms, twelve Beauforts took off on 17 May to join a similar formation from 86 Squadron to intercept the *Prinz Eugen* off Mandal. The Flight Commander of 42 Squadron, Squadron Leader Johnny Dinsdale, took the first wave through intense flak from the cruiser and its escorts and dropped his torpedo, only to be confronted by the fighters as he flew clear of the target. Within a few minutes three squadron aircraft were lost and the unlucky 86 Squadron lost four. The *Prinz Eugen* sailed on with only minor damage. Despite a strong and co-ordinated attack and the assistance of escorts, the Beauforts had failed to inflict significant damage when confronted by heavy flak and fighter opposition. This was the last big Beaufort operation in NW Europe, but the attack on the *Prinz Eugen* was to point the way forward for the future tactics of the Strike Wings which would prove so successful.

The summer months of 1941 were taken up with convoy escorts and Rover Patrols along the Norwegian coast. On 13 June, Branton and his crew dropped a 'cucumber' (sea mine) on a minelaying sortie, codenamed 'Bottle', off the Norwegian coast at Karmsund. On 12 September, the docks at Haugesund were bombed with 250 lb and eleven-second-delay 500 lb GP bombs and the people ran into the streets to wave to Peter Branton and his crew as he swept over their town. In early October, flying Beaufort W 6476, Branton and his crew set couse from Leuchars for Egersund where three merchant vessels of 1,000 tons were sighted tied up to the docks. Pulling up from 100 feet, the Beaufort rolled into a dive at 1,000 feet and the four bombs were released at 200 feet. The intense flak necessitated violent evasive action and the results could not be observed.

It was during this period that one of the Squadron's most experienced pilots, Flight Lieutenant Oliver Philpot DFC, was shot down and forced to ditch his Beaufort just off the Norwegian coast. After his capture he eventually found himself at *Stalag Luft III* at Sagan from where, in November, 1943, he reached Sweden with two colleagues after their epic 'Wooden Horse' escape.

On 2 December, 1941, the now Flight Sergeant Peter Branton took off in Beaufort L 9965 for his thirty-second and final sortie with 42 Squadron to patrol off the South Norwegian coast. As was so often the case following sorties by Coastal Command aircraft, the post-mission report was a simple 'Nothing sighted'. Such a report does not of course tell the full story of the devotion, skill and patience of the Beaufort crews. It was their job to safeguard the vital convoys and to keep the enemy shipping off the seas while the nation built up its strength before going over to the offensive. During his second tour Branton would get more than his fair share of action.

Passing on hard-won experience to new crews at 5 (Coastal) OTU, first at Chivenor and then at Turnberry, was to occupy the next eighteen months. A Flying Instructors' course at the Central Flying School and the award of a commission were to feature during this period. A posting to 1 Torpedo Training Unit was a prelude to a return to operations. On 4 September, 1943, Peter Branton returned to Leuchars and joined 489 (NZ) Squadron, commanded by his old Flight Commander, Wing Commander Johnnie Dinsdale DSO, DFC.

The concept of combined strikes against surface shipping had been developed by the Beaufort squadrons operating from Malta under the brilliant leadership of Wing Commander Pat Gibbs DSO, DFC, as they attacked Rommel's resupply convoys in the Mediterranean. Together with the hard-won experience of the UK based Beaufort and Blenheim anti-shipping squadrons during 1941-42, the Coastal Command Strike Wings – the integrated force of torpedo and anti-flak escort Beaufighters training and operating together as one unit – were introduced during 1943.

By the end of 1943, the already established North Coates Wing was joined by similar Wings forming at Wick and Leuchars. As part of the reorganisation, 489 (NZ) Squadron gave up its old Hampden torpedo bombers for Beaufighter Mk Xs and were joined by the Australian 455 Squadron to form the Leuchars Wing, known throughout the Command as the Anzac Wing.

Beaufighter TFX (Torbeaus) of 489 Squadron armed with torpedoes. (Andy Thomas)

A 489 Squadron Beaufighter fires 3 inch 25 lb rockets at a merchant vessel off the Norwegian coast. (MOD)

Conversion to the Beaufighter occupied the last few weeks of 1943 with over 450 training hours being flown during the short Scottish December days. By mid-January the Anzac Wing was ready to start operations.

With the intensive training programme complete, eight aircraft of 489 Squadron took off at mid-day on 14 January, 1944, to fly its first operation with the Beaufighter. Peter Branton, with his regular navigator Flying Officer P. Leach, was at the controls of Z (NE 217) flying as number two in the torpedo section . With five anti-flak aircraft in support, the Squadron set heading for Lister off the Norwegian coast on a Rover Patrol. Immediately landfall was made, a convoy of a 5,000 ton merchant vessel, a smaller vessel and four escorts, including an M Class minesweeper, were sighted on a south-easterly heading.

The anti-flak aircraft attacked the escorts with cannon, scoring hits on all the escorts as the torpedo aircraft headed for the largest merchant vessel encountering heavy flak from shore batteries and the escorts. Flying at 100 feet, Branton dropped his 18 ins torpedo at 1,500 yards from the starboard bow of the target. All three aircraft in his section dropped successfully and after a short time there was an explosion just forward of amidships and a large mushroom of smoke developed. The lead torpedo aircraft was hit by flak; the nose fell off on landing without injury to the crew. German radio later admitted the loss of the vessel attacked by Branton. This action-packed and highly successful first sortie by the re-armed squadron is well summed up in the Squadron Record Book: 'The work done by the Squadron and the crews on our first operation was magnificent.' HQ Coastal Command agreed and commented that 'great credit is due to the crews for their success'.

A week later an almost identical sortie was flown with equally successful results. This time Branton was flying in the anti-flak section when a heavily escorted convoy steaming at twelve knots was attacked off Lister. Heavy damage was inflicted on the escorts, which included an 'M' class minesweeper, and the torpedo section scored hits on the major merchant vessel. Branton and a fellow pilot reported 'a terrific convulsion' of water aft of amidships. Subsequently, the German Home News radio admitted a torpedo had caused serious damage to the ship.

There was more excitement for the Branton/Leach crew on 6 March. Flying in the torpedo section, they were lined up on their target, another large merchant vessel, and were about to drop when they were attacked head-on by two Me 109 fighters. The attack was aborted, and, taking violent evasive action, they sought the nearest cloud. Other aircraft were attacked and some suffered damage, but there were no losses. Deployed to Skitten in the Orkneys for a short period later in the month, the Squadron flew many anti-shipping patrols off the Norwegian coast with some engagements but no major successes.

Early in April the two Anzac squadrons moved south to Norfolk to form the Langham Wing . This was part of a major reorganisation in preparation for operations in support of the lead-up to the invasion of France later in the year. Shipping recces and anti-shipping patrols in squadron strength became the normal routine through May and early June. The Squadron achieved a spectacular success on 14 May when it inflicted heavy damage on a large convoy off the Dutch coast but Peter Branton missed out, being on a well-earned leave. He was back in action in time for D-Day. Operating from Manston on 6 June, 489 Squadron remained at instant readiness all day waiting to attack any surface ships threatening the great armada. As dusk approached, Branton, at the controls of NE 209, was patrolling between Boulogne and Fécamp in search of E-Boats. The Squadron spent the rest of the month on similar patrols along

A Beaufighter scores a direct hit on a M-Class minesweeper flak ship off the Frisian Islands on 8 July, 1944. (MOD)

the French and Dutch coasts. Few engagements were made, which is testimony to the effectiveness of the Beaufighter Wings as a deterrent. The success of D-Day, and the crucial build-up phase that followed, was in no small part due to the excellent work of the crews of the Coastal Strike Wings.

By mid-July, Peter Branton and his navigator were one of the most experienced crews on the Squadron and they were regularly leading sections of six aircraft on anti-shipping strikes. However, on 21 July, they were involved in a much bigger formation, a combined strike by the Langham and Strubby Wings. Flying in the anti-flak role, twenty cannon-armed Beaufighters of the Langham Wing formed up with ten rocket-armed and eleven torpedo-carrying Beaufighters from Strubby. As the formation reached the East Frisian Islands a large convoy was leaving the Weser estuary on a westerly heading. Three miles ahead of the main convoy were five M Class minesweepers. This was by far the largest convoy seen by the Squadron. There were nine large merchant vessels in two columns. The escort was particularly heavy with eight M Class

It was dangerous work attacking shipping in the Norwegian fjords. Two merchant ships under attack in Fede Fjord in 1944. (MOD)

minesweepers, ten armed trawlers, a *Rendsburg* vessel, two R-boats and four other assorted escorts; a formidable target and clearly an important one on the basis of the size and firepower of the escort. Branton in NE 826 was on the port side of the anti-flak section and on turning south towards the target took the rear minesweeper as his target, scoring cannon strikes and leaving the vessel smoking. Nearly all the ships were flying balloons and there was accurate and intense light flak. Numerous aircraft were damaged and one brought back fifty feet of balloon cable, but all 489 Squadron aircraft landed safely. Two of the largest merchant vessels were left on fire after torpedo hits and photographs showed the vessels sinking. Four others were left on fire and three minesweepers and four armed trawlers were burning furiously.

This highly successful operation involving forty aircraft flying complex and closely co-ordinated tactics serves to show the devastating firepower of the Coastal Strike Wings and the advances made since Peter Branton battled his way to Norway in his lone Beaufort almost four years earlier.

July had been an epic month for the Strike Wings with combined strikes becoming the order of the day. The increased availability of long-range fighter escorts, usually Mustangs, gave the Beaufighters greater freedom of action and the devastating effect of the anti-flak aircraft became a telling factor. The 25 lb 'J' type head rocket was used on every occasion and the results were excellent, as the many low-level photographs testified. The worth of the rocket as an anti-shipping weapon against even big ships was irrefutably established.

By early August, the Strike Wings were again fully committed to attacks against the coastal convoys and 489 Squadron were to mount some of their biggest attacks of the war so far. Operating from North Coates on 8 August and escorted by USAAF Mustang long-range fighters, fifteen Squadron aircraft, together with nine of the Australian 455 Squadron, all armed with cannon for anti-flak duties, took off in support of twelve Torbeaus of 254 Squadron for an anti-shipping strike off Norway. Just after making landfall at Oberstad, a northbound convoy was sighted close inshore. The four large merchant vessels had a heavier than normal escort, including a *Rendsburg*. The majority of 489, including Branton, attacked this formidable escort. Torpedo hits were registered and the Torbeau crews commented on the effectiveness of the anti-flak section. Photographs showed all the escorts attacked to be on fire and one of the merchant vessels was left burning furiously. Sadly, 489 Squadron lost two crews, including Squadron Leader P. Hughes DFC, who had led the raid.

Two days later it was 489 Squadron's turn to be in the torpedo role with 455 and 254 providing twenty-five aircraft for anti-flak support. An 'outrider' Beaufighter had taken off ahead of the main force on a reconnaissance and marked an area with high intensity 'Drem' flares after locating a nearby convoy. An hour after the strike force had taken off, and guided by the 'Drem' flares, the westbound convoy was sighted, having just sailed from the Weser. The five merchant vessels had no less than twelve escorts, including a 1,600 ton *Artvelde* Class flak ship and six M Class minesweepers. Flying NE 826, Peter Branton launched his torpedo against a 6,000 ton merchant vessel. Despite the intense and accurate light flak from the ships and heavy flak from the *Artvelde*, at least two torpedos hit the merchantman. The anti-flak aircraft concentrated on the *Artvelde*, which was seen to blow up after being hit by a salvo of rockets.

An early morning strike three days later by the Langham and North Coates Wings brought further success. Armed with cannon and rockets, Branton and his eleven squadron colleagues attacked the minesweeper escorts to an eastbound convoy along the East Frisian Islands. Two minesweepers were left on fire and the North Coates squadron scored at least one torpedo hit on a large merchantman.

The frenetic pace of operations continued, more successes were achieved and by mid-September Peter Branton and his long-time navigator Leach were leading joint strikes by the Langham and North Coates Wings. Returning from a sortie with the now rare debrief of 'No shipping sighted', Flight Lieutenant Peter Branton was informed that he had been awarded the Distinguished Flying Cross and the citation encapsulated his distinguished and sustained record: '*He*

The Prime Minister of New Zealand visits 489 (NZ) Squadron at Langham in August 1944. Peter Branton is the pilot on the right in the back row. The Prime Minister is flanked by Group Captain A E Clouston, the station Commander (with pipe) and Wing Commander J Dinsdale the Squadron Commander. (Author's collection)

A 489 Squadron Beaufighter attacks a merchant vessel and flak ship off the Norwegian coast during a Wing Strike on 8 August, 1944, when Branton was in the anti-flak section armed with cannons. (MOD)

has completed many anti-shipping sorties. He has sunk at least two enemy merchant vessels and participated in the sinking of three others. On more than one occasion his aircraft has been attacked by enemy aircraft but these were successfully evaded. The operational record of this officer is outstanding and he has delivered his attacks with great skill by day or night and in all weather.'

Within a few days of the announcement of his award Branton was in the anti-flak section of a sixty-five-strong Beaufighter strike against shipping off Den Helder. With five others of his section he attacked the M-Class minesweeper escorts and went on to attack the shore flak batteries which were putting up a very intense barrage. Four ships were left in flames, but the flak had taken its toll, with many aircraft returning badly damaged and one aircraft lost

On 30 October, Peter Branton took off in NE 213 on his seventy-second and final operational sortie. He headed for the Norwegian coast on a Rover patrol. By an amazing coincidence he made his landfall within a mile or two of his first

Beaufighters attacking M-Class minesweeper flak ships off Den Helder on 25 August, 1944, when Branton flew in the anti-flak section. (MOD)

sortie almost exactly four years earlier. His mission report, 'No shipping sighted', could have been taken from that first sortie. However, although the results of his first and his seventy-second sortie were identical, there had been an enormous change in the capability of the Coastal Strike Wings and Peter Branton had been involved throughout. From the lone patrols of single aircraft of modest performance and capability, the Strike Wings had developed into one of the most powerful attack forces seen and no enemy ship was safe from the marauding Beaufighters and their even more capable successor, the Mosquito. The disruption suffered by the German war and industrial machines as a result of attacks against the surface ships carrying crucial raw materials from Scandinavia is rarely acknowledged, yet it was complementary to the bombing offensive which concentrated on attacking enemy industries.

Branton's operational war was over, but he continued to make an important contribution to the Strike Wings' capabilities by training the new blood at 5 (Coastal) OTU at Turnberry. Shortly after being released from the service at the end of 1945 he was given the Air Efficiency Award.

CHAPTER TWENTY TWO

Master Bomber – Dennis Witt

Shortly after 1300 hours on 28 April, 1941, Dennis Witt turned his giant four-engined Stirling I towards Emden to begin his bombing run towards the dock area. Most of the flight had been made with the protection of cloud cover, but Witt and his crew had broken out into open skies as they approached the target. They were greeted by a heavy barrage of flak as the eighteen 500 lb delay-fused bombs were released from just 900 feet. With his two gunners returning fire throughout the run, Witt regained the safety of the clouds as soon as the 'Bombs Gone' call came from his navigator, Keith Deyell, and he headed the bomber for home. Ten aircraft had been detailed to attack Emden but he must have wondered why he appeared to attract all the enemy fire. It became clear during the de-brief held after he landed safely back at Oakington; he was the only captain to reach the target and press home an attack. This incident is just one of the very many that marked out Dennis Witt as one of the outstanding heavy bomber pilots of the war.

Dennis Witt's medals are, Distinguished Service Order, Distinguished Flying Cross, Distinguished Flying Medal, 1939-45 Star, Aircrew Europe Star with France and Germany Clasp, Africa Star, Defence Medal, War Medal, General Service Medal (Malaya clasp), Coronation Medal EIIR.

Witt completed a full bomber tour flying Whitleys on 10 Squadron. Two of the Squadron aircraft in formation. (Author's collection)

Dorset-born Dennis Witt started his long and distinguished career as an aircraft apprentice arriving at Halton on 20 January, 1931. Having enlisted as an instrument maker, he carried out his training at the Electrical and Wireless School at Cranwell. He graduated three years later as a Leading Aircraftman and spent the next two years serving on bomber squadrons, gaining accelerated promotion to Corporal in August, 1935. He was recommended for training as an airman pilot but he had to wait eighteen months before starting his flying training.

Witt reported to 9 Flying Training School in March, 1937, and gained his wings and promotion to Sergeant at Hullavington on 23 October, when he was posted as a bomber pilot to 10 Squadron, based at Dishforth. This Yorkshire airfield, situated on the Great North Road, was opened in September, 1936, during the rapid expansion of the Royal Air Force, and 10 Squadron was the first flying unit to arrive there. Dennis Witt arrived six months later and began training as a second pilot.

10 Squadron was the first to be equipped with the twin-engined Whitley bomber and it operated the Mark I for almost two years before it was re-equipped with the much improved Merlin-engined Mark IV. The Whitley was a significant advance on its predecessors, the Heyford, Harrow and Wellesley but its rapid introduction into service was beset by numerous difficulties and

teething problems. The aircraft operated with two pilots, the second pilot being responsible for navigation. With war looming and the pace of training increasing, Witt attended a course at the School of Navigation at Manston, returning to 10 Squadron in May, 1939, just in time for the Squadron's annual bombing and gunnery training camp at Evanton on the Moray Firth.

Shortly after the Squadron's return from Scotland to Dishforth, war was declared and the Whitley bomber squadrons of 4 Group were put on immediate readiness. Air Plan No 14, the propaganda war, was implemented and leaflet raids over German cities began on the first day, but 10 Squadron crews had to wait a few days before embarking on their first war sortie. On the night of 8/9 September, 1939, eight squadron aircraft were tasked for a 'Nickel' raid and Dennis Witt took his second-pilot's seat in K 9021, with Sergeant Chandler as his captain. The port of Lübeck was their target, which they found successfully, dropped their leaflets and returned after a six-hour flight. Three weeks later 10 Squadron despatched four aircraft to Hamburg and Bremen. They completed the task despite severe weather, but three aircraft got lost on the return, with two landing in North Scotland and the third crashed. Dennis Witt's crew was the only one to find Dishforth. The inadequacy of the aircraft's navigation equipment had been abundantly clear from the outset. The ebullient and courageous Squadron Commander, 42-year-old Wing Commander Bill Staton, who had fought with distinction during the First World War, described it aptly as 'groping'. This amazing man knew of only one way to command – from the front. He had won a Military Cross and a Distinguished Flying Cross during the First World War, to which he was to add a Distinguished Service Order and a bar to the Distinguished Flying Cross during the Second. He eventually retired as an Air Vice-Marshal.

After more 'Nickel' sorties, the Whitleys were tasked in mid-December to carry out security patrols at night over the seaplane bases of Northern Germany and Witt flew sorties to Sylt, Borkum and Norderney with his regular captain, Flight Sergeant H. Cattell. The dreadful winter of 1940 seriously curtailed operations, with the airfield at Dishforth covered in ice and snow – later to become water-logged as the thaw set in. In February new instructions came from Bomber Command tasking the Whitley squadrons to carry out reconnaissance sorties against the German transportation system. On 16 March, Witt and his crew flew down the River Rhine as far as Wesel, using flares to assist with target identification.

After an attack against the *Luftwaffe*-held airfield at Stavanger in Norway during April, the bombing war over the German mainland began as a direct reprisal for the indiscriminate bombing of Rotterdam. The 'Phoney War' was over, but targets were restricted to those associated with the oil industry and the transportation system. This coincided with the re-equipment of 10

Squadron with the Whitley Mark V and Witt took off in P 4955 to bomb the railway yards at Jülich on 21 May. While over the target at 5,000 feet the aircraft was caught by searchlights and attacked repeatedly by four single-engined fighters. On landing, bullet holes were found in the fuselage. Over the next three weeks Witt bombed seven more targets in Germany. During this period bomber crews chose their own routes, timings and bombing heights and, without the aid of night cameras, it was very difficult to assess the effectiveness of the bombing.

After eighteen operational sorties as a second pilot, the majority with the recently decorated Pilot Officer Cattell DFC, the newly promoted Flight Sergeant Witt was made an aircraft captain. He took off with his crew in N 1497 on 11 June to bomb the road junctions outside Amiens in support of the retreating remnants of the British Expeditionary Force. Two similar sorties soon followed before France capitulated and the Whitley Force returned to the bombing of targets in Germany.

The first of Dennis Witt's many sorties over Germany as a captain was to the oil plant at Gelsenkirchen on 17 June. The target was attacked successfully from 10,000 feet despite very heavy anti-aircraft fire and searchlight activity, and Witt had to take evasive action to shake off an enemy fighter. Over the next week he flew five more sorties, visiting the Hamm marshalling yards three times, where the enemy defences had increased significantly.

Throughout July targets for the Whitley Force were regularly switched and appeared to lack a cohesive policy, causing one squadron wag to speculate that the planners were choosing the targets with a hat-pin! Over a three-week period Witt and his crew attacked the *Germaniawerft* at Kiel, the aircraft park at Diepholz and an aircraft factory at Bremen, followed by a return to the marshalling yards at Hamm – a target which had gained the reputation of being a 'hot one'.

A similar pattern of raids followed in early August with a successful attack against the Dornier aircraft factory at Weismar and a blast furnace at Gelsenkirchen, and it was during this period that Bomber Command casualties started to rise as the German defences improved. However, Dennis Witt's next sortie was to a less well-defended target in Italy when ten aircraft each from 10 and 51 Squadrons were detailed to attack the Fiat works at Turin on the night of 13 August. To increase their reach, the bombers positioned at Abingdon before setting off on the long flight over the Alps. Despite this arrangement, the bombers were still operating at the maximum limit of their range. Eight of 10 Squadron's Whitleys reached the target, including Witt's aircraft P 4967. He dropped his 500 lb bombs and incendiaries from 5,000 feet, hitting the objective which was left in flames, and then turned to begin the long flight home in the inadequately heated aircraft landing after a nine-hour sortie. Two nights later Witt completed another nine-hour trip when his aircraft was one of ten to attack the Zeiss optical works at Jena deep into Germany.

On 24 August, the target was an electrical equipment factory at Milan and Abingdon was used again to refuel the bombers. As the crews lazed on the grass in the afternoon sunshine, it was difficult for them to appreciate the desperate battle being fought by their fighter pilot colleagues over the fields of Kent. At 1800 hours Witt climbed into his Whitley P 4967 for the last time and for yet another nine-hour sortie. Four aircraft returned early, but Witt pressed on and arrived over Milan to find most of the target obscured by cloud. He remained long enough to find the target before setting a direct course for home. With his fuel tanks almost dry, he landed at Abingdon at the end of his thirty-ninth and final operational sortie on his first bomber tour.

During his tour Witt had developed a reputation as a captain who allowed nothing to deter him from his objectives. He had the rare distinction of never abandoning a sortie and he frequently remained over the target to obtain positive confirmation of his aiming point before starting his bombing runs, and on many targets he made numerous attacks. It came as no surprise a few weeks later when it was announced that he had been awarded the Distinguished Flying Medal. His Station Commander commented: '*His integrity and devotion to duty is worthy of the highest praise.*' The Air Officer Commanding the Group added, '*His work has been marked by the greatest zeal and courage and his devotion has been a consistent example to other members of the Squadron.*' Dennis Witt had established the pattern of excellence and courage that became the hallmark of his distinguished career. Two weeks after the announcement of his award he was commissioned as a Pilot Officer.

At the end of an arduous bomber tour aircrew were normally posted to an Operational Training Unit (OTU) for a 'rest' as instructors. However, as Dennis Witt ended his time with 10 Squadron, the first of the four-engined bombers was entering service and experienced pilots were required to join the first Stirling squadron which was forming at Leeming. He was posted to this Squadron, which had been given the added responsibility of conducting proving trials before the Stirling was cleared for operations.

7 Squadron had six Stirling Mk Is on strength when it moved to the Cambridgeshire airfield at Oakington on 1 November to begin a programme of development and training flying. Teething troubles with the new bomber restricted the amount of flying, although the ground crew were kept very busy, particularly with the many undercarriage problems. Pilots with four-engined flying experience were in short supply and most of the early training was geared to converting Witt and his colleagues, who had previously flown only twin-engined aircraft.

Training for Witt and his Canadian navigator, Keith Deyell, was interrupted

Dennis Witt and his 7 Squadron naviga-tior Keith Deyell at Duxford on the occa-sion when they received their DFMs from His Majesty The King. (Keith Deyell)

on 16 January,1941, when they attended an Investiture held at the nearby fighter airfield at Duxford where they each received their Distinguished Flying Medals from His Majesty The King. After lunch the Royal party travelled to Oakington to inspect the new bomber and meet the 7 Squadron personnel. The following day, the first opera-tional Stirling was delivered to the Squadron, but difficulties with the massive undercarriage of the bomber continued to limit the amount of flying severely.

Problems with the aircraft continued, but the senior echelons of the Air Force were becoming impa-tient with the delays and, more in desperation than in an acknowledge-ment that the aircraft was ready, 7 Squadron was ordered to start opera-tions in February. After a number of false starts, the Stirling finally flew on its first bombing operation of the war when three aircraft attacked Rotterdam on 14 February. The following day it was Witt's turn when he flew as second-pilot to Flight Lieutenant G. Bennett in N 3641 to bomb Boulogne docks with sixteen 500 lb GP bombs. Ten days later three Stirlings joined a larger force to bomb the German battle-cruiser *Scharnhorst*, berthed in the docks at Brest, and Witt flew his second Stirling operation with former civil airline pilot Gordon Bennett.

After two further sorties as a second pilot, Witt assumed command of his own crew and they took N 6012 to Kiel for their first operation on 7 April. Sorties by the Stirlings increased during April and Witt paid two visits to Brest as Bomber Command continued to be pressed into operations against maritime targets. On the second of these sorties a USAAF Major flew as an observer and

Dennis Witt and his Stirling crew at Oakington. Keith Deyell is in the back row on the left.
(Keith Deyell)

witnessed the intense flak and searchlight activity. After dropping the five 2,000 lb armour-piercing bombs, Witt's aircraft was hit by flak and the rear turret was damaged. Witt took violent evasive action, finally departing the scene at 2,000 feet. His American passenger had not anticipated such a hostile sortie and could only comment that he was impressed with 'how cool the Brit crew had been'.

On 28 April, the Stirlings mounted their first daylight cloud-cover sortie of the war when three aircraft were tasked to bomb Emden. Witt was at the controls of N 6010 when he took off at mid-day with eighteen 500 lb bombs. He arrived over the target two hours later, breaking cloud at 900 feet to be met by a hostile reception from the light flak. Keith Deyell dropped the bombs over the dock area as both of the Stirling's gunners returned the enemy's fire. On return to Oakington Witt and his crew discovered that they were the only crew

A 7 Squadron Stirling I - N 3641. Witt flew this aircraft on his first bombing sortie on 7 Squadron when he attacked Boulogne docks on 15 February, 1941. (Author's collection)

to reach the target, so had the dubious distinction of completing the first successful daylight attack by the Stirling.

Witt's next sortie took him and his crew to Berlin for the first time. Theirs was one of only two Stirlings to reach the target and they dropped a mixed load of 1,000 and 500 lb GP bombs. Two weeks later they carried out another sortie to the 'Big City'. The pace of operations increased through June and by early July, the Stirlings flying with heavy fighter escort on daylight 'Circus' raids against the Channel ports in addition to night raids against Germany.

Witt's skill and tenacity were in evidence again on 1 July when he led three aircraft on a daylight attack against the seaplane base at Borkum. The bombs were seen to strike the concrete slipway and the harbour area just as a strong force of enemy fighters closed in for an attack. The Me 109Fs soon shot down one of the Stirlings and Witt withstood four separate attacks by a single fighter. The rear gunner, Pilot Officer J Mills, was wounded but he insisted on remaining in his turret and eventually shot down the German fighter. He was leaving his turret when another attack developed and he courageously returned to his post and engaged the enemy which was last seen diving vertically and emitting black smoke.

During July, Witt led a number of daylight attacks and was attacked again by fighters when he bombed the coking plants at Béthune. The flak was intense and the fighter escort remained high while the Stirlings attacked the target. As the bombers pulled away, Me 109s appeared and shot down one of the Stirlings. Witt's gunners engaged another enemy fighter, claiming a 'damaged' before the Spitfire escorts came down to drive off the enemy fighters. Coasting out on the return flight, the second Stirling was engaged by flak and was shot down, leaving Witt to return alone. Five days later he led another daylight attack against Béthune and saw one of his formation shot down by flak and blown to pieces as they began the bombing run. He continued to lead the attack despite the intensity of the anti-aircraft fire and his bombs were seen to hit the marshalling yards. Reconnaissance photographs taken later highlighted the extensive damage caused by Witt's attack.

Immediately following the debrief of this operation, Witt's Squadron Commander submitted a glowing recommendation for the immediate award of the Distinguished Flying Cross, describing the circumstances of the attack and quoting details of his successful engagement with enemy fighters a few days earlier. He concluded his recommendation: *'The success of this attack is attributed to the tenacity, skill and determination of this pilot. He is an outstanding captain who has gained signal success in operations against the enemy.'* His Station Commander commented on his *'conspicuous courage, skill and devotion to duty'*, and Air Vice-Marshal J. Baldwin, who continued to fly on operations himself, added that *'Flying Officer Witt continues to show the same courage, zeal and deter-*

mination that he showed at the commencement of his operational tour in spite of the large number of sorties he has now completed.' These outstanding citations speak for themselves. A week later the Commander-in-Chief of Bomber Command approved the immediate award.

The run of daylight attacks was interrupted in mid-July and the bombers returned to attacks against targets in Germany. On the 14th, Witt took off in N 6022 to bomb Hanover with a load of 1,000 and 500 lb bombs and 420 incendiaries. The stick was seen to burst across large sheds and started a major fire and explosions. En route home, the Stirling was engaged by flak over the Dutch coast and two engines were put out of action, with a third causing trouble shortly afterwards. With a ditching in the North Sea a strong possibility, Witt and his second pilot, Sergeant L. Bolton, struggled to keep the stricken bomber airborne. Almost out of fuel, they eventually staggered over the English coast near Cromer and Witt ordered the crew to bale out. Holding the crippled bomber steady for his crew to make their escape, he finally jumped and landed without injury. His friend and navigator, Keith Deyell, broke his leg and did not fly again on 7 Squadron and the Flight Engineer sustained back injuries. The Stirling was last seen by the navigator as it left a trail of sparks with the engines faltering finally crashing seven miles south of Norwich.

Witt and his crew were given a few days' rest, but they were in the thick of the action on their very next trip on 23 July. Although the planning staffs at Bomber Command had decided to discontinue the daylight attacks by Stirlings, reconnaissance had shown that the *Scharnhorst* had slipped her moorings at Brest and an attack with armour-piercing 2,000 lbs was organised. Further intelligence indicated that the German battle-cruiser had moved to the French port of La Pallice and three Stirlings of 7 Squadron were briefed to join other bombers for the daylight attack. Witt took off in W 7434 at 1745 hours and joined up with his two colleagues as they headed out towards the Bay of Biscay. Each aircraft dropped three of the armour-piercing bombs from 13,000 feet scoring at least one hit. Other hits by a force of Halifax bombers ensured that the *Scharnhorst* would have to return to Brest for repairs, thus delaying her deployment into the Atlantic. As the three Stirlings turned away they were attacked by six Me 109 fighters and three turned in on Witt's aircraft. He immediately dived to sea level and the fighters broke off the attack, enabling him to return safely to Oakington.

By the middle of August, Witt was coming to the end of his second tour and he had no wish to join an OTU as an instructor. Two colleagues who were also due for posting had discovered that this could be avoided by volunteering for a 'specialist' course so one applied for an armaments course, the second for an engineering course and Witt for navigation. A few days later, he attended a 'navigation course for aircraft captains' at Cranage and, on completion, he returned to fly two more operations.

On 18 August, his was one of only two Stirlings to reach Magdeburg. Encountering complete cloud cover, he flew to the secondary target of Hanover and dropped his bombs. On returning to Oakington, the weather had become almost impossible for landing. One aircraft had already made an emergency landing at Gravely and the Squadron Commander had crashed on landing at Oakington. With fuel low, Witt was committed to an approach and he carried out a successful crash landing which badly damaged the aircraft, but the crew escaped injury.

Duisburg was the target for seven Stirlings of 7 Squadron on the night of 28 August when they joined a mixed force of 118 bombers. Witt was one of the captains on this, his sixty-fourth bombing operation, and the last of his second tour. Flying an old Stirling I (N 3669), he dropped his five 1,000 lb and eight 500 lb bombs on the target and returned to base after one of the few routine sorties of his highly successful and dangerous tour on the first of the Stirling squadrons. He had deserved his rest. By the middle of 1941 he had established himself as one of the most experienced and outstanding bomber pilots in the Royal Air Force.

Having left 7 Squadron Witt completed the Specialist Navigation Course before sailing for Canada where he was loaned to the Canadian Government to assist in the establishment of the British Commonwealth Air Training Plan. The plan, which was devised to train many thousands of young aircrew cadets, was one of the outstanding feats of organisation achieved during the war and Witt was heavily involved in establishing the early navigation schools.

In August, 1942, he returned to the United Kingdom and was posted to

A Lancaster of 635 Squadron with the H2S radome and the automatic gun laying radar in the rear turret clearly visible. (Author's collection)

Headquarters Bomber Command as a Squadron Leader to join the staff of the newly formed Pathfinder Force as a specialist navigator. With his unique experience of two bombing tours as a pilot, allied to his specialist navigation qualifications, he was an ideal candidate to be intimately involved in the early development of one of the most remarkable forces assembled during the war. He soon joined the Headquarters of Air Commodore Don Bennett at 8 Group, based at Wyton near Cambridge, as the Group Training Inspector with the rank of acting Wing Commander. This marked the period when the Pathfinder techniques were being developed with the introduction of new navigation and bomb-aiming aids and target-marking equipment. Within a few months he began trying to return to operational flying.

Having completed two bomber tours he could have completed the rest of the war in a comfortable ground appointment, but that was not in his nature and he finally persuaded the Air Officer Commanding to allow him to return to a bomber squadron. The AOC insisted that he complete a series of refresher flying courses first and that he should attend the War Staff College Course where he could 'convert' those who doubted the value of the Pathfinder Force. He reverted to the rank of Squadron Leader and, in April, 1944, he finally joined 635 Pathfinder Squadron, equipped with Lancasters, at Downham Market.

At that time, Bomber Command was formally committed to General Eisenhower for operations in support of Operation Overlord. However, Witt initially had to complete his conversion training for Pathfinder operations before flying his first sortie just after D-Day. Immediately following the Allied landings in Normandy, the priority given to Bomber Command was to attack the German flying-bomb sites in the Pas de Calais area of Northern France.

Three days after the first flying-bomb landed on English soil, Dennis Witt took off on the night of 16 June from Downham Market in his Lancaster III (ND 809) with fifteen other Lancasters to bomb the 'construction works' at Rennescure. Cloud obscured the target but the 500 lb bombs were dropped on the glow of the red TIs.

Each crew joining a Pathfinder squadron flew their first few sorties as 'Supporters'. They carried only high explosive bombs and the aim was for them to arrive at zero hour exactly, in order to create the right conditions for the incendiaries of the follow-up waves of bombers from the Main Force. On Witt's next sortie the Squadron carried out the first attack directed against a V-1 site. Sixteen Squadron Lancasters were employed in the Supporter role against Coubronne and Witt dropped his 1,000 lb bombs on the red TIs which the Master Bomber had confirmed as accurate. Sadly, after directing an excellent attack, the Master Bomber failed to return.

Witt flew three more sorties in the bombing role against V-1 sites before

A Lancaster over Trossy St Maxim on 4 August, 1944, when Witt flew in the bomber role and Ian Bazalgette failed to return and was subsequently awarded a posthumous Victoria Cross. (MOD)

Bomber Command was called on to bomb the city of Caen which was proving to be a major bottleneck for the armies endeavouring to break out of the Normandy bridgehead. On 7 July, 457 heavy bombers delivered almost 2,400 tons of bombs in the space of 38 minutes. The destruction of Caen was almost total and within a few days the army were able to make progress.

After two more attacks against V-1 sites, Witt flew his first sortie as an 'Illuminator' on 14 July when the Squadron attacked Revigny marshalling yard. White flares were dropped accurately from 12,000 feet but the 'Backers Up' failed to identify the target positively. To avoid casualties to the French civilian population in the surrounding built-up area, the Master Bomber finally called off the attack.

During the latter part of July, Bomber Command were given clearance to mount a number of attacks against Germany targets. Witt took his Lancaster to Kiel on 23 July and to Stuttgart the following night when 4,000 lb HC Minol bombs were dropped. The target was covered by a blanket of strato-cumulus cloud at 5,000 feet, but a diffused glow from the red TIs was clearly visible. Flares were dropped for a 'Wanganui' sky-marker attack which achieved a good concentration, and the Master Bomber gave instructions to bomb the flares. Some crews reported seeing explosions in the target area and Witt, who was among the last to leave the area, reported that a good glow was clearly visible through the cloud. Four nights later Witt led off 635 Squadron Lancasters to attack Hamburg with 2,000 lb bombs. He was flying in the 'Blind Backer-up' role which involved going out with the main bomber stream and dropping further sky markers using the H2S radar. Night fighters were very active and over 7% of the bomber force was lost.

Early August marked a return to attacks on the Battle Area and the V-1 sites. On 4 August, 635 Squadron launched fourteen aircraft on a daylight raid against the main V-1 stores area at Trossy St Maxim. Leading the 635 Squadron contingent was Squadron Leader Ian Bazalgette DFC who had been a Flight Commander since the Squadron's formation some months earlier. He had regularly carried out the duties of Master Bomber. Dennis Witt was flying as a 'Backer-up' with yellow TIs. These landed close to the red TIs which were right of the aiming point and the Master Bomber instructed the crews to bomb on the reds. The flak was intense and the Master Bomber's aircraft was badly damaged, but he continued to direct the attack until the target was completely obscured by smoke. Bazalgette's Lancaster was hit soon after he started his run-up, a fire broke out in the starboard wing and he lost both starboard engines. Two of his crew were badly injured, and once it became apparent that the remaining crew could not quell the fires he ordered them to bale out at 1,000 feet. Aware that his two seriously injured colleagues were unable to operate their parachutes, he elected to stay and attempt a crash-landing. He steered the burning bomber away from a French village and made a good landing. Within seconds the Lancaster exploded killing the three men on board. So died a very gallant pilot. A few months later it was announced that Ian Bazalgette had been awarded a posthumous Victoria Cross, the first of only three awarded to the Pathfinder Force.

After the tragic loss of Bazalgette, Dennis Witt was made the Flight Commander and within a few days he acted as Master Bomber against a V-1 construction site at La Breteque. The OBOE-equipped Mosquitos had one of their rare failures when they put their markers down six miles from the aiming point. It took some time for this error to be realised, and in the meantime the Deputy Master Bomber had backed up the errant red markers. Witt marked the correct target with his greens but he had great difficulty communicating this to the Main Force and it was estimated that only 25% of the Force attacked the correct target.

After a daylight attack on the railway centre at Lens, 635 Squadron made two attacks against the Opel Factory at Russelheim. This had been one of Germany's biggest automobile factories before the war but it had been developed as a military vehicle and aircraft components factory. The first raid on 12 August was moderately successful, but two weeks later a concentrated attack caused considerable damage. Witt led off the 635 Squadron force of sixteen Lancasters. His bomb-aimer, Squadron Leader P. Lester, identified the target visually, following an accurate attack with hooded flares, and he dropped his TIs and a 4,000 lb HC Minol bomb together. A good concentration was achieved and the fires from the target could be seen for over 100 miles.

The following night the Squadron suffered three losses from a force of sixteen when it attacked Kiel. Again Witt carried a 4,000 lb HC bomb, together with 1,000 lb armour-piercing bombs. He dropped his TIs using H2S, but the raid was hampered by an effective smoke-screen; nevertheless the raid was acknowledged by the German authorities as 'a very serious raid' with extensive damage. Ten days after this successful attack Witt acted as a 'Blind Illuminator' on a very concentrated attack against Frankfurt. Two Mosquitos from 608 Squadron, who shared Downham Market with 635, preceded the attack and dropped Window, which added to the confusion for the defences. It was three days before all the fires had been extinguished.

By mid-September the Channel ports of Boulogne and Calais had failed to fall to the advancing Armies and their non-availability to the Allies was causing major resupply problems for Montgomery's Army which was advancing into Holland. The batteries of large-calibre coastal guns were also still in operation and they posed a serious threat to Allied shipping. A number of large daylight raids were mounted and Witt acted as Deputy Master Bomber when 762 heavy bombers attacked Boulogne on 17 September and again when 646 attacked Calais on the 20th. The bombing was very concentrated and the German garrisons surrendered shortly afterwards. A week later he acted as the Longstop Master Bomber on a daylight raid in the Calais area. Following these raids, Bomber Command was able to return to Germany in force for what the Commander-in-Chief of Bomber Command described as 'The Second Battle of the Ruhr'.

Dennis Witt was promoted again to Acting Wing Commander on 7 October and, with almost thirty Pathfinder operations, he was one of the most experienced captains in the Force. He flew all his remaining sorties in the blind marker role against the most heavily defended targets in Germany. The role of the blind marker was only undertaken by the most capable crews and they were responsible for the success or failure of the raid. They located the target on H2S, dropped the appropriate ground or sky markers and remained in the target area to re-centre the attack if 'creep back' developed as the raid progressed. They also carried a heavy load of bombs to add to the weight of the Main Force.

After marking the target at Stuttgart with 'Wanganui' sky markers on 19 October, Witt flew as a blind marker on a daylight raid to Essen on 25 October. With almost complete cloud cover, it was once again necessary to use the 'Wanganui' sky markers which were placed accurately. His Lancaster (PB 585) was subjected to heavy anti-aircraft fire and the aircraft was damaged, but he remained in the area to provide further marking. Considerable damage was

Dennis Witt attended No 8 Course at the RAF Flying College, Manby in 1956. (RAF College Cranwell)

inflicted on the giant Krupps industrial complex and much of the activity of this important target had to be dispersed to other sites. Five days later he dropped his markers over Cologne which suffered very heavy damage, and once again he brought back a damaged bomber, having been hit by flak over the heavily defended target.

Excellent weather conditions prevailed on 2 November when Witt and his crew carried out a 'Paramatta' ground-marking attack with their green TIs on Düsseldorf, after the OBOE-equipped Mosquitos had placed their red TIs close to the aiming point. For the third consecutive sortie, Witt's Lancaster suffered flak damage, but he remained in the target area to drop his 4,000 lb HC and 1,000 lb bombs. Over 900 heavy bombers attacked and this proved to be the last major raid against Düsseldorf, which suffered extensive damage after this accurate attack.

After two successful blind marker sorties against Münster and Neuss, Dennis Witt and his long-standing crew rolled down the main runway at Downham Market at 1710 hours on 30 November in their recently repaired Z for Zebra (PB 585) en route to Duisburg. Complete cloud cover dictated a 'Wanganui' attack after the OBOE Mosquitos had dropped their red TIs which disappeared into cloud, leaving a glow which indicated a good concentration. Five minutes later, Witt's green flares went down and the Main Force began their attack which appeared to be well delivered.

Dennis Witt landed his Lancaster at 2120 hours and taxied back to the dispersal pan. As the engines gently windmilled to a stop, a small crowd gathered by the aircraft to greet the captain. He had returned safely from his 100th heavy-bomber sortie. He was informed that Air Vice Marshal Don Bennett, the Pathfinder leader, had decided that it was also to be his last and he was screened from any further operations. A few days later he was awarded his Permanent Pathfinder Badge.

So ended the operational career of one of the outstanding bomber pilots of the war. Just before he left for a flying instructors' course at the Empire Central Flying School, it was announced that an immediate award of the Distinguished Service Order had been approved. The recommendation, written personally by Air Vice-Marshal Bennett, epitomises the dedication and gallantry of this officer and it is reproduced opposite.

Dennis Witt clearly led an outstanding crew who had flown with him throughtout his tour. They too received well deserved awards with the navigator, Squadron Leader R. W. Coutts, receiving the Distinguished Flying Cross. There were Distinguished Flying Medals for the two air gunners, Flight Sergeants C. Shaw and R. S. Stuart.

After completing a flying instructors' course, Witt flew on the Pathfinder Navigator Training Unit at Warboys until the end of the war when he reverted

Christian Names: DENNIS THEODORE   Surname: WITT, D.F.C., D.F.M.

Rank: F/L (Acting Wing Commander)   Official No: 44867

Command and Group: BOMBER 8 (PFF)   Unit: No. 635 Squadron, R.A.F.
DOWNHAM MARKET, NORFOLK

Total hours flown
on operations: 540.15   Since last award: 159.50

Total number of
sorties carried out: 100   Since last award: 40

Appointment held: PILOT   Recognition for which
recommended: D.S.O.

Particulars of meritorious service:

On 25.10.44 this officer was captain of an aircraft detailed to carry out blind marking on the heavily defended target of Essen. On 30.10.44 he was again detailed for a similar role on Cologne, and on 2.11.44 on Dusseldorf. It was absolutely imperative that, irrespective of the odds, this officer should fly his aircraft with absolute precision in order to mark accurately.

On each of these three attacks his aircraft was engaged and hit by heavy and accurate flak which made his job extremely difficult, and on one occasion his aircraft hard to handle. Disregarding these heavy odds on each of these occasions, this officer pressed home his attacks with the utmost determination and with excellent results. His handling of the aircraft and total disregard for his personal safety in these circumstances set a rare example which has seldom been surpassed.

This officer has now completed 100 operational sorties against the enemy's most heavily defended objectives, including Hamburg, Kiel, Stuttgart, Duisburg and Berlin.

As captain and pilot he has pressed home his attacks with the utmost determination and vigour. No defences have proved too formidable, and any task, however arduous, alloted to him has been carried out in a cheerful, cool and confident manner. As flight commander his leadership co-operation and strong sense of duty have been an inspiration to all and of the utmost value to his Squadron.

I strongly recommend him for the award of the Distinguished Service Order.

Air Vice Marshal, Commanding,
27th December, 1944.   Path Finder Force (No. 8 Group).

AWARDED THE DISTINGUISHED SERVICE ORDER
(IMMEDIATE AWARD)

Air Chief Marshal,
Commanding-in-Chief,
8th January, 1945.   BOMBER   COMMAND.

The recommendation for the award for the DSO written by Air Vice-Marshal Don Bennett the Commander of the Pathfinder Force.

to the rank of Squadron Leader. In March, 1946, he assumed command of XV Squadron which was partially equipped with Lancaster B1 (Specials), originally used by 617 Squadron and modified to carry the 22,000 lb 'Grand Slam' bombs. To reduce weight, the front and dorsal gun turrets had been removed.

During May the Squadron took part in Operation Front Line a combined exercise with USAAF B-29 Superfortresses. (The US authorities called the operation Ruby). This involved trials against the former U-boat pens at Farge near Bremen when the 'Grand Slam' and the smaller 12,000 lb 'Tallboy' bombs were dropped, using the Mark XIV bombsight and the H2S radar bombing aid.

From June, 1947, Dennis Witt spent three years on the Joint Planning Staff at Headquarters Air Command Far East during which time he qualified for the General Service Medal with Malaya clasp. On return to the United Kingdom, he completed a flying refresher course before assuming command of 109 Squadron at Hemswell flying Mosquito B 35s. In November, 1951, he moved to Scampton on promotion to Wing Commander and a year later he started a series of appointments in the operations division at Headquarters Bomber Command.

In April, 1956, he converted to jet aircraft before attending the Flying College Course at Manby where he flew a variety of aircraft, including the Meteor and Canberra. On graduation from the course he was posted to command

Lancaster B1 (Special) - PD 131 - of XV Squadron flown by Witt on Operation Front Line dropping Grand Slam and Tallboy bombs. The enlarged bomb bay is clearly visible.
(Norman Roberson)

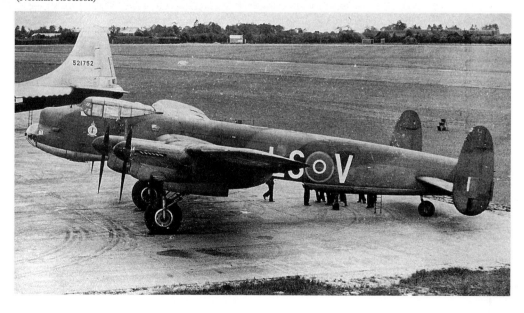

Dennis Witt, third from right, and his crew pose in front of a XV Squadron Lancaster B1 (Special) (Author's collection)

88 Squadron equipped with the Canberra B 8 and operating from its German base at Wildenrath. His two-and-a half year tour was punctuated by many exercises and practice alerts when the 'Alarm' was sounded at any time, day or night, and aircrew would sometimes rush from their beds and be airborne within thirty minutes. In those days the majority of aircrew were young and on their first tour and keen to be the first to arrive at the Squadron in order to fly one of the few available aircraft. One has recounted how he was too late to be allocated a 'quick reaction' aircraft, only to stand on the dispersal and see through the early morning gloom 'The Boss' taxi past wearing his wartime leather helmet and with a life jacket over a raincoat. Even on peacetime exercises, he was 'leading from the front'. His young crews described him as 'charismatic'. At the end of his tour, he was promoted to Group Captain and posted to the Air Ministry to serve in the Operational Requirements Branch.

Dennis Witt commanded 88 Squadron equipped with the Canberra B 8 at Wildenrath. Here he poses with the Flight Commanders and the ground crew of 'A' shift. (Barry Collins)

In February 1962, Dennis Witt was selected to attend the prestigious senior officer's course at the NATO Defence College in Paris. Towards the end of the course he became ill and was admitted to the RAF Hospital at Uxbridge. On 26 December, 1963, this modest and courageous ex-Halton apprentice who rose to be a Pathfinder Master Bomber died.

It is fitting that this chapter should be the last in this book which has related the stories of many gallant aircrew. Few who flew during the war could have contributed more than Dennis Witt. He flew from the very first days of the war and survived three tours in the bomber role which claimed the lives of over 55,000 brave young men. His contribution to the bomber effort was prodigious and he ended at the very pinnacle of his profession; a Master Bomber in the elite Pathfinder Force. Yet, those who knew him would say that this modest, un-assuming and courageous man simply thought that he was doing his job and just happened to receive some recognition. In that respect, he is typical of The Many.

The final word should rest with his Canadian navigator who flew with him on those early and extremely dangerous daylight raids in the Stirling and who wrote: *'I can think of few others more worthy of tribute than Dennis Witt. He set a sterling example of skill and courage under fire and inspired great confidence in those around him. He deserves to be remembered.'*

Bibliography

Extensive use has been made of primary sources held at the Air Historical Branch and at the Public Record Office. The most frequenly used were in the AIR series in particular AIR 2,14, 26,27,28,29,40,41,50. Other primary sources included aircrew flying log books, personal diaries, many interviews and BBC transcripts.

Published works

Air Ministry	Wings of the Phoenix.	HMSO
Bingham V	Bristol Beaufighter.	Airlife 1994
Blanchett C	From Hull, Hell and Halifax.	Midland Counties
Bowyer C	Bristol Blenheim.	Ian Allen 1984
Bowyer C	Beaufighter.	William Kimber 1987
Bowyer M	No 2 Group.	Faber 1974
Bowyer M	The Stirling Bomber.	Faber & Faber 1980
Brookes A	Fighter Squadron at War	Ian Allen 1980
Delve K	Source Book of the RAF	Airlife 1994
Donnelly G L	Whitley Boys.	Airlife 1991
Embry Sir Basil	Mission Completed.	Methuen 1957
Franks N	Valiant Wings.	Crecy 1994
Franks N	First in the Indian Skies.	Life Publications 1981
Goulter C J M	A Forgotten Offensive.	Frank Cass 1995
Gunby D	Sweeping the Skies.	Pentland Press 1995
Hastings M	Bomber Command.	Michael Joseph 1979
Jefford C G	RAF Squadrons.	Airlife 1993
Jefford C G	The Flying Camels.	Jefford 1995
Johnson J E	Wing Leader.	Chatto & Windus 1956
Kennedy L	Pursuit.	Wm Collins 1975
Lloyd Sir Hugh	Briefed to Attack.	Hodder & Stoughton 1949
Mason F	Battle over Britain.	RAF Museum 1990
Mason F	The Hawker Hurricane.	Aston 1990
Mason F	The Avro Lancaster.	Aston 1989
Maynard J	Bennett and the Pathfinders.	Arms and Armour 1995
Middlebrook M	The Berlin Raids.	Viking 1988
Middlebrook & Everitt	Bomber Command War Diaries	Viking 1985
Millington G Air Cdr	The Unseen Eye.	Panther 1961
Morgan & Shacklady	Spitfire, The History.	Key 1993

Moyes P	Bomber Squadrons of the RAF	Macdonald 1964
Musgrave G	Pathfinder Force.	Crecy 1992
Nesbit R C B	Torpedo Airmen.	Wm Kimber 1983
Nesbit R C B	Strike Wings.	Wm Kimber 1984
Pelly-Fry J	Heavenly Days.	Crecy 1994
Probert H	The Forgotten Air Force	Brasseys 1995
Ramsey W G	The Battle of Britain – Then and Now.	After the Battle 1989
Rawlings J D R	Fighter Squadrons.	Macdonald & Janes 1978
Rawlings J D R	Coastal, Support and Special Squadrons.	Janes 1982
Richards D	Hardest Victory.	Hodder & Stoughton 1994
Richards&Saunders	Royal Air Force 1939–1945 Vols I–III.	HMSO 1953
Sarkar D	Bader's Tangmere Spitfires.	Patrick Stephens Ltd 1996
Sharp & Bowyer	Mosquito.	Faber & Faber 1967
Shores C	Fledgling Eagles.	Grub Street 1991
Shores C	Dust Clouds in the Middle East.	Grub Street 1996
Shores & Cull	Air War for Yugoslavia, Greece and Crete.	Grub Street 1987
Shores & Cull	Malta. The Hurricane Years.	Grub Street 1987
Shores & Cull	Malta. The Spitfire Years.	Grub Street 1991
Shores & Ring	Fighters Over the Desert.	Neville Spearman 1969
Tavender I	The Distinguished Flying Medal.	Hayward 1990
Terraine J	The Right of the Line.	Hodder & Stoughton 1985
Thetford O	Aircraft of the Royal Air Force since 1918.	Putnam 1995
Webster & Frankland	The Strategic Air Offensive against Germany.	HMSO 1961